Purpose Publishing
1503 Main Street #168 ♪ Grandview, Missouri
www.PurposePublishing.com

Sound the Alarm
Copyright © 2018 Cindy Alexander
ISBN: 978-17326832-0-4

Editing by PP Editing Team and Cindy Alexander
Book Cover Design by Drew Sky
Cover photograph provided by www.Depositphotos.com

All scriptures referenced are taken from the King James Version of the bible. *The Holy Bible © 1982 by Thomas Nelson, Inc.*

All books, articles, websites, and references have been noted in citation and included in extensive reference section included in the back of this book.

Printed in the United States of America.

Sound The Alarm

"Surely the Lord GOD will do nothing, but he revealeth his secret unto his servants the prophets." (Amo. 3:7)

Vital Info:

According to the above scripture God reveals secrets, secrets of the future, to His prophets. I am not claiming to be a prophet. No, not at all but with the help of God and His servants, and my very strong passion for the truth, I have come to understand many secret things. Things that God wants His people to know. I searched hard after the truth, and finally admitted I couldn't find it without God's help. I gave it up to Him, put it in His hands and *our Heavenly Father gave me understanding*. He added puzzle piece after puzzle piece, every time I followed the understanding He had just given me, until I had the whole puzzle put together. I understood the vision. And you will too. The revelations are extreme, so extreme you need all the puzzle pieces in order be able to believe some of them.

When you've read all of the book, all the puzzle pieces are connected and show the big picture of many secret things, secret things that have been changed, secret things that have been added, secret things that have been taken out, secret things that are going to happen, the image of the beast, how Mystery Babylon's leader is the antichrist and his crown has an inscription that equals 666 in Roman Numerals, another sure way to know who he is and a lot more that you need to know. The key is, do not stop reading even if you cannot believe what you've just read. Be determined to continue reading to the end because all the pieces fit together like a perfect puzzle. If you stop before you have all the puzzle pieces you may not be able to believe it. This is a vision that you and your family need to understand, for we are in the end times now.

God brought me step by step to the vital info that is in this book. With God's help I understood **_great and terrible revelations, truths, some so terrible, I didn't believe them at first_**. I continued following hard after each clue. Each clue, each step brought me deeper into the truth. I couldn't stop. God's people needed to know what had been hidden from them. I was determined with God's help I would bring it to them.

In Revelation 12:9 we find that Satan deceives the whole world. I was amazed to find out that the whole world includes God's people. In reading: **Sound The Alarm**, you will see how Satan has been very busy deceiving the world, including Christians. That's why **_God is calling His people (Christians) out of Mystery Babylon_, that His people receive not her plagues in Rev 18:4.** God is calling His people out of Mystery Babylon that they receive her judgment.

1 Pet. 4:17 says the church must be judged first and God is warning His people in Rev 18 to come out of Mystery Babylon, *that they receive not her plagues*, i.e. THAT THEY RECEIVE NOT HER JUDGMENT, THAT THEY BE NOT JUDGED with her.

- "And the great dragon was cast out, that old serpent, called the Devil, and Satan, which **_deceiveth the whole world_**: he was cast out into the earth, and his angels were cast out with him." (Rev 12:9)
- "For the time is come *that judgment must begin at the house of God*:..."(1Pe 4:17)
- "And I heard another voice from heaven, saying, **_Come out of her, my people_**, that ye be not partakers of her sins, and **_that ye receive not of her plagues_**." (**Rev 18:4**)

Some of the revelation of who Mystery Babylon is, will be very hard to read or even offensive. Please forgive me but this is urgent info, vital info, *truth*, that everyone needs to know. I love you and in no way am I judging or condemning anyone. Satan started deceiving God's people way before we were born, many generations ago. Actually right after the death of Jesus' apostles. You will see why it is not our fault. Many will find, to their shock, they have family in Mystery Babylon or even that they are in Mystery Babylon. This revelation may look false but keep reading to the end and you will see it is true. There are more revelations than you can imagine,

i

on each page, right up to the end of the book. This book is very detailed because we cannot have any doubt who Mystery Babylon is. God's people must know who Mystery Babylon is because God will judge Mystery Babylon very soon. God is warning us, His people, to come out of her before He judges her (see Rev 18:4). God does not take it lightly when His people refuse to hear. God warned Israel, God gave Israel many opportunities to hear Him but they refused. God not only divorced His people Israel because they committed spiritual adultery (following after Baal of Babylon) but He also judged them and dispersed them from their promise land to all nations of the earth.

- "And I saw, when for all the causes whereby **backsliding Israel committed adultery I** had put her away, and **given her a bill of divorce**; yet her treacherous sister Judah feared not, but went and played the harlot also." (Jer 3:8)

- "Thus saith the Lord of Hosts; Behold I will send upon them the sword, the famine, and the pestilence, and I will make them like vile figs, that cannot be eaten, they are so evil. And I will persecute them with the sword, and with famine, and with pestilence **and will deliver them to be removed to all the kingdoms of the earth,** to be a curse, and an astonishment, and hissing, and reproach, among all the nations whither I have driven them: **Because they have not hearkened to my words, saith the LORD**, which I sent unto them by my servants the prophets, rising up early and sending them; **but ye would not hear, saith the LORD.**" (Jer. 29: 17- 19)

I show clearly that we are in the end times now. You will see that the nations God foretold to be ruling right before He comes, are ruling now. Time is very, very short.

We must not close our ears to God's warnings of judgment (as Israel did) but we must come out of Mystery Babylon before God judges her. It sounds so unbelievable but it fits **God's description** of Mystery Babylon, found in the book of Revelation, to a tee. Mystery Babylon adopted over 35 doctrines from Babylon and people are unknowingly following the same doctrines that Israel was cast out of her promise land for following, the same doctrines that God judged Israel for. To close our ears to God's warning means to be judged with Mystery Babylon. We still have time to come out of her now, if we open our ears to hear.

- "And I heard another voice from heaven, saying, **Come out of her, my people**, that ye be not partakers of her sins, and ·**that ye receive not of her plagues**." (Rev 18:4)

- "**My people are destroyed for lack of knowledge: because thou hast rejected knowledge, I will also reject thee** ..." (Hos 4:6)

Hosea 4:6 says: "My people are destroyed for lack of knowledge". The knowledge in this book is vital knowledge. When you see these terrible revelations, take note that they all fit perfectly together, like a perfect puzzle, a perfect mystery revealed so that you will receive the vital knowledge you need for you and for your family. Great multitudes are in Mystery Babylon and do not know it, that's why it is called Mystery Babylon.

I want to thank the many people God used: Rev. Baxter Jr., Jonathan Cahn, John McTernan, Tim Spincer, the many websites, and images God used to bring understanding in this step by step revelation. Thank you for your boldness in sharing the truth. Thank you to all the people who came to the same conclusion to sound the alarm, although from different viewpoints, all sounding the alarm: WARNING, WARNING, WARNING!

And finally you'll have to make your own conclusion what to do with these terrible revelations of truth, close your eyes and ears to them or Sounds the Alarm, with us: WARNING, WARNING, WARNING!

TABLE OF CONTENTS

Chapter 1   WARNING, WARNING, WARNING
Many Alarms Are Sounding!

Hi, I'm Cindy Alexander and I've got so much to tell you. (Please go back and read **Vital Info** if you skipped past it. It is **Vital.**) The revelations of Mystery Babylon and the Mystery of God are shocking. I urge you do not stop when you read some of the terrible revelations that do not seem possible because some of them are only understood when you see the whole picture. In these end times we need to understand both: the revelation of Mystery Babylon and the Mystery of God and how they fit together. Let me start at the beginning.

I always looked forward to Sunday. I love Jesus and I love to worship Him. I remembered the Senior Pastor, saying: "Always check for yourself to see if the doctrine is scriptural, don't just believe everything you hear, even check my teachings." That is what they did in Acts 17:11.

- Act 17:11 says: "These were more noble than those in Thessalonica, in that, they received the word with all readiness of mind, and searched the scriptures daily, whether those things were so."

I didn't just believe the things preached about the rapture but I studied extremely hard trying to understand for myself whether the rapture is to be: pretribulation, mid-tribulation, or post tribulation. I couldn't figure it out. I finally gave up after much study. I prayed "Jesus, I give it up to you. You'll have to show it to me." And I stopped studying. He would have to give me understanding. And believe it or not, He did.

After giving up the understanding of when the rapture would be, to Jesus, I simply let it go. Weeks later, I turned on the radio. I put on a Christian station. A man was talking about the end times. I kept listening. Because I had studied about the end times so hard, I could tell this man really knew the scriptures, and that this was the man that would give me the understanding that I so desperately needed. I needed the truth.

Day after day I listened. It all fit, everything he said, fit the scriptures. This was the answer to my prayer. I watched all his DVD's. He was not a date setter. That was good. It wasn't long and I really, really understood. I understood that we were already in the end times and it wouldn't be long before Jesus comes for His people, it wouldn't be long before He comes for me, and I smiled.

I even found a time line of the end times called the Events of the Final Seven Years, in his magazine, called End Time Magazine. I understood Matthew 24 said that all these things happen in one generation...

- "Verily I say unto you, **this generation** shall not pass, till **all these things be fulfilled**." (Mat 24:34)

I was really shocked, I understood so much in such a short time. WOW OMG I have to share it with my brother's and sister's in Christ. I understood the Mystery of God, who Mystery Babylon is, who the beast is, who the antichrist is (although I had learned previously who the antichrist is), that we are in the end times now and what prophecy says will happen next.

I sat down at my desk and started to write... I kept listening daily to Rev. Baxter, the man that God used to open my eyes, the man who brought me so much enlightenment and understanding, the answer to my prayer. I could see the signs. Everything was getting ready to be fulfilled...***this is the generation to see it all fulfilled.***

I also had heard other men sounding the alarm: Warning, warning, warning, sounding the alarm from very different views.

- Rabbi Jonathan Cahn's book: <u>The Mystery of the Shemitah</u> was warning America that we are following the same patterns of Israel (<u>rejecting God and His word</u>) and we are being warned of God, as Israel was warned of God before He judged Israel.
- John McTernan's book: <u>As America Has Done To Israel</u> shows clearly many disasters happening in the USA on the same day as the USA pushed to divide Israel (a two state solution). These disasters clearly show God is warning America to stop trying to divide Israel.
- Tim Spincer's <u>Secret USA Navy</u> map showing America divided by water, warning us that our government knows America could be divided, split in half.
- The first one I heard sounding the alarm, the answer to my prayer for understanding: Rev. Irvin Baxter Jr. on his radio show, <u>Politics and Religion</u> (Now on TV called: End of the Age) and his <u>End Time DVD's</u>, warning that we are in the end time now.
- And I heard about the <u>Blue Beam Project</u>, a very real hologram project, of the USA and a plan to deceive the world with a False Rapture and or fake Aliens, using the Blue Beam Project. (A hologram with sound that is so real you can't tell it's not real) God warns us in several places there will be signs and wonders that deceive.
- "For there shall arise *false Christs, and false prophets*, and shall shew *great signs* and wonders; insomuch that, if *it were* possible, they shall deceive the very elect." (Mat 24:24)

I could clearly see that they were all sounding an alarm: WARNING, WARNING, WARNING.

These were all very, very real. Connection after connection and I remembered God's word says in 2 Tim. 2:15

- "Study to shew thyself approved unto God, a workman that needeth not to be ashamed, rightly dividing the word of truth."

Well we really, really need to do that, I let out a breath. Not only are these men: Rabbi Jonathan Cahn, John McTernan, Tim Spincer, and Rev Baxter Jr. sounding the ALARM, but *there is a great warning in God's word*, for the end times, that we are in right now, *that the whole world will be deceived*. We must study because there has already been a great deception put on the Christian world that very, very, few are aware of.

God loves His people and is calling **_His people_** out of Mystery Babylon in Revelation 18, before it is too late, before He judges Mystery Babylon the Great. He's calling His people out of Mystery Babylon before He pours out His wrath, the plagues of judgment on Mystery Babylon. Remember 1 Pe. 4:17 says judgment must begin at the house of God.

- "And I heard another voice from heaven, saying, **Come out of her, _my people_**, that ye be not partakers of her sins, and **_that ye receive not of her plagues (judgments)_**." (**Rev 18:4**)

- "For the time is come **_that judgment must begin at the house of God_**: ..." (1Pe 4:17)

Great multitudes do not know who Mystery Babylon is. Some believe that Mystery Babylon is America or New York but I will show beyond a shadow of a doubt that is it not America or New York. Simply everyone must know, who Mystery Babylon is. And we, God's people, must know who Mystery Babylon is that we heed God's warning to come out of her, that we receive not her plagues, that we do not receive her judgments. This is why we must obey and study (*and receive this revelation*) before it's too late.

First let me tell you about what I found out from:

- Rabbi Jonathan Cahn's book,
- Rev. Baxter's End times videos,

- John McTernan's book,
- And Tim Spincer's, Secret Navy map.

I had just finished reading, The Mystery of the Shemitah by Rabbi Jonathan Cahn and I knew it. It was another warning. I knew the things happening in America were really warnings. They were not coincidences at all.

I went through what I had learned in my mind: The Shemitah can be a blessing or a judgment from God [1]. 9-11 was on the climax of the Shemitah [1]. I had seen in the Bible that God judged His own people, Israel, using other countries to bring judgment. God took His protection off of them and allowed His Temple, the Jewish Temple to be destroyed twice. The Jewish Temple was destroyed in 586 B.C.E. and again in 70 AD. Wow, OMG, I understood God had took His protection off of America the same way He did with His people, and allowed America's financial towers to be destroyed. It was a symbol. It was a very strong warning of coming financial judgment if America doesn't turn back to Him.

Then I remembered a scripture that said God would heal our land if we: humble ourselves, pray, seek his face, and turn from our wicked ways. Oh Heavenly Father, open our eyes that we may turn from our wicked ways. God revealed to me, what we need to do, what wicked ways we, His people, need to turn from. You will see in the chapters to come.

- **"If my people**, which are called by my name, shall humble themselves, and pray, and seek my face, and **turn from their wicked ways**; then will I hear from heaven, and will forgive their sin, and will heal their land." (2Ch 7:14)

Then I watched Rev. Baxter's End times video: The Seven Trumpets. [2] It shows clearly that the first 5 trumpets have taken place already and we are in the time period of the 6th Trumpet war now. I watched his series Understanding the End Times and learned how to understand the book of Revelations. He explains how the book of Revelations is written in the same manner as the first four books of the New Testament. The four gospels tell essentially the same story four times and the book of Revelations essentially tell the same story three times: a long version, a shorter version, and a very short version. I highly recommend his DVD's. He gives a much clearer understanding than I do. Call 1-800-EndTime or go to https://www.endtime.com/ [3] to order The Seven Trumpets or the set: Understanding the Endtime. I highly recommend them.

On The Next Page are my notes from Rev. Baxter Jrs' video

THE SEVEN TRUMPETS:[2]

I have listed very briefly the seven trumpets from the book of Revelations on the left side of the page and how they are fulfilled on the right side of page. Read them simultaneously. **5 of the 7 trumpets are wars**: WWI, WWII, The Gulf War, WWIII (The Euphrates River War) that kills 1/3 of mankind, that we are in now, and Armageddon. Trumpets are a sound to prepare for war, a sounding of the alarm.

- "Again, if the trumpet does not sound a clear call, who will get ready for battle?" (1 Cor. 14:8)

---

[1] The Mystery of the Shemitah by Rabbi Jonathan Cahn
[2] Rev. Baxter's End times video: The Seven Trumpets
[3] Rev. Baxter 1-800-Endtime https://www.endtime.com/

SCRIPTURES Explained Very Briefly	And the Fulfilment Explained Very Briefly
The 1st Trumpet - (Rev 8:7) "...there followed hail and fire mingled with blood, and they were cast upon the earth: and the third part of trees was burnt up, and all green grass was burnt up."	**The 1st Trumpet** - Bombings and the first biological weapons, the scorched earth policy to destroy everything- trees and grass burnt. More than 9 million combatants and 7 million civilians died...**WWI 1914-1918**
The 2nd Trumpet - (Rev 8:8-9) "... as it were a great mountain burning with fire was cast into the sea: ... the third part of the ships were destroyed"	**The 2nd Trumpet** - An atomic explosion could look like a mountain on fire to someone who had never seen one. Since it happened in Japan, it could look like it was a burning mountain cast into the sea to John the revelator...105,127 ships participated, 36,387 were destroyed = 1/3 of the ships destroyed and 52 Million died......................... **WWII 1939-1945**
The 3rd Trumpet - (Rev 8:10-11) "... And the name of the star is called Wormwood: and the third part of the waters became wormwood; and many men died of the waters, because they were made bitter."	**The 3rd Trumpet** - Wormwood in Russian is Chernobyl, the fire burn for 3 weeks, the nuclear reaction was 10 times as much as the bombs of Hiroshima in WWII, it rained for 5 days and the water flowed through the rivers in Europe and many died because of the water... **Chernobyl Nuclear Power Plant Accident 1986**
The 4th Trumpet - (Rev 8:12) "...the third part of the sun was smitten, and the third part of the moon, and the third part of the stars; so as the third part of them was darkened, and the day shone not for a third part of it..." (Mat 24:22) "...those days shall be shortened"	**The 4th Trumpet** - Days and Nights shortened The Theory of Relativity in Action - Time Sped Up Rev. Baxter Jr explains this very well.
The 5th Trumpet - (Rev 9:1-11) (Rev 9:2) "And he opened the bottomless pit; and there arose a smoke out of the pit, as the smoke of a great furnace; and the sun and the air were darkened by reason of the smoke of the pit." (Rev 9:7) "And the shapes of the locusts ... and their faces were as the faces of men." (Rev 9:11) "And they had a king over them, which is the angel of the bottomless pit, whose name in the Hebrew tongue is Abaddon, but in the Greek tongue hath his name Apollyon."	**The 5th Trumpet** – Saddam Husain set 700 oil wells on fire that darkened the noon air to look like middle of the night, for 3 months $5 Million Dollars of oil burnt up per day-the smoke of a great furnace, and to John, who never had seen a helicopter, seeing the men's faces through the windshields, it could look like locust having faces of men. See Rev. Baxter's video, Helicopters really can look like locusts. Angel can mean messenger. Abaddon and Apollyon mean the destroyer. Saddam Husain's first name Saddam, means the destroyer (Abaddon and Apollyon) ....**The Gulf War 1090-1991**
The 6th Trumpet - (Rev 9:13-16) "... Loose the four angels which are bound in the great river Euphrates." (Rev 9:15) "And the four angels were loosed, which were prepared for an hour, and a day, and a month, and a year, for to slay the third part of men. (Rev 9:16) And the number of the army of the horsemen were two hundred thousand thousand..."	**The 6th Trumpet** – starting from the Euphrates River, 1/3 of men to die, 2 Billion people to die in this war, **We are in this war Now.**
The 7th Trumpet, (Rev 11:15-18) and (1 Co 15:52) "...**at the last trump:** for the trumpet shall sound, and the dead shall be raised..." (1 Thess. 4:16) "...with **the trump of God**: and the dead in Christ shall rise first: ...17) Then we which are alive *and* remain shall be caught up together with them...	**The 7th/ the Last Trump, The last War- Armageddon** Jesus raptures His saints and clothed in fine linen white and clean they ride on white horses to rescue the Jews at Armageddon (See Rev 19:14). (Rev 11:15) The kingdoms of this world are become *the kingdoms* of our Lord, and of his Christ...

Then I learned about the pattern of the Jubilees on the video called The End of Shemitah – You Tube (The Official 700 Club) [4]

- Rabbi Jonathon Cahn explained about the supper Shemitah, **the seventh Shemitah ushers in the Jubilee, a restoration**. Whatever you lost you get it back. If you lost your home you get it back. Israel lost its home 2000 years ago, it's land and according to Endtime prophecy they have to come back to their land, which they have done. God restored the land to His people with the Balfour declaration. **This was the Jubilee.** The next seventh Shemitah September 1966 to September 1967, gave another prophetic restoration, the six day war happened. (During the 19 years when Jordan occupied eastern Jerusalem and its holy sites (1948-1967), Jerusalem was divided. Jews were expelled from eastern Jerusalem and barred from visiting their holy places. As a result of the Six Day War, the entire city of Jerusalem and its holy sites came under Jewish control. Israel reunified the city, ***Jerusalem was restored.*** If the cycle continues, *every time it has meant war in the Middle East and ending in a prophetic restoration. (Jubilee- restoration)* **The Jubilee *always* begins on Yom Kipper**.

Phil Richardson explains the dates for the Jubilee according to Lev. 25:10.[5]

- "And ye shall hallow **the fiftieth year**, and proclaim liberty throughout *all* the land unto all the inhabitants thereof: **it shall be a jubilee unto you**; and ye shall return every man unto his possession, and ye shall return every man unto his family." (Lev 25:10)

- According to Phil Richardson **This would make Yom Kipper September 2017, the beginning of the Solar 50th Year of Jubilee**.

So watch for a war in Middle East *that brings prophetic restoration to Israel during the year of Jubilee September 2017 to September 2018.*

We are in the prophesied six trumpet war now, a Middle East war, called the Euphrates River War because it emanates from the Euphrates River, also called WWIII. According to Rev. 9:13 it will kill 1/3 of mankind. Following the previous pattern, that **the Jubilee comes after a war**, I believe this war will bring about the seven year peace agreement of Daniel 9:27. The peace agreement then enables the Jewish Temple to be rebuilt. **This Jubilee brings the restoration of the Jewish Temple and the restoration of the daily sacrifice and oblation** which stopped 2000 years ago when the Jewish Temple was destroyed.

Our Saviour's return is very near but first the six trumpet war that kills 1/3 of mankind. I must share all our Heavenly Father has revealed to me. Keep reading and He will give you great and terrible revelations that we, His people, must know.

After I read Jonathan Cahn's book, I read: John McTernan's As America has done to Israel [6] showing disaster after disaster after disaster happening in the USA, even on the same day, to America's pressuring Israel to divide her God given land.

Here I show seven examples from the many disasters listed in John Mc Ternan's Book: As America Has Done to Israel[6]. You will be able to clearly see that these are not coincidences and that God's word and His warnings are true. Gen. 12:3 And I will bless them that bless thee, and curse him that curse thee... (God was speaking to Abraham and his descendants- Israel, so those that bless Israel will be blessed and those that curse Israel will be cursed.)

---

[4] The End of Shemitah – You Tube (The Official 700 Club) https://www.youtube.com/watch?v=t6v2D36oCvc
[5] Phil Richardson http://september2021.com/book-september-2021-graphs-and-images/
[6] John McTernan's, As America has done to Israel

My Notes from <u>John Mc Ternan's Book</u>: *As America Has Done To Israel* [6]

- President George Washington, Abraham Lincon, Woodrow Wilson all helped in the beginnings of Israel. America saved Israel from imminent destruction several times. **America became a Great Nation**
- 9-1938 Pres. Roosevelt called for conference, Chamberlain speech: "Peace in our time" caused Millions of Jews soon to die. **The Great Hurricane of 1938, Meteorological equiv. to Pearl Harbor**
- 10-30-1991 President George Bush announced USA official Policy to divide the land of Israel and make a Palestine state. **While President Bush gave that speech his house in Maine totally destroyed by the Perfect storm-A very strong warning.**
- 8-2005 President Bush met with Prime Minister Sharon in White House, pressuring him to pull out of Gaza, divide the land of Israel, President Bush congratulated Sharon for making the decision. **Hurricane Katrina formed. When the last Jew was out of Gaza, Sharon had stroke.**
- 7-16-2007 Pres. Bush gave speech regarding dividing land of Israel and Jerusalem, calling outpost illegal and America prepared to lead discussions. **7-20-2007 Stock Market Falls** worst decline in years, 2008 Housing crisis, Foreclosures, Illegal banking deals for houses/land
- 5-22-2011 President Obama gave speech, Israel to go back to 67 boarders- **Joplin Missouri Tornado**
- 3-11-2011 Japanese came against Israel, telling them to go back to pre-67 boarders **Great Earth Quake 2nd greatest in History**

And John McTernan listed warnings from God's word:
- Gen. 12:3 And I will bless them that bless thee, and curse him that curse thee: and in thee shall all families of the earth be blessed. (God was speaking to Abraham and his descendants-Israel)
- Obadiah 1:15 For the day of the LORD is near upon all the heathen: as thou hast done, [To Israel] it shall be done unto thee: thy reward shall return upon thine own head.

Through these and the many John McTernan listed in his book, God is clearly giving warnings, warnings of judgment, for America to stop trying to divide His land, Israel. In the Old Testament, God warned the people through Noah of the coming judgement of a flood that would cover the earth but they thought he was crazy. They didn't believe Noah and ignored his warnings. In the Old Testament, God allowed the Jewish Temple to be destroyed by their enemies twice, and His people to be carried off as slaves by their enemies. God caused the earth to open her mouth and swallow His people and the fire of the Lord was kindled and consumed those at the utter most parts of the camp. God sent a great plague upon some. He persecute His people (the Jews) with the sword, with the famine, and with the pestilence, and delivered them to be removed to all the kingdoms of the earth, to be a curse, and an astonishment, and an hissing, and a reproach **because they refused to hear His word**. They refused to hear His warnings. Rom 15:4 tells us whatever was written aforetime was written for our learning. We must remember to heed God's warnings to us.

- "For whatsoever things were written aforetime were written for our learning, that we through patience and comfort of the scriptures might have hope." (Rom 15:4)

One example is that we learn about the 70th week, the time of trouble, the great tribulation from Daniel in the Old Testament. Here are a few of the scriptures aforetime also written for our learning:

- "And, behold, **I, even I, do bring a flood of waters upon the earth, to destroy all flesh**, wherein *is* the breath of life, from under heaven; *and* every thing that *is* in the earth shall die." (Gen 6:17)
- "And what he did unto Dathan and Abiram, the sons of Eliab, the son of Reuben: how **the earth opened her mouth, and swallowed them up**, and their households, and their tents, and all the substance that *was* in their possession, in the midst of all Israel:" (Deu 11:6)
- "And *when* **the people complained**, it displeased the LORD: and the LORD heard *it;* and **his anger was kindled; and the fire of the LORD burnt among them, and consumed *them that were* in the uttermost parts of the camp.**" (Num 11:1)
- "And while the flesh *was* yet between their teeth, ere it was chewed, **the wrath of the LORD was kindled against the people, and the LORD smote the people with a very great plague**." (Num 11:33)
- "17) **Thus saith the LORD of hosts; Behold, I will send upon them** the sword, the famine, and the pestilence, and will make them like vile figs, that cannot be eaten, they are so evil. 18) And **I will persecute them with the sword, with the famine, and with the pestilence, and will deliver them to be removed to all the kingdoms of the earth, to be a curse, and an astonishment, and an hissing, and a reproach, among all the nations whither I have driven them**: 19) <u>**Because they have not hearkened to my words, saith the LORD**</u>, which I sent unto them by my servants the prophets, rising up early and sending *them;* but ye would not hear, saith the LORD." (Jer 29:17-19)

From the previous scriptures we see that God judged *His* people. The Holocaust was part of the fulfillment of Jer. 29:17-19. The antisemitism that Jews have suffered is a part of the judgment of Jer. 29:17-19. And through John McTernan's many examples in his book: <u>As America Has Done To Israel</u>[6], we repeatedly and clearly see that God still warns and judges. Many of God's people have been affected in the disaster warnings God has given America to stop trying to divide Israel. Although as Americans, we think we are helping to bring peace but God has told Israel not to make deals (covenants) with those around them.

- "And I will set thy bounds from the Red sea even unto the sea of the Philistines, and from the desert unto the river: for I will deliver the inhabitants of the land into your hand; and thou shalt drive them out before thee. 32) **Thou shalt make no covenant with them**, nor with their gods." (Exo 23:31)

- "When the LORD thy God shall bring thee into the land whither thou goest to possess it, and hath cast out many nations before thee, the Hittites, and the Girgashites, and the Amorites, and the Canaanites, and the Perizzites, and the Hivites, and the Jebusites, seven nations greater and mightier than thou; 2) And when the LORD thy God shall deliver them before thee; thou shalt smite them, and utterly destroy them; **thou shalt make no covenant with them**, nor shew mercy unto them:" (Deu 7:1)

In Revelations 18:4, four chapters from the end of the book of Revelations, God is speaking to His people, Christians, warning us, of the judgment coming to Mystery Babylon. God is calling us, His people, to come out of Mystery Babylon that we receive not her plagues, her judgments. He is warning His people of coming judgment. We are still here and His judgment has not come yet. We are in the end times now, right before God judges Mystery Babylon and God will judge His people (Christians) if we refuse to hear his warning as Israel refused to hear God. They told God they would keep their vows to the Queen of heaven (Semiramis, the goddess of Babylon) which was Baal worship and in Jer. 44:28 God said *"**shall know whose words shall stand, mine, or theirs**". This is very serious. Mystery Babylon adopted the same Baal worship that God judged and divorced Israel for.* Mystery Babylon adopted over 35 traditions of Babylonian Baal worship. Mystery Babylon is a Mystery that God's people must understand now for great multitudes of God's people are in Mystery Babylon and do not know it. God's is calling us to come out of her that we receive not her plagues, that we receive not her judgments. We must understand who Mystery Babylon is and warn God's people and if we find we are in Mystery Babylon we must hear and heed God's warning to come out of her.

- "And I saw, when for all the causes whereby backsliding **Israel committed adultery** I had put her away, and **given her a bill of divorce**; yet her treacherous sister Judah feared not, but went and played the harlot also." (Jer 3:8)

- "25) Thus saith the LORD of hosts, the God of Israel, saying; Ye and your wives have both spoken with your mouths, and fulfilled with your hand, saying, **We will surely perform our vows that we have vowed, to burn incense to the queen of heaven,** and to pour out drink offerings unto her: ye will surely accomplish your vows, and surely perform your vows. 26) **Therefore hear ye the word of the LORD,** all Judah that dwell in the land of Egypt; Behold, **I have sworn by my great name**, saith the LORD, that my name shall no more be named in the mouth of any man of Judah in all the land of Egypt, saying, The Lord GOD liveth. 27) Behold, I will watch over them for evil, and not for good: and all the men of Judah that *are* in the land of Egypt **shall be consumed by the sword and by the famine,** until there be an end of them. 28) Yet a small number that escape the sword shall return out of the land of Egypt into the land of Judah, and all the remnant of Judah, that are gone into the land of Egypt to sojourn there, **shall know whose words shall stand, mine, or theirs**." (Jer 44:25-28)

They refused to hear God's warning. We dare not close our eyes and our ears to God's warning.

- "And I heard another voice from heaven, saying, **Come out of her, my people**, that ye be not partakers of her sins, and **that ye receive not of her plagues**." (**Rev 18:4**)

Who Mystery Babylon is has been a Mystery to most people for centuries but because we are in the end times now, just before God judges Mystery Babylon and God is calling His people out of Mystery Babylon that we receive not her plagues, that we receive not her judgment, we must know who Mystery Babylon is. Chapter 3 reveals who Mystery Babylon is beyond a shadow of a doubt but I must mention a few other important things first.

Tim Spincer's *Secret USA Navy Map with America Divided by Water*[7]

It wasn't long after reading John McTernan's book that I heard a warning from a radio broadcast (sorry, I do not remember the radio station or date it aired or where I got the map), the broad caster said: Tim is my neighbor. Tim is a Veteran of the United States Sub Marine Cor. He lives a few minutes drive from me. Then he asked Tim why he moved... and Tim replied: In 1986, I was working in Adair Federal Building in New Orleans, Louisiana in the Sub Marine Manning Shop and directly across the hall from there I saw a map of the United States colored in with yellow highlighter. I asked the Master Chief what the map was about. He told me, when I get out of the Navy, I should move to one of the areas in white.

I remembered seeing a map of the New Madrid Fault Line full of pipe lines for gas and oil after I saw all the disasters from: As America has done to Israel, that showed the very strong WARNINGS for America's to stop pressuring Israel to divide her land. Wow, if America continues pushing Israel into dividing her land, God could allow our land to easily be divided, like the U.S. Navy map I saw from Tim Spincer Navy Sub Marine Vet. with America divided in two and most of California under water. What did the Navy already know? See the two maps: one with the New Madrid Fault Line full of pipe lines and the Navy Map with America divided.

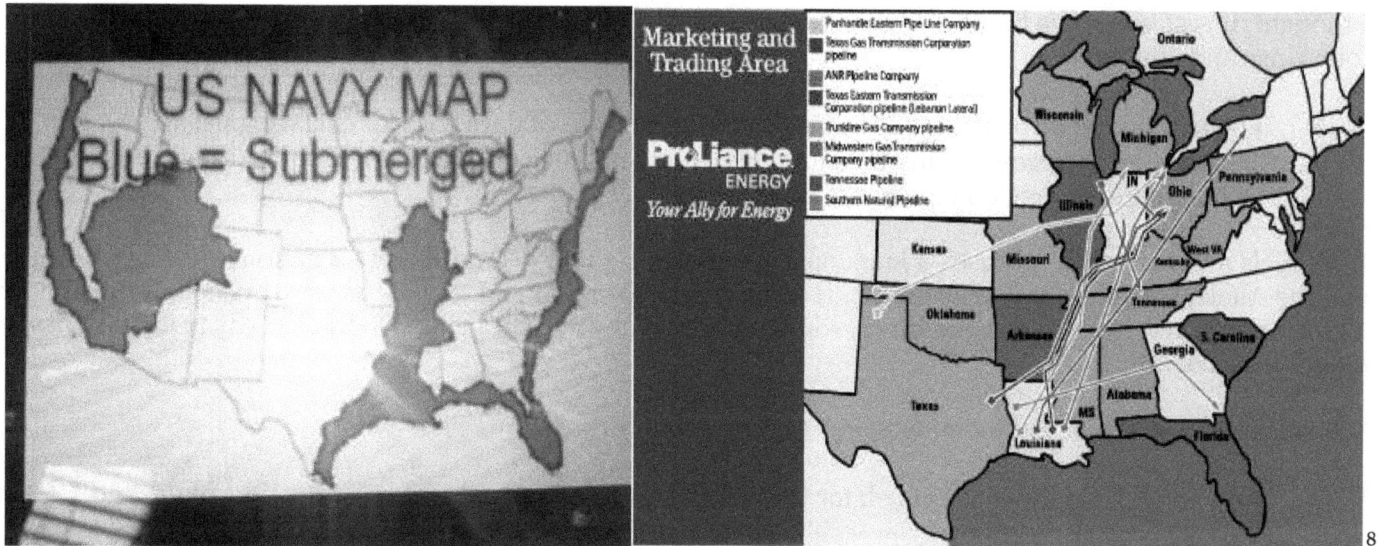

New Madrid Seismic Zone graphics, illustrations, diagrams Natural gas pipelines & NMSZ This Company (above right) delivers Billions of cubic feet of gas per year through 19 major pipelines. Note how the pipelines cross the New Madrid Seismic Zone. ... [8]

"You have four of the five major natural-gas pipelines come right through the soup in New Madrid, the soft alluvial soil," says Gray. "They carry gas all the way to Detroit, Chicago, Indianapolis and Pittsburgh. If (the earthquake) happened during the winter, you're going to have major-league problems on your hands. Try to explain to somebody why you cannot heat a nursing home or keep a hospital warm."
Ed Gray, Missouri State Emergency Management Agency (SEMA) [8]

Riverfront Times: An earthquake in the middle of the country, along the precarious New Madrid fault, could have enormous fiscal and energy consequences. **"Virtually every natural gas pipeline in the nation is built over that fault," Geller says. "You'll see the explosion reflected off the moon.**
insurancenewsnet.com[8]

I have so much more to share with you. If it didn't fit together so perfectly, I would not believe it myself. But everything fits together, like a perfect puzzle. I have only told you a small part of what Rev Baxter Jr. taught me and the others sounding the alarm. I will share with you as much as I can. You will need all of the puzzle pieces to understand. It all fits, perfectly with the scriptures, one after another, after another, after another. The next puzzle piece is, America is in the Bible!

America is in the Bible!

I thought about the first thing I understood from Rev. Baxter's End Time DVDs. It was that the United States of America was in the Bible. You see nations have symbols. God of course knew the nations that would be in the end times. God used the symbols we use for nations but instead of calling them animals, God's word calls them beasts. The birth of the USA is in Daniel, Chapter 7. (I understood this because of watching Endtime Ministries DVD- United States Discovered in the Bible by Rev. Baxter Jr. [9])

- "And four great beasts came up from the sea, diverse one from another." (Dan 7:3)
- "These great beasts, which are four, are four kings, ..." (Dan 7:17)
- "Thus he said, The fourth beast shall be the fourth kingdom ..." (Dan 7:23)

---

[8] Ed Gray, Missouri State Emergency Management Agency (SEMA) http://www.showme.net/~fkeller/quake/maps3.htm
[9] https://www.endtime.com/united-states-discovered-in-the-bible/

I thought, it is so awesome how the Bible interprets itself. Daniel 7: 17 and 23 explain that the four beasts are four kings and kingdoms.

- "I beheld till the thrones were cast down, and the Ancient of days did sit, ..." (Dan 7:9)
- "... thousand thousands ministered unto him, and ten thousand times ten thousand stood before him: the judgment was set, and the books were opened." (Dan 7:10)

In Daniels dream, he saw 4 beasts, 4 kingdoms, 4 nations. He watched until these 4 nations were cast down and the Ancient of Days sat on His throne. It was the time for judgment, the books were opened. Daniel saw the 4 kingdoms that reigned in the end times, which were cast down, right before God was ready to judge! *These kingdoms exist now!*

When Daniel had asked God for understanding, God told him:

- "And he said, Go thy way, Daniel: for the words are closed up and sealed till the time of the end." (Dan 12:9)

This is why we can understand it now, the words were closed up till the end times and we are in the end times now. I understood 3 of the 4 (beasts) nations clearly, of the 4 nations that Daniel saw, that were cast down right before the judgment.

The 1st beast is in Daniel 7:4

- "The first was like a lion, and had eagle's wings: I beheld till the wings thereof were plucked, and it was lifted up from the earth, and made stand upon the feet as a man, and a man's heart was given to it." (Dan. 7:4)

In Daniel's dream he saw a lion with eagle's wings. Are there any nations using these beasts (*animals*) for symbols now? Yes. Great Britten's symbol is the Lion and America's symbol is the Eagle. Daniel watched till the wings of the Eagle were plucked from the Lion. That was the birth of America from Great Britten being foretold in the Bible. America, the Eagle, come off of Great Britten, the Lion. Then it was given a heart and made to stand as a man. That was Uncle Sam! I was amazed. This was awesome. I was ready to find out more. And I did. The web address to get the very informing DVD's that I watched is https://www.endtime.com/united-states-discovered-in-the-bible/

The 2nd beast is in Daniel 7:5

- "And behold another beast, a second, like to a bear, and it raised up itself on one side, and it had three ribs in the mouth of it between the teeth of it: and they said thus unto it, Arise, devour much flesh." (Dan 7:5)

The bear is Russia's official symbol! I remember seeing the Winter Olympics in 2014 and Russia had the mascot of a white bear, then I started seeing it in the news: the Russian bear... over and over. I remember when the Russian bear stood up against the Ukraine was in the newspaper.

The 3rd beast is in Dan. 7:6

- "After this I beheld, and lo another, like a leopard, which had upon the back of it four wings of a fowl; the beast had also four heads; and dominion was given to it." (Dan 7:6)

The leopard had four heads. Each head stood for each time it reigned. There was one nation that had reigned 3 times already, Germany.

The term Third Reich, originally coined by Arthur Moeller van den Bruck as the title of his 1923 book Das Dritte Reich, was used by the Nazis for propaganda purposes to legitimize their regime as a successor state to the retroactively-renamed First Reich (the Holy Roman Empire, 962–1806) and the Second Reich (Imperial Germany, 1871–1918). The terms First Reich and Second Reich were never used by historians. [10]

The term "Fourth Reich" has been used in a variety of different ways. Some neo-Nazis have used it to describe their envisioned revival of Nazi Germany, while conspiracy theorists have used it to refer to what they perceive as a covert continuation of Nazi ideals. It has also been used by critics who believe that Germany exercises a dominant role in the European Union. [10]

And Germany has a tank called the Leopard, the Leopard 1 and the Leopard 2. More than 3,480 Leopard 2s have been manufactured. The Leopard 2 was used in Kosovo. [9]

The last beast is in Dan. 7:7

- "After this I saw in the night visions, and behold a fourth beast, dreadful and terrible, and strong exceedingly; and it had great iron teeth: it devoured and brake in pieces, and stamped the residue with the feet of it: and it was diverse from all the beasts that were before it; *and it had ten horns*." (Dan 7:7)

This forth beast had 10 horns and it was a harder to understand.

I remembered that I had heard from Rev. Baxter Jr, on the End Times[5], that in Revelation 13:1-2, showed the same beasts (nations) as in Daniel. The Lion- Great Britten, The Bear- Russia, the Leopard- Germany, and the 10 horned beast but in Revelations 13:1-2 they were all merged into one beast, they were all merged into one nation, **the one world order**, **except the Eagle- America, was not mentioned in this beast.**

- "And I stood upon the sand of the sea, and saw a beast rise up out of the sea, having seven heads and *ten horns*, and upon his horns ten crowns, and upon his heads the name of blasphemy." (Rev 13:1)

- "And *the beast* which I saw was like unto a *leopard*, and his feet were as the feet of a *bear*, and his mouth as the mouth of a *lion*: *and the dragon gave him his power*, and his seat, and great authority." (Rev 13:2)

This is very important to know: **the dragon, the Devil, gave this beast, the one world government its power** and great authority.

- "And **the great dragon** was cast out, that old serpent, **called the Devil**, and Satan, which deceiveth the whole world: he was cast out into the earth, and his angels were cast out with him." (Rev 12:9)

I had already understood that Great Britten, Russia, Germany, are in the one world government foretold in Rev. 13 then one day I was on the internet and I saw a map. This map showed the world, divided into ten kingdoms, just as God's word had just describe- *the ten horns*. I must be honest and admit, I truly do not know if this map showing the world divided into ten will be the fulfillment of Rev. 17:12. Rev. Baxter teaches that these ten Kings must come from Europe. My next resource tells about the Club of Rome and how they divided the world into ten kingdoms but these kings were not from Europe. The name, The Club of Rome, gives you a clue who is behind this organization, Rome. We can only know for sure as we continue to watch to see where

---

[10] https://en.wikipedia.org/wiki/Fourth_Reich

the ten horns, kings, rulers come from. (But as for the identity of Mystery Babylon, I am completely sure, beyond a shadow of a doubt and you will be too.)

- "And the ten horns which thou sawest are ten kings, which have received no kingdom as yet, but receive power as kings one hour with the beast." (Rev. 17:12)

The Club of Rome [11]

The Ten Kingdoms - *The ten regions originated with the Club of Rome "think tank", and was established by the United Nations.* The Club of Rome was given the task of uniting Europe, and dividing the world into manageable blocks. Here's a map of the world, divided into the ten economic regions, *which the United Nations and the Club of Rome call "The Ten Kingdoms".*
From Gary Kah's En Route to Global Occupation, page 40: "The Club of Rome had its beginnings in April of 1968...The Club of Rome has been charged with the task of overseeing the regionalization and unification of the entire world; the Club could therefore be said to be one step above the Bilderbergers in the one world hierarchy...On September 13, 1973, the Club released one such report entitled "Regionalized and Adaptive Model of the Global World System"...The document reveals that the Club has divided the world into ten political/economic regions, which it refers to as "kingdoms". As the ten kingdoms/regions come together even more in preparation for the reign of the world ruler, we will see the regionalizing of money, then a globalization of monetary exchange or the "cashless society". (Revelation 13) Regarding the world and its division into economic regions: Here are the countries for each region: Since this map was drawn in 1973, the first region also includes Mexico. 1. NAFTA (America, Canada and Mexico) 2. The E.U. – countries of the European Union, Western Europe as a whole 3. Japan 4. Australia, New Zealand, South Africa 5. Eastern Europe, Pakistan, Afghanistan, Russia and the former countries of the Soviet Union 6. Central and South America, Cuba and Caribbean Islands 7. The Middle East and North Africa 8. The rest of Africa, except South Africa 9. South and Southeast Asia, including India 10. China (Mongolia is now included with China) the islands of the seas, for the most part, fit in with the closest region.[11]

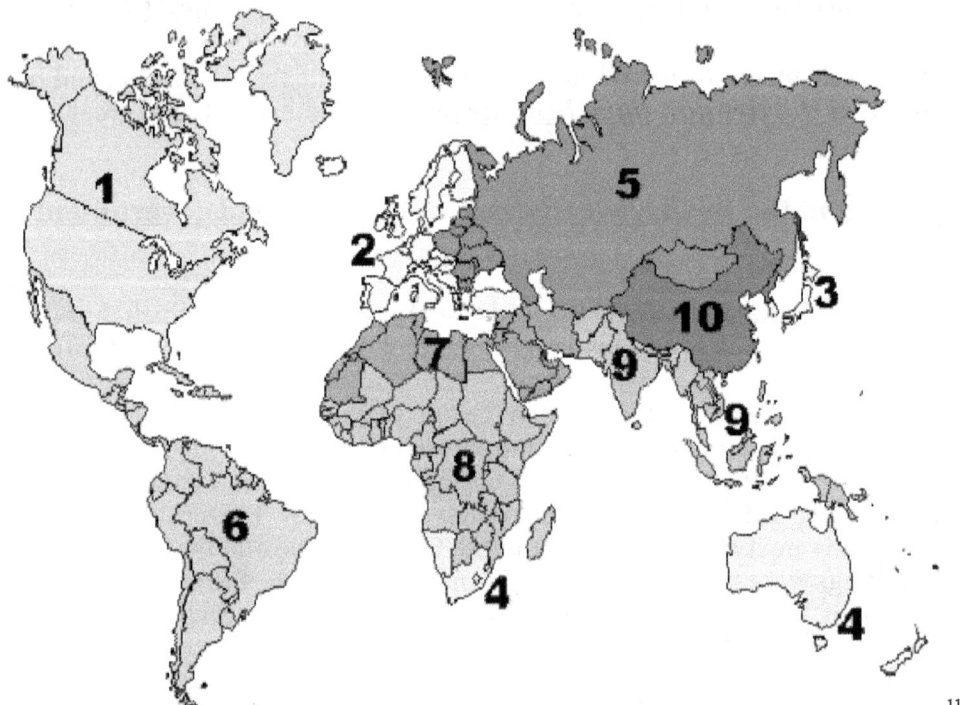

[11] http://www2.ministries-online.org/biometrics/rome.html

I had learned so much in such a short time: that beast was a symbol for a kingdom, a nation and its leader, like the Eagle is the symbol for America and how the book of Revelations show the beasts come together to form one great beast, one great world government in the end time and this world government receives its power is from the dragon, the old serpent, called the Devil, and Satan. This is the one world government that causes the world to take the mark of the beast, three and a half years after the confirmation of the covenant (the signing of the peace agreement).

God had shown the one world kingdom right before He opens the books to judge! But the Eagle wasn't in that merged beast, America wasn't in the one world government, thank God! But where was the Eagle? Where was America? I didn't know, I didn't know yet. I had to find out. I kept studying.

Chapter 2   The Timeline Jesus Gave for the End Times

I continued thinking, I even understood the time line Jesus gave in Matthew 24. Who would have thought I could understand so quickly. Jesus gave us the exact order in His answer to His apostles. I had asked for understanding. God had given it. It was all answered prayer.

God's word is perfect and the timeline Jesus gave in Matthew 24 will be fulfilled. But first let me tell you about the image prophesied in Daniel 2. Ninety percent of the image has already been fulfilled, its history. The rest will be fulfilled in our generation. It is proof from God's word that we are in the End Time now.

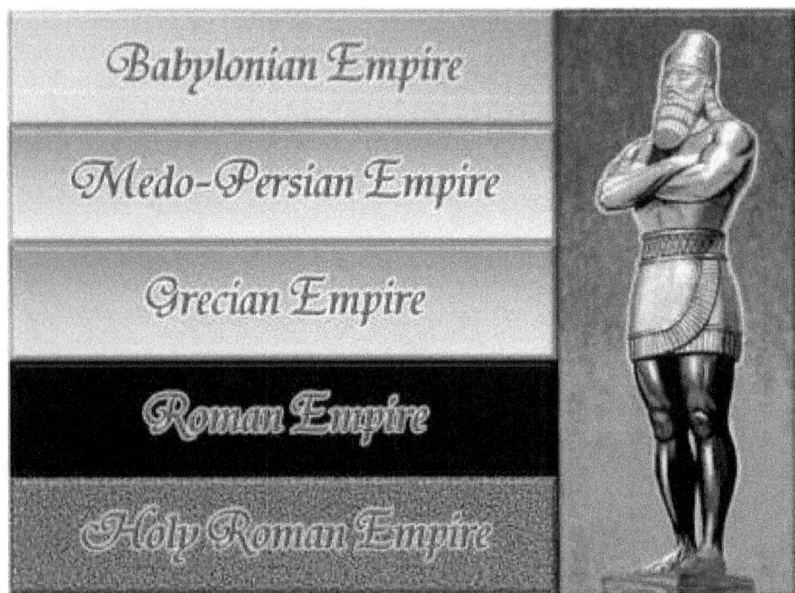

12

I looked back through my notes from Rev. Baxter's Understanding the Endtime (from an earlier DVD series). [13] Here's what I had learned: The prophecy about the Holy Roman Empire is found in Daniel 2. **King Nebuchadnezzar's dream is the most incredibly accurate prophecy in the entire Bible.** In this dream, God listed the powers that rule the world, from the time of Daniel till God establishes His kingdom. The key verse is 39 "...which shall bear rule over all the earth". (bear rule over all the earth = World Empires, One World Governments, Global Powers) God had shown King Nebuchadnezzar and us the world powers that will reign till God comes and casts down the kingdoms and sets up His own, at Armageddon. Dan 2:31-34 are shown here with a number next to the five world empires, then I explain who they are on the next page.

Thou, O king, sawest, and behold a great image. This great image, whose brightness was excellent, stood before thee; and the form thereof was terrible. (Dan 2:31)
1) This image's head was of fine gold,   (Dan 2:32)
2) his breast and his arms of silver,   (Dan 2:32)
3) his belly and his thighs of brass,   (Dan 2:32)
4) His legs of iron,   (Dan 2:33)
5) his feet part of iron and part of clay.   (Dan 2:33)
Thou sawest till that a stone was cut out without hands, which smote the image upon his feet that were of iron and clay, and brake them to pieces. ...and the stone that smote the image became a great mountain, and filled the whole earth. (Dan 2:34)

---

[12] http://kenraggio.com/KRPN-Statue-Of-Nebuchadnezzar.html
[13] https://www.endtime.com/understanding-the-endtime/

1) *Head of Gold* - King Nebuchadnezzar ruled Babylon **around 600 BC**. Babylon ruled the entire world at that time. King Nebuchadnezzar's grandson lost the kingdom to the Medes and Persians as scripture foretold.

- "TEKEL; Thou art weighed in the balances, and art found wanting." (Dan 5:27)
- "PERES; Thy kingdom is divided, and given to the Medes and Persians." (Dan 5:28)

2) *Arms & Breasts of Silver* - The Medes and the Persians ruled the entire world from approx. **539 BC to 331 BC**, for close to 200 years.

3) *The Belly & the Thighs of Brass* - The world government of Alexander the Great, the Grecian Empire ruled from **331BC to 197BC.**

4) *The Legs of Iron: The Roman Empire* - ruled from **197 BC to 248 AD**, almost 500 years. The Romans ruled during the time of Jesus Christ. That's why the Roman soldiers were in Israel for the crucifixion. They were the occupying soldiers enforcing the world community in that day.

5) *The Feet of Iron & Clay* - The Iron is carried over from the legs into the feet, but now clay is added to the iron. The Iron in the legs stood for Roman Empire. Now the Iron and clay stand for the Holy Roman Empire.

The Roman Empire ended around 300 AD. The Holy Roman Empire didn't exist till 800AD. **800 AD officially marks the birth of the Holy *Roman* Empire.**

The Holy Roman Empire's political leader of the day combined with the religious leader of the day always happened to be the Pope of the Vatican.

God foretells **The Feet of Iron & Clay in Dan 2:33,** *the Holy Roman Empire, which rules the world, by its leader- the Pope and a political leader.* The next verse tells us the stone (representing God- Jesus coming to rescue Israel) casts down this world kingdom and sets up His kingdom, at Armageddon. Yes, this sounds unimaginable but after you read chapter 3 you will understand.

- "Thou sawest till that a stone was cut out without hands, which **smote the image upon his feet that were of iron and clay**, and brake them to pieces." (Dan 2:34)

- "And **in the days of these kings** shall the God of heaven set up a kingdom, which shall never be destroyed: and the kingdom shall not be left to other people, but it shall break in pieces and consume all these kingdoms, and it shall stand for ever." (Dan 2:44)

Charlemagne, The First Holy Roman Emperor, was crowned December 25th 800 AD. The European Union adopted one money called the Euro. The Euro *is in scripted with Charlemagne* the founder of the Holy Roman Empire.

In November 1989 Pope John Paul II along with President Bush and Gorbachave came out of the meetings announcing the birth of the New World Order. (The 5th world empire, foretold by God in His word, which actually is the Holy Roman Empire)

I remember listening to Rev. Baxter's radio show, Politics and Religion, one day and a Roman Catholic lady called in and told him: "Our prophecy books tell us that there is a false Pope coming. All of us Catholics know there is a bad Pope coming." When I heard this, I thought to myself wow, if she only knew. Keep reading and you will know.

Daniel's dream of the beasts in Dan 7:9 says: "I beheld till the thrones were cast down, and the Ancient of days did sit" This is the same event in Dan. 7 as Dan 2:44, 45 and Rev. 11:15

- "And the seventh angel sounded; and there were great voices in heaven, saying, The kingdoms of this world are become the kingdoms of our Lord, and of his Christ; and he shall reign for ever and ever." (Rev. 11:15)

- "Forasmuch as thou sawest that the stone was cut out of the mountain without hands, and that it brake in pieces the iron, the brass, the clay, the silver, and the gold; the great God hath made known to the king what shall come to pass hereafter: and the dream is certain, and the interpretation thereof sure." (Dan 2:45)

God's word says this prophecy is sure. The first 4 kingdoms (world governments) happened exactly as God's word foretold. It is history and we are in the time of the 5th one world government. President Bush along with Pope John Paul II called it the New World Order. Revelations 13:1-2 describe this world government as a beast and says the dragon, (the Devil) gives it his power and authority. Daniel 2:31-34 shows this world government as ten toes mixed with iron and clay which is the Holy Roman Empire and rules the one world government by its leader the Pope. (I know this sounds unbelievable but chapter 3 will bring understanding. All the puzzle pieces are needed to understand this.)

"Thou sawest till that a stone was cut out without hands, which smote the image upon his feet that were of iron and clay, and brake them to pieces." (Dan 2:34)

This is when Jesus comes with His saints riding on white horses and rescues the Jews from the one world government at Armageddon and sets up His kingdom.

Jesus gives us a time line in Matthew 24. In Matthew 24:32-42 Jesus is telling a parable explaining when His coming is. Explaining that all the end time events in the Matthew 24 happen in one generation, then His coming is at the door. We are in that generation now. In the list of signs in Matthew 24, the 15th verse, the abomination of desolation, (when the antichrist sits in the temple in Jerusalem claiming to be God) is the key sign to watch for. Jesus tells us to watch in Matt 24:42 and Mar 13:37.

- "So likewise ye, when **ye shall see all these things**, know that it is near, *even* at the doors. 34) Verily I say unto you, **This generation shall not pass, till all these things be fulfilled**." (Mat 24:33,34)
- "But ye, brethren, are not in darkness, that that day should overtake you as a thief." (1Th 5:4)
- "**Watch** therefore: for ye know not what hour your Lord doth come." (Mat 24:42)
- "And what I say unto you I say unto all, **Watch**." (Mar 13:37)

Notice God's word says: Brethren we are not in darkness that the day should overtake us as a thief, and notice, Jesus said: we know not what "*hour*". We know not the hour but we do know that we are in the season of His coming and can estimate very, very, closely from His word, that it is at the door, when we obey to *watch* the signs fulfilling His word.

---

[14] http://guide.discoveronline.org/discover/guide07/7sec4.htm

The Timeline Jesus Gave for the End Times Matt. 24:3 What shall be the sign of thy coming ... Notice the numbers. *Jesus answered in order*, with		
The Beginning	**The Middle of the seven years**	**After the Tribulation**
"the beginning of sorrows" **Matt.24:8** But He said **"The end is not yet" Matt. 24:6** (The antichrist) he shall confirm the covenant with many for one week = 7 years **Daniel 9:27**	"in the midst of the week", (in the middle of the 7yrs) **Daniel 9:27** "when ye shall see the abomination of desolation" (the antichrist sitting in the temple in Jerusalem calling himself God) "*spoken of by the prophet Daniel*" **Matt. 24:15** "*then* shall be Great tribulation" *Matt. 24:21*	"Immediately after the tribulation of those day…" **Matt. 24:29** The very next verse says: "**then** they shall see **the Son of man coming in the clouds**…" **Matt. 24:30** "*And He shall send His angels to gather His* **chosen** *with a great sound of trumpet*" **Matt. 24:31**

Matt.24:34 "**When ye shall see *all* these things** know it is near even at the doors … *this generation shall not pass, till* ***all*** *these things be fulfilled.*"
Matt. 24:42 Jesus said: "**Watch**…"
"But ye are a ***chosen*** generation, a royal priesthood, an holy nation, a peculiar people; that ye should shew forth the praises of him who hath called you out of darkness into his marvelous light:" **1Pe 2:9**

Matthew 24
The Timeline Jesus Gave for the End Times

- **Matt. 24:3** "**What shall be the sign of thy coming…**" (Jesus answered in order. He started with the beginning)
- **Matt. 24:6** "**The end is not yet**"
- **Matt. 24:8** "…**the beginning** of sorrows"
- **Matt. 24:15** "the abomination of desolation, *spoken of by Daniel*" *(Dan.9:27 **in the midst of the week**)* The middle of the seven years, the antichrist sits in the temple of God calling himself God)
- **Matt. 24:21** "**then** shall be Great Tribulation",
- **Matt. 24:29** "**Immediately after the tribulation** of those day…" , in the very next verse
- **Matt. 24:30** "**then** they shall see **the Son of man coming in the clouds**…"
- **Matt. 24:31** "*And He shall send His angels to gather His chosen with a great sound of trumpet*" (1 Co 15:52 "**at the last trump**")
- **Matt.24:34** "When ye shall see ***all*** these things know that it is near even at the doors … this generation shall not pass, till ***all*** these things be fulfilled."
- **Matt. 24:42** Jesus said: "**Watch**…"
- **1Pe 2:9** "But ye are a ***chosen*** generation, a royal priesthood, an holy nation, a peculiar people; that ye should shew forth the praises of him who hath called you out of darkness into his marvelous light:"

I thought how very orderly Jesus gave His answer to His disciples. He told exactly when His coming will be, saying: then, then, then, and immediately after… He started with the beginning, then the middle and then, the end. He said, immediately after the tribulation, He shall come in the clouds and sends His angels to gather His chosen people. Remember He said: "**When ye shall see *all* these things know** that it is near even at the doors" He was talking about His coming. When ye shall see all these thing, His coming is at the door. *All* these things shall happen in one generation. The one generation that is here at His coming will see all these things.

Jesus was talking to His disciples, those He was going to save with His own blood, the first Christians and He explained: **when *ye shall see* the abomination of desolation … then shall be great tribulation**. The abomination of desolation starts the great tribulation, the worst tribulation since the beginning of time or ever shall be. Would there be a specific sign that starts the beginning of the great tribulation? Yes, Yes, Yes, I found it, it was in one of Rev. Baxter's earlier End Time Ministries DVDs, called The Road to Armageddon.[15] Now he has a new DVD called: From Here To Armageddon. We can understand what starts the final countdown from the word of God. The answer to: Is there a specific sign that starts the great tribulation, is found in Daniel 9:27.

- "And he shall confirm the covenant with many for one week: and **in the midst of the week he shall cause the sacrifice and the oblation to cease**, and for ***the overspreading of abominations he shall make it desolate***, even until the consummation, and that determined shall be poured upon the desolate." (Dan 9:27)

---

[15] From Here To Armageddon https://store.endtime.com/?s=from+here+to+armageddon+DVD

That was the abomination of desolation that Jesus spoke of in Matt. 24:15

- "**When ye therefore shall see the abomination of desolation**, spoken of by Daniel the prophet, stand in the holy place, (whoso readeth, let him understand:)" (Mat 24:15)
- "For **then shall be great tribulation**, such as was not since the beginning of the world to this time, no, nor ever shall be." (Mat 24:21)

Daniel 9:27 says: "he (the antichrist) shall confirm the covenant with many for one week". Week is symbolism standing for seven years. He confirms the covenant with many, with Israel, Palestine, and the United Nations, the UN. Then Daniel 9:27 says: "in the midst (middle) of the week". Symbolism meaning in the middle of the seven year covenant (agreement). Then Daniel 9:27 tells what the antichrist will do in the middle of the seven year agreement; that he will cause the sacrifice to stop (this is when the antichrist stands in the Jewish Temple in Jerusalem and claims to be God and causes the sacrifices to stop) this is what Jesus calls the abomination of desolation in Mat 24:15 and then Jesus says in Mat 24:21 then shall be great tribulation. So the first sign to watch for is the signing and confirming of the Peace agreement, confirming the Abrahamic covenant (Israel's right to the land) and the making of a Palestinian State where the Jews are allowed to continue to live there. Then the Jewish temple will be built in Jerusalem, the sacrifices will start and then 3 ½ years after the confirmation of the covenant, in the midst of the covenant, in the middle of the peace agreement, the abomination of desolation. We will see the antichrist, the one who confirmed, agreed with the peace covenant, we will see him stand in the temple and claim to be God. This will start the great tribulation and is when the mark of the beast, 666 will be required in the right hand or the forehead to buy and sell.

Scriptures are not clear which happens first, the Euphrates River War, the war that kills 1/3 of mankind or the peace agreement. It could happen that prophesied Euphrates River War, WWIII comes first and then the peace agreement, and then **the Jubilee will restore the Jewish Temple,** and the daily sacrifice and oblation will be restored (started for the first time in 2000 years) to Israel (a lamb of the first year without spot offered, killed, one in the morning and one in the evening, the oblation which God instructed them to do in the Old Testament). In the middle of the seven years the antichrist stands in the Jewish Temple claiming to be God, the abomination of desolation, which starts the great tribulation and the mark of the beast. As Jesus said: "Watch", watch for these signs.

The year of Jubilee starts (with Yom Kipper September 29th 2017) and goes through September 18, 2018. Watch for the restoration of the Jewish Temple and sacrifices to start during this time.

- "So likewise ye, when *ye shall see all these things*, know that it is near, *even* at the doors. 34) Verily I say unto you, **This generation shall not pass, till all these things be fulfilled**." (Mat 24:33,34)
- "But ye, brethren, are not in darkness, that that day should overtake you as a thief." (1Th 5:4)
- "**Watch** therefore: for ye know not what hour your Lord doth come." (Mat 24:42)
- "And what I say unto you I say unto all, **Watch**." (Mar 13:37)

You will find out who the antichrist is that sits (rules) in the Jewish Temple, beyond a shadow of a doubt later in this book.

Most Christians have been taught that the rapture will be before these things. But remember the first thing Jesus said when His disciples asked Him in Matt 24:3: ...what shall be the sign of thy coming and the end of the world. The very first thing Jesus answered was "take heed that no man deceive you", people will say Christ is here, low Christ is there (so Christ hasn't come yet or they wouldn't be deceived that he is here or there). He warns, not to let the false prophets working great signs and wonders deceive you (Christ hasn't came yet or he wouldn't tell us not to be deceived be these great signs.) When ye shall see *all* these things, know that it is near, even at the doors. He was saying we shall see **all these things** then **know His coming is at the door** and the end of this age.

- "Jesus answered and said unto them, **TAKE HEED THAT NO MAN DECEIVE YOU**." (Matt. 24:4)

- "23) Then if any man shall say unto you, Lo, here is Christ, or there; believe it not. 24) For there shall arise false Christs, and false prophets, and ***shall shew great signs and wonders***; insomuch that, if it were possible, they shall deceive the very elect. 25) Behold, I have told you before." (Mat 24:23-25)
- "13) ... **he doeth great wonders**, so that he maketh fire come down from heaven on the earth in the sight of men, 14) And **deceiveth them that dwell on the earth by *the means of* those miracles**..." (Rev 13:13, 14)

Jesus was talking to those who believed in him, in Christ. He wasn't talking too Jews, although they were probably Jewish. He was talking to believers and warning believers, those looking for His coming. Jews are not looking for Jesus return. He was giving us, those that would be here, Christians, looking for his return, these warnings because He knew we would still be here and would see all these things, including the great wonders that deceiveth those on the earth by *the means of* the miracles and the antichrist sitting in the Temple of God in Jerusalem, calling himself God.

They are ready to deceive the world with the coming of God, a false rapture, or fake Aliens using the Blue Beam Project, a U.S. governmental **holographic** project with picture and sound. I recommend you see these after finishing this book. These may not be believable without the complete revelation of Mystery Babylon first.

- Project Blue Beam in Action. MUST SEE THIS !!! You Tube [16]
- Government Plans Fake Alien Invasion To Usher in World Peace - You Tube By Mark Dice 8-9-13 [17]
- Anonymous!!! Project blue beam and fake rapture agenda -You tube By Daniel Fitzpatrick 06-10-2014 [18]
- Project Blue Beam REVEALED! THIS IS HOW THEY PLAN TO UNVEIL THE FALSE MESSIAH! By TruthUnveiled777 12-242015 [19]
- The secret Vatican Alien Connection Tom Horn-You tube By Icelandic Watchman 02-14-2015 [20]

In Matt 24 **Jesus warns to be not deceived**. He gives the order of things to happen, showing the rapture last, warning not to be deceived by false Christs who work great wonders making fire come down from heaven, it's not Him.

2 Thess. 2:2-4 gives another warning not to be deceived about the timing of the rapture.

- "That ye be not soon shaken in mind, or be troubled, neither by spirit, nor by word, nor by letter as from us, as that the day of Christ is at hand. 3) Let no man deceive you by any means: for ***that day shall not come, except there come a falling away first, and that man of sin be revealed***, the son of perdition; 4) Who opposeth and exalteth himself above all that is called God, or that is worshipped; ***so that he as God sitteth in the temple of God, shewing himself that he is God***." (2Th 2:2-4)

This clearly says: that the day of Christ, speaking of the rapture, let no man deceive you, that day, the rapture shall not happen till the antichrist is revealed, (at the abomination of desolation) where the antichrist sits in the temple claiming to be God.

Many preachers have said that we, God's people must be raptured before the tribulation, for God's word says we are not appointed to the wrath of God. Jesus paid it all and God is not mad or wrathful toward us, those who He has cleansed us with His blood. Yes, yes, yes, I agree 100 % that those of us who are saved, we are not appointed to the wrath of God. Those of us who are saved by the blood of the Lamb (Jesus blood) are not appointed to wrath. Jesus paid it all but **Please Notice WHOSE Great wrath it is in Rev. 12:12.**

---

[16] https://www.youtube.com/watch?v=61Ij8JcrSGY
[17] https://www.youtube.com/watch?v=7NdC4a4tDD4
[18] https://www.youtube.com/watch?v=el1TXBwfw3k
[19] https://www.youtube.com/watch?v=BjqaMJrfq5U
[20] https://www.youtube.com/watch?v=vHxqoDnmHlg

It is not God's wrath but it is the devil's great wrath knowing he has a short time.

- "Therefore rejoice, ye heavens, and ye that dwell in them. Woe to the inhabiters of the earth and of the sea! for **the devil is come down unto you, having great wrath, because he knoweth that he hath but a short time.**" (Rev 12:12)

And notice who he wears out in Daniel 7:25

- "And he shall speak great words against the most High, **and shall wear out the saints of the most High**, and ...*they shall be given into his hand until a time and times and the dividing of time*." (Dan. 7:25)
- "And it was given unto him *to make war with the saints, and to overcome them*: and power was given him over all kindreds, and tongues, and nations." (Rev 13:7)

Rev 12:12 is not God's wrath, it is the great wrath of the devil. God's wrath has not come yet. Since it is the devil's wrath and not God's wrath, Christians (saints- those who the Son of God has cleansed from all unrighteousness with his blood) can still be here. In Daniel 7:25 the antichrist wears out the saint (Christians, those cleansed by the blood of the lamb) and they are given into his hand for a time and times and a dividing of times. A time, times and a dividing of times is symbolism for three and a half years, the three and a half years the antichrist rules. In Rev. 13:7 the antichrist make war with the saints (Christians) and overcomes them. In Rev. 18:4 God is still calling, warning, His people come out of Mystery Babylon that they do not receive Mystery Babylon's plagues, so that they do not receive God's wrath, His judgment. God's judgment has not come yet in Rev. 18:4. In Revelation 15:1 it says the wrath of God is full in the seven last plagues.

- "And I saw another sign in heaven, great and marvelous, seven angels having **the seven last plagues; for in them is filled up the wrath of God**." **(Rev. 15:1)**
- "And I heard another voice from heaven, saying, ***Come out of her, my people***, that ye be not partakers of her sins, and **that ye receive not of her plagues**." **(Rev 18:4)**

Revelation 18, is four chapters from the end of the Bible. In Rev. 18:4 God is calling His people out of Mystery Babylon that they receives not her plagues, that they receive not God's wrath, God's judgment. Chapter 3 gives very clear understanding of who Mystery Babylon is so that we can heed God's warning to come out of her.

God's word tells us we (those who are saved by the blood of the Lamb) are not appointed to the wrath of God but to obtain salvation.

- "For God hath not appointed us to wrath, but to obtain salvation by our Lord Jesus Christ," (1Th 5:9)

Yes, 100% yes, those saved by the blood of the Lamb are not appointed to wrath, we are not appointed to God's judgement. God put on flesh to pay our sin debt, with His death on the cross.

- "So Christ was once offered to bear the sins of many; and ***unto them that look for him shall he appear the second time*** without sin unto salvation." **(Heb 9:28)**

Jesus 1st coming, He came as Saviour, born in a manger and gave his life on the cross to save us from our sins.

Jesus 2nd coming, He shall appear the second time, he comes to get those he saved (called the rapture) and to judge those who rejected and refused His salvation.

Jesus 2nd coming is the first resurrection (also known as the rapture- See above Heb. 9:28).
The first resurrection is in Revelation 20:6.

- "Blessed and holy is he that hath part **in the first resurrection**: on such the second death hath no power, but they shall be priests of God and of Christ, and shall reign with him a thousand years." **(Rev 20:6)**

The last chapter of the Bible is Rev. 22. Just four chapters before the end of the Bible, in Rev. 18:4 ***God is calling his people to come out of Mystery Babylon***, that they receive not her plagues, her judgments and then in Rev 20:6, two chapters later, He is talking about the rapture, the ***first resurrection.***

The next chapter explains thoroughly who Mystery Babylon is. God's people must have clear understanding of who Mystery Babylon is that they may heed God's warning to come out of her before He judges her. Jesus has paid our sin debt and therefore we are not appointed to the wrath of God. God does not want us to receive Mystery Babylon's plagues, her judgments and is calling us out of Mystery Babylon that we receive not God's wrath against her. We must heed God's warning to come out of her because if we do not come out of her, God will judge us with her. We make the choice weather to be judged. If we do not heed God's warning to come out of her, He will judge us along with Mystery Babylon.

- "And I heard another voice from heaven, saying, ***Come out of her, my people***, that ye be not partakers of her sins, and **that ye receive not of her plagues**." **(Rev 18:4)**

In the Old Testament, God warned people through Noah of the coming judgement of a flood that would cover the earth but they thought he was crazy. They didn't believe Noah and ignored his warnings. God allowed the Jewish Temple to be destroyed by their enemies twice, and His people to be carried off as slaves by their enemies. God caused the earth to open her mouth and swallow His people and the fire of the Lord was kindled and consumed those at the utter most parts of the camp. God sent a great plague upon some. These were judgments. God persecuted His people (the Jews) with the sword, with the famine, and with the pestilence, and delivered them to be removed to all the kingdoms of the earth, to be a curse, and an astonishment, and an hissing, and a reproach **because they refused to hear His word**. They refused to hear His warnings. In chapter 1 we saw from John McTernan's book, <u>As America Has Done To Israel</u>[6], that God still clearly and repeatedly warns and judges. Many of God's people have been affected in the disaster warnings God has given America to stop trying to divide Israel.

We are in the end times now, right before God judges Mystery Babylon and God will judge His people (Christians) if we refuse to hear His warning as Israel refused to hear God. They told God they would keep their vows to the Queen of heaven (Semiramis, the goddess of Babylon) which was Baal worship and in Jer. 44:28 God said ***"shall know whose words shall stand, mine, or theirs"***. *Mystery Babylon adopted over 35 traditions of Babylonian Baal worship, the same Baal worship that God judged and divorced Israel for.* Mystery Babylon is a Mystery that God's people must understand for great multitudes of God's people are in Mystery Babylon and do not know it. God's is calling us to come out of her that we receive not her plagues, that we receive not her judgments. We must understand who Mystery Babylon is and warn others and if we find we are in Mystery Babylon we must hear and head God's warning to come out of her.

- "25) Thus saith the LORD of hosts, the God of Israel, saying; Ye and your wives have both spoken with your mouths, and fulfilled with your hand, saying, **We will surely perform our vows that we have vowed, to burn incense to the queen of heaven,** and to pour out drink offerings unto her: ye will surely accomplish your vows, and surely perform your vows. 26) **Therefore hear ye the word of the LORD,** all Judah that dwell in the land of Egypt; Behold, **I have sworn by my great name**, saith the LORD, that my name shall no more be named in the mouth of any man of Judah in all the land of Egypt, saying, The Lord GOD liveth. 27) Behold, I will watch over them for evil, and not for good: and all the men of Judah that *are* in the land of Egypt **shall be consumed by the sword and by the famine,** until there be an end of them. 28) Yet a small number that escape the sword shall return out of the land of Egypt into the land of Judah, and all the remnant of Judah, that are gone into the land of Egypt to sojourn there, **shall know whose words shall stand, mine, or theirs**." (Jer 44:25-28)

They refused to hear God's warning. We dare not close our eyes and our ears to God's warning.

- "And I heard another voice from heaven, saying, **Come out of her, _my people_, _that ye be not partakers of her sins_**, and **that ye receive not of her plagues**." (Rev 18:4)

Chapter 3   Mystery Babylon the Great

You can solve this Great And Terrible Mystery!

WARNING, WARNING, WARNING,

In Hosea 4:6 God gives a very strong WARNING, that God's people are destroyed for lack of knowledge, and He will forget our children if we forget His law.

- "My people are destroyed for lack of knowledge: **because thou hast rejected knowledge, _I will also reject thee, that thou shalt be no priest to me: seeing thou hast forgotten the law of thy God, I will also forget thy children_**." (Hos 4:6)

This is a very serious warning. God tells us in His word that we are a royal priesthood, kings and priests unto God.

- "But ye _are_ a chosen generation, _**a royal priesthood**_, an holy nation, a peculiar people; that ye should shew forth the praises of him who hath called you out of darkness into his marvellous light:" (1Pe 2:9)

- "And hath made us _**kings and priests**_ unto God and his Father; to him _be_ glory and dominion for ever and ever. Amen." (Rev 1:6)

- "And hast made us unto our God _**kings and priests**_: and we shall reign on the earth." (Rev 5:10)

Jews and Christians are God's people. **God is warning His people, very strongly, not to reject knowledge** for His people are destroyed for lack of knowledge and if we reject knowledge He shall reject us. Also stating that thou shalt be no priest to Him because we have forgot His law, He will forget our children!

And here is the shock of all shocks but true. When the whole puzzle is put together you will see how Mystery Babylon adopted over 35 of Babylon's traditions and taught God's people the Babylonian traditions as her doctrines and traditions **_and thereby caused them to forget two of God's commandments_**. I know this seems impossible but it is true, keep reading.

In the book of Revelation, chapter 12:9 God's word says: Satan deceives the whole world. Amazingly, the whole world really does include God's people. That's why **_God is calling His people (Christians) out of Mystery Babylon_**, that His people receive not her plagues, that His people receive not her judgments, in Rev 18:4.

- "And the great dragon was cast out, that old serpent, called the Devil, and _**Satan, which deceiveth the whole world**_: he was cast out into the earth, and his angels were cast out with him." (Rev 12:9)

- "... _**Come out of her, my people, that ye be not partakers of her sins**_, and **that ye receive not of her plagues.**" (**Rev 18:4**)

Please forgive me, some of the revelation of who Mystery Babylon is, may be very, very, hard to read or even offensive but this revelation of who Mystery Babylon is, is true. Please forgive me but **this is urgent info, vital info, a must in these end times for everyone**. I love the people in Mystery Babylon. I love you. It is a great mystery, an extreme mystery. So extreme that at first you will probably not think it is correct but if you keep reading all the way to the end, it will all come together, an extreme mystery revealed, like a 1000 piece puzzle all put together, it takes time for the picture to come together. After these many puzzle pieces fit perfectly together, you'll see a clear image of who Mystery Babylon is, you'll see the truth clearly.

... Assyria, Babylon, Meads and Persia, Greece and Rome, were the "world civilizations" of the old world-and the Aztecs, Incas, Mayas, Toltec culture and Sioux of the new world all, **all worshiped the SUN!** ... the **whole wide world** was <u>ruled</u>, <u>governed</u>, **controlled** and **compelled to worship** according to "**Lucifer Sun Worship**", and that is all the people of the world ever knew, including even, the nation of Israel, God's people, who wanted nothing less, and did also **worshiped the SUN**, and God destroyed them because of it. (Read Ezekiel chapters 8 and 23) [21] Mystery Babylon has its roots in this same Sun worship.

Please remember, I love the people in Mystery Babylon. I even have family in Mystery Babylon. God loves the people in Mystery Babylon. The people in Mystery Babylon are devoted people that love God. This mystery is a great shock, so please bear with me as we go through the hard part of starting this puzzle and putting it all together.

God gives all the clues we need in the book of Revelation, to know who Mystery Babylon is. Some teach that America is Mystery Babylon. America does fit some of the clues for Mystery Babylon but not all. There is only one that fits all the clues perfectly, that God has given us, in His word. If you read this book with an open mind, seeking truth, when all the scripture clue puzzle pieces are put together, along with all of Babylon's doctrines that she adopted, you will clearly see and know who Mystery Babylon is and who the antichrist is, beyond a shadow of a doubt, that you may heed God's warning to come out of her. When *all* the puzzle pieces are put together, you will know the truth.

- Mystery Babylon and the Perfect Match
- The Secret of Mystery Babylon
- Quick Overview
- 33 of Babylon's Doctrines Adopted by Mystery Babylon
  detailed Explanations and Pictures
- Mystery Babylon Admits They Changed This! (34)
- Another, Babylonian Doctrine of the Sun God, Brought into the Church (35)
- Mystery Babylon actually worships Satan as Babylon Did (Seen on Video)
- Mystery Babylon's Leader, the Antichrist, and 666 The Mark of the Beast Match Perfectly

---

[21] http://granddesignexposed.com/sun/baal.html

Mystery Babylon
And the Perfect Match

God describes Mystery Babylon so everyone can know who she is. God even defines the symbols of His word[2] so we can be sure beyond a shadow of a doubt.

First, God's people (His Church) are always described in His word as woman because we are His Bride, we are His Wife.

- "**<u>For your husband is your Maker</u>**, whose name is the LORD of hosts" (Isaiah 54:5)
- "19) And **<u>I will betroth thee unto me for ever</u>**; yea, I will betroth thee unto me in righteousness, and in judgment, and in lovingkindness, and in mercies. 20) I will even betroth thee unto me in faithfulness: and thou shalt know **the LORD**." (Hos 2:19,20)
- "7) Let us be glad and rejoice, and give honour to him: for ***the marriage of the Lamb*** is come, and **<u>His wife</u>** hath made herself ready. 8) And to **<u>*her*</u>** was granted that she should be arrayed in fine linen, clean and white: for the fine linen is the righteousness of saints. 9) And he saith unto me, Write, Blessed *are* they which are called unto the marriage supper of the Lamb. And he saith unto me, These are the true sayings of God." (Rev 19:7-9)

God's word describes His Bride, His Wife as either a Virgin (Pure and Faithful to Him) or as a Whore, a Harlot (Unfaithful, committing *Spiritual Adultery – Idolatry, the worship of another god*).
Israel was God's Wife but God gave Israel a bill of divorce in Jer 3:8 for her spiritual adultery.

- "For I am jealous over you with godly jealousy: for **<u>I have espoused you to one husband</u>**, that I may present *you as* a **<u>chaste virgin to Christ</u>**." (2Co 11:2)
- "And I saw, when for all the causes whereby backsliding ***<u>Israel committed adultery</u>*** I had put her away, and given ***<u>her a bill of divorce</u>***; yet her treacherous sister Judah feared not, but went and played the ***harlot*** also." (Jer 3:8)

<u>For *spiritual adultery* God describes Mystery Babylon *as a great whore* in Rev 17:1.</u>

- "And there came one of the seven angels which had the seven vials, and talked with me, saying unto me, Come hither; I will shew unto thee the judgment of the ***<u>great whore</u>*** that sitteth upon many waters:" (Rev 17:1)
- "And I gave her space to repent of ***<u>her fornication</u>***; and she repented not. Rev 2:22 Behold, I will cast her into a bed, ***<u>and them that commit adultery with her</u>*** into great tribulation, except they repent of their deeds." (Rev 2:21)

God calls Mystery Babylon the mother of harlots. She has taught *her* fornication, spiritual adultery to her daughter Churches.

- "And upon *her* forehead was a name written, MYSTERY, BABYLON THE GREAT, *THE **MOTHER** OF HARLOTS* AND ABOMINATIONS OF THE EARTH." (Rev 17:5)

- "For true and righteous *are* his judgments: for he hath judged ***<u>the great whore, which did corrupt the earth with *her* fornication</u>***, and hath avenged the blood of his servants at her hand." (Rev 19:2)

God refers to Mystery Babylon as a great whore, which corrupted ***the earth with her (spiritual) fornication*** (going after another other than her husband, the one true God). You may believe Mystery Babylon has not corrupted you or your Church with her fornication and idolatry but God says, she corrupted the earth, not just part of the earth and she truly has. You may not be in Mystery Babylon but you may unknowingly be in one of her daughter Churches that she has corrupted with her spiritual fornication. There is not an organized Church today that she has not corrupted with at least one of her Babylonian doctrines. The majority of God's people are in Mystery Babylon or one of her daughter Churches, *unknowingly* partaking of her sins, the doctrines of Babylon. God divorced Israel for this and is getting ready to judge Mystery Babylon for it.

Israel was actually following the doctrines of Babylon, worshiping Baal, the sun god, also called Tammuz and they worshiped the queen of heaven. "**They made cakes used in the wordhip of the queen of heaven, the goddess Easter**, as early as the days of Cecrops, the founder of Athens – that is, 1500 years before the Christian era." [21] **1500 years before the Virgin Mary, who is now called the queen of heaven.** God's prophets warned them not to do this but they chose to do so any way saying: "...**we will not harken unto thee.** But **we will certainly do whatsoever thing goeth forth out of our own mouth, to burn incense unto the queen of heaven**..." (Jer 44:16,17)

They were committing spiritual adultery. You will see God takes this very seriously. They were God's Wife, just as we are His Bride, His Wife. Mystery Babylon has caused God's people to follow the same doctrines of Babylon, to commit the same spiritual adultery. God calls Mystery Babylon, Mystery Babylon *the great* in Rev 17:5. Mystery Babylon is a great adulterous Church who adopted over 35 Babylonian doctrines and spread the Babylonian doctrines over the earth, that is why she is called a great whore.

The terrible thing is, God's people do not know they are following the Babylonian doctrines, that Mystery Babylon has spread over the earth. That is why her name is called Mystery, because it is a Mystery, hidden, even to the people in Mystery Babylon, that they are following doctrines of Babylon.

You will be shocked at the resemblance of Babylon's trinity: the invisible Father, Nimrod, Nimrod's reincarnation as the son, Tammuz, in the lap of Semiramis, and Semiramis, the goddess of spring, who is called the queen of heaven. There are many historical examples shown in the next section.

In the New testament God tells us, adultery is the only reason acceptable for divorce. In the Old Testament God even divorced His people for this *spiritual adultery* and in the New Testament God is warning His people to come out of Mystery Babylon that they receive not her plagues.

God hates Baal worship. God's people are His wife, so when they follow doctrines of Baal, it is spiritual adultery. He said "shall know whose words shall stand, mine, or theirs" when they said they would burn incense to the queen of heaven (1500 years before the virgin Mary was born), and when they cried for Tammuz, worshiping Tammuz the son, in the door of the house of God, God said: Therefore will I also deal in fury: mine eye shall not spare, neither will I have pity: and though they cry in mine ears with a loud voice, yet will I not hear them. This is serious.

- "18) The children gather wood, and the fathers kindle the fire, and the women knead their dough, **to make cakes to the queen of heaven,** and to pour out drink offerings **unto other gods, that they may provoke me to anger.** 20) **Therefore thus saith the Lord GOD; Behold, mine anger and my fury shall be poured out** upon this place, upon man, and upon beast, and upon the trees of the field, and upon the fruit of the ground; and it shall burn, and shall not be quenched." (Jer 7:18,20)

- "18) And I will persecute them with the sword, with the famine, and with the pestilence, and will deliver them to be **removed to all the kingdoms of the earth**, to be a curse, and an astonishment, and an hissing, and a reproach, **among all the nations whither I have driven them:** 19) **Because they have not hearkened to my words,** saith the LORD, which I sent unto them by my servants the prophets, rising up early and sending *them;* but ye would not hear, saith the LORD." (Jer 29:18,19)

- "15) Then all the men which knew that their wives had ***burned incense unto other gods***, and all the women that stood by, a great multitude, even all the people that dwelt in the land of Egypt, in Pathros, answered Jeremiah, saying, 16) *As for* the word that thou hast spoken unto us in the name of the LORD,

we will not hearken unto thee. 17) But **we will certainly do whatsoever thing goeth forth out of our own mouth, to burn incense unto the queen of heaven,** and to pour out drink offerings unto her, ... 27) Behold, I will watch over them for evil, and not for good: and all the men of Judah that *are* in the land of Egypt **shall be consumed by the sword and by the famine, until there be an end of them. 28)** Yet a small number that escape the sword shall return out of the land of Egypt into the land of Judah, and all the remnant of Judah, that are gone into the land of Egypt to sojourn there, _**shall know whose words shall stand, mine, or theirs.** 29) **And this shall be a sign unto you, saith the LORD, that I will punish you in this place**,_ that ye may know that my words shall surely stand against you for evil:" (Jer 44:15-17,28,29)

- "13) He said also unto me, Turn thee yet again, *and* thou shalt see greater abominations that they do. 14) Then he brought me to **_the door of the gate of the LORD'S house_** which *was* toward the north; and, behold, **_there sat women weeping for Tammuz._** 15) Then said he unto me, Hast thou seen *this,* O son of man? turn thee yet again, *and* thou shalt see greater abominations than these. 16) And he brought me into the inner court of the LORD'S house, and, behold, **at the door of the temple of the LORD,** between the porch and the altar, *were* about **_five and twenty men_**, with their backs toward the temple of the LORD, and their faces toward the east; and **they worshipped the sun toward the east.** 17) Then he said unto me, Hast thou seen *this,* O son of man? Is it a light thing to the house of Judah that **they commit the abominations** which they commit here? for they have filled the land with violence, and have returned to provoke me to anger: and, lo, they put the branch to their nose. 18) **_Therefore will I also deal in fury: mine eye shall not spare, neither will I have pity: and though they cry in mine ears with a loud voice, yet will I not hear them._**" Eze 9:6 "Slay utterly old *and* young, both maids, and little children, and women: but come not near any man upon whom *is* the mark; and begin at my sanctuary. Then they began at the ancient men which *were* before the house." (Eze 8:13-18, 9:6)

God's people are always referred to as a female, as a woman, as a her, because we are God's Bride, His Wife. This is the first thing we need to understand in understanding Mystery Babylon. *Mystery Babylon is God's Wife (a Church)* that has went whoring after Babylonian traditions, adopted over 35 doctrines of Babylon into the Church and spread them over the earth. That is why God's word describes Mystery Babylon as a great whore and her daughters as harlots for following their mother's Babylonian teachings. God is a jealous God. We are God's Bride, His wife. God hates this spiritual adultery and is going to judge Mystery Babylon for it.

- "And there came one of the seven angels which had the seven vials, and talked with me, saying unto me, Come hither; I will shew unto thee the judgment of the **_great whore_** that sitteth upon many waters:" (Rev 17:1)
- "And upon **her** forehead was a name written, **MYSTERY, BABYLON THE GREAT**, THE **MOTHER** OF HARLOTS AND ABOMINATIONS OF THE EARTH." (Rev 17:5)

Rev. 17:3 says: a woman rode on a beast having seven heads. This is more symbolism.
- "So he carried me away in the spirit into the wilderness: and I saw **a woman** sit upon a scarlet coloured beast, full of names of blasphemy, **_having seven heads_** and ten horns." (Rev 17:3)
Rev. 17:9 explains **the seven heads are seven mountains.** [2]
- "And here *is* the mind which hath wisdom. **_The seven heads are seven mountains_, on which the woman sitteth.**" (Rev 17:9)

So God describes Mystery Babylon the Great, as a woman (a Great Church), a great *whore* (A great Church following the *adulterous* doctrines of Babylon), **that sets on (rules from) seven mountains.**

Tiber River (Tiberis)

Vatican

Quirinal Hill (Collis Quirinalis)

Field of Mars (Campus Martius)

Viminal Hill (Collis Viminalis)

Capitoline Hill (Collis Capitolinus)

Esquiline Hill (Collis Esquilinus)

Tiber Island (Insula Tiberina)

Palatine Hill (Collis Palatinus)

Caelian Hill (Collis Caelius)

Aventine Hill (Collis Aventinus)

Servian Wall (Murus Servii Tullii)

The Seven Hills of Rome: 1) Quirinal Hill, 2) Viminal Hill, 3) Capitoline Hill, 4) Esquiline Hill, 5) Palatine Hill, 6) Caelian Hill, 7) Aventine Hill. **The Seven Hills of Rome is the headquarters (called the Vatican) for the Great Roman Catholic Church.** [22]

Please remember I am not the one saying Mystery Babylon sits on (Rules from seven hills) Rome. These are God's descriptions. This may seem very far-fetched but it does fit scripture perfectly. This is a Mystery that can be understood clearly if we look at all of God's scripture clues and all the puzzle pieces.

Note: Some have said that America or New York is Mystery Babylon but America and New York do not fit this scripture clue or the others. God is calling His people out of Mystery Babylon. God is not calling us out of New York or America.

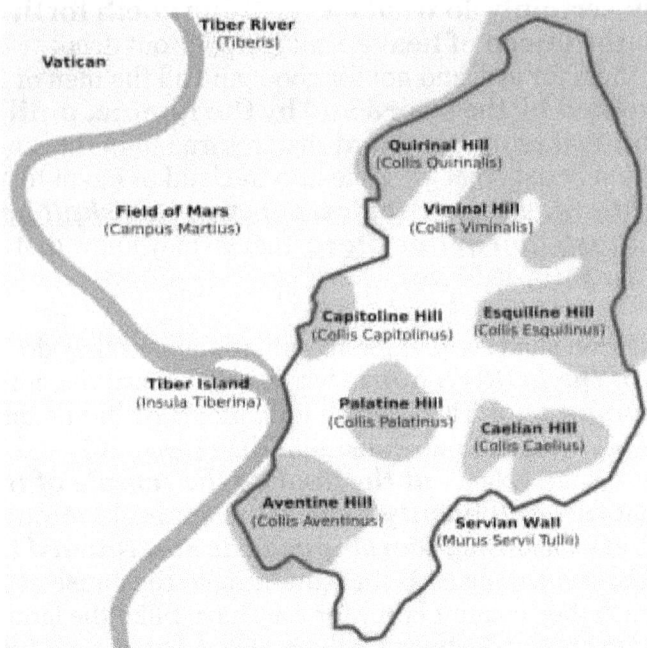

Rev. 17:18 explains that the ***woman is also a great city***.
- "And the woman which thou sawest ***is that great city***, which reigneth over the kings of the earth." (Rev 17:18)

Rome is the great city that sitteth on seven hills, and that has reigned over the kings of the earth, through the Roman Catholic Church.

The next scriptures explain that the great whore (the great adulterous church) has international power and influence over people.

Rev. 17:1 says, "I will show you the judgment of the great whore ***that sitteth on many waters"*** then explains it in Rev 17:15.
- "And there came one of the seven angels which had the seven vials, and talked with me, saying unto me, Come hither; I will shew unto thee the judgment of **the great whore *that sitteth upon many waters:*"** (Rev 17:1)
- "And he saith unto me, ***The waters which thou sawest, where the whore sitteth, are peoples, and multitudes, and nations, and tongues***." (Rev 17:15)

God calls the woman a great whore, (a great adulterous wife, Church (Rev. 17:1) I show 35 adulterous Babylonian doctrines she follows in this chapter, she has international power and influence (Rev 17:15), she is a great city (Rev.17:18), that sits on seven mountains- *hills* (Rev 17:9). Rome is the great city that sits on seven hills, where she reigneth over kings and has influence over the world through the Roman Catholic Church's Headquarters (The Vatican). [2] I'm sorry to say, the Roman Catholic Church continues to fit all God's scripture clues. Please keep reading, for this is an extremely urgent Mystery to understand for God is judging Mystery Babylon in our day and ***all*** the scripture clues that God gave fit perfectly.

Rev.17:5 explains the woman had a name written on her forehead, Mystery Babylon the great...
- "And upon her forehead *was* a name written, **MYSTERY, BABYLON THE GREAT,** and THE MOTHER OF HARLOTS AND ABOMINATIONS OF THE EARTH." (Rev 17:5)

---

[22] https://en.wikipedia.org/wiki/Seven_hills_of_Rome

God calls this Church, **BABYLON THE GREAT, MYSTERY BABYLON THE GREAT** (Because it is a Mystery (It is hidden). It is hidden that she adopted all the Babylonian doctrines and spread them over the earth (Rev 19:2 ***the great whore, which did corrupt the earth with her fornication***).

Rev.17:5 also explains the woman had a name written on her forehead, …. ***the mother of harlots…***

- "And upon her forehead *was* a name written, MYSTERY, BABYLON THE GREAT, and **THE MOTHER OF HARLOTS** AND ABOMINATIONS OF THE EARTH." (Rev 17:5)

The Roman Catholic Church is the only Church that claims to be the Mother Church.

The Roman Catholic Church proclaimed, "We, the Mother Church are opening our arms to all of our daughters to return home." in the 1960's under the Vatican Counsel 2.[15]

At the time of the reformation, many departed from the Catholic Church but they departed taking with them many of their Mother's teachings, taking many Catholic teaching with them, which (you will see) were Babylonian doctrines. This is why God's calls the daughters, harlots, because they have the mother's doctrines, which the mother adopted from Babylon. This is how Mystery Babylon corrupted the earth with her fornications. The next chapter shows historical proof, dates and images, etc.

Rev.17:4 says that the woman, (Mystery Babylon- *the Church*), ***is arrayed in purple and scarlet.***

- "And the woman was ***arrayed in purple and scarlet colour***, and decked with gold and precious stones and pearls, having a golden cup in her hand full of abominations and filthiness of her fornication:" (Rev 17:4)

The two ruling bodies of ***the Roman Catholic Church*** are the Cardinals and the college of the Bishops and Archbishops. ***The Cardinals wear red (scarlet) and the Bishops wear purple.***[2]

[23]

I love the people in the Catholic Church and her daughter Churches. I love them and I don't want them to receive Mystery Babylon's plagues (judgments). She is called Mystery Babylon because it is a Mystery. It has been hidden even from those that are in Mystery Babylon. God is warning His people to come out of Mystery Babylon before He judges her, in Rev. 18:4. I love those in Mystery Babylon. God loves them more than I do.

I know these are terrible revelations, please forgive me but these are very urgent revelations. We must know who Mystery Babylon is that we may heed God's warning to come out of her.

---

[23] https://www.worldslastchance.com/end-time-prophecy/who-is-the-beast.html

In Rev 17:6 God describes Mystery Babylon as drunk with the blood of the saints... (saints here is referring to Christians, those made righteous by the faith in the blood of the Lamb).

- "And I saw the woman drunken with the blood of the saints, and with the blood of the martyrs of Jesus..." (Rev 17:6)

Over 60 million saints, those who have faith in Jesus alone (Christians), have been martyred by the Roman Catholic Church through the last 1500 years. See Fox's Book of Martyrs, it explains in great detail, how the Roman Catholic Church has been drunk with the blood of the saints, if you can bare the terrible details.

The Inquisition

Executioner's block in the Tower of London

[24]

[24]

Urn for heating brands and pokers for torture in The Hague, Netherlands.
Note: Since the doctrine, "Compel them to come in," was developed in the 4th Century by Augustine of North Africa, forced conversion through torture and persecution at the hands of secular authorities was carried out among most Christian nations until the birth of the American Republic. [24]

Mask of the Executioner

[24]

Note: When the papacy reached the height of its power under Pope Innocent III, the monstrous council of the Inquisition was established about the year 1200 A.D. This institution spread throughout Europe, resulting in the death of over 60 million Christians during its bloody history. According to the sure word of God, similar Roman Catholic tribunals and persecutions will reappear before the return of our Lord. (Revelation 12:17; 13:15.) [24]

[24] **This Irish example of a dungeon is typical of those found beneath the medieval church of Europe.**

Darryl Eberhart, ... (as recently as the 1940s we find Roman Catholic Ustashi military units in Croatia, led and urged on by Franciscan priests, monks, and friars, slaughtering from 600,000 to one million innocent Serb Orthodox Christian men, women, elderly, and children – many of the victims being first brutally tortured);[24]

---

[24] http://www.mindserpent.com/American_History/religion/pope/rc_images.html

So according to God's word, Mystery Babylon is:

1) a woman (Rev.17: 1,3,4,6,7,9,18), **a whore** (Rev. 17:1,15,16) - ***God's* people (His Church)** are always described as a woman, ***a her***, because we are His Bride, His Wife. We are described as either a Virgin: Pure and Faithfully following Him or a Whore and a Harlot: Unfaithful, committing *Spiritual Adultery*, *Idolatry*. God describes this woman, this Church as a whore, one who is committing spiritual adultery.

2) The woman, (the Church) sitteth on (rules from) **seven Hills** (Rev 17:3,9). The woman is also **a great city which reigneth over the kings of the earth** (Rev. 17:18) – Rome is the great city of seven hills and the seat of authority for the Roman Catholic Head Quarters where she has reigned over kings.

3) The woman (the Church) sits on waters, - peoples, and multitudes, and nations, and tongues (Rev 17:1,15). **This woman (this Church) has influence over the World** – The Roman Catholic Church has influence over the world through her Head Quarters in Rome, the Vatican.

4) Mystery Babylon, Babylon the GREAT (Rev. 17:5). You will see in this chapter how this woman (this Church), the Roman Catholic Church, adopted over 35 Babylonian sun worship doctrines, so that God calls her Babylon the Great. She spread the Babylonian doctrines over the earth fulfilling Rev 19:2 ***the great whore (Church), which did corrupt the earth with her fornication*** (spiritual fornication-idolatry).

5) According to the word of God, this woman (this Church) is **The Mother of harlots** (Rev.17:5) – The Roman Catholic Church is the only Mother Church. God calls Mystery Babylon the great whore in Rev. 17:1 and calls her daughters harlots because they have the mother's Babylonian's doctrines, that they took with them at the reformation.

6) The woman (the Church) is arrayed in Purple and Scarlet (Rev 17:4) – The Roman Catholic Cardinals wear scarlet (red) and the Bishops wear purple.

7) The woman (the Church) is drunken with the blood of the saints, and with the blood of the martyrs of Jesus (Rev 17:6) – The Roman Catholic Church has killed over 60 Million Christians (saints- those cleansed by the blood of the Lamb) *those who refused her doctrines*.

Mystery Babylon is a Church. According to God's word she is a Mother Church, that sits on (rules from) seven Hills (*the great city of Rome*), is influential over the world from the Vatican in Rome, arrayed in Purple and Scarlet, drunk with the blood of the saints, is called Babylon the Great (because she adopted the Babylon's doctrines of worship), and corrupted the earth with the fornication of these doctrines. But you say, the Roman Catholic Church did not adopt the doctrines of Babylonian worship. And I respond, I will show you 33 of them in the next section called **Quick Overview**.

The Secret of Mystery Babylon

My grandma was a devoted Catholic and others in my family too. I remembered enjoying going to Church with my grandma, eating fish on Fridays, and learning the Apostle's Creed. I had a lot of good memories with my grandma. I love the people in the Catholic Church that's why I have to share the secret of Mystery Babylon now, before the plagues come, before God judges Mystery Babylon. The plagues in Rev. 18:4 are God's judgments. Time is very short. God is calling His people out that they receive not her plagues.

- "... **Come out of her, my people**, *that ye be not partakers of her sins*, and **that ye receive not of her plagues.**" (Rev 18:4)

There were many more examples of secrets of Mystery Babylon but I will only list five here.

- Cardinal Newman lists many examples of things of "pagan origin" which *the papacy brought into the church "in order to recommend the new religion to the heathen:"*... "The use of temples, and these dedicated to particular saints, and ornamented on occasions with branches of trees; incense, lamps, and candles; holy water; asylums [hermitages, monasteries and convents]; **[pagan] holy-days**

..."--Cardinal J. H. Newman, An Essay on the Development of Christian Doctrine, 1920 edition, p.373 [Roman Catholic]. [25]

- "Confiding then in the power of Christianity to resist the infection of evil, and to transmute the instruments and appendages of ***demon worship to an evangelical use*** ... ***the rulers of the church*** from early times were prepared should occasion arise, ***to adopt, or imitate, or sanction the existing rites and customs of the populace.***"- Development of Christian Doctrine, Cardinal Newman. p. 372 [25]

- "... **Pagan festivals dear to the people, reappeared as Christian feasts, and pagan rites were transformed into Christian liturgy** . . . The Christian calendar of saints replaced the Roman 'fasti' [gods]; ancient divinities dear to the people were allowed to revive under the names of 'Christian saints' . . . Gradually the tenderest features of Astarte, Cybele, Artemis, Diana, and Isis were gathered together in the worship of Mary"--Wil Durant, The Age of Faith, 1950, pp. 745-746. [25]

- Two dominant elements brought into Christianity from paganism by Rome were ***Sun worship symbols*** and the religious ***practices of ancient Babylon*** "The solar theology of the Chaldaeans [***Babylonians***], had decisive effect . . . [upon the] final form reached by the religion of the pagan Semites, and following them, by that of ***the Romans*** when [the Roman emperor] Aurelian, the conqueror of Palmyra, had ***raised 'Sol Invictus' [the invincible sun-god] to the rank of supreme divinity*** in the Empire"--The Cambridge Ancient History, vol. 11, pp. 643, 646-647. [25]

- The penetration of the religion of Babylon became so general and well known that Rome was called the "New Babylon." - Faith of our fathers 1917 ed. Cardinal Gibbons, p. 106 [25]

I was astonished. The traditions of the Roman Catholic Church came from Babylon! We just saw God's description of Mystery Babylon fits the Vatican perfectly and the traditions the Roman Catholic Church teaches that are equal to the word of God or higher than the word of God, were actually of pagan origin and are rituals worshiping the Babylonian pagan sun god, the pagan rites were transformed into Christian liturgy. I know it is very hard to believe but continue with me and you will see that it is true and this is still the tip of the ice burg.

This is the secret of Mystery Babylon, that the doctrines of Babylon were adopted into the Church and given Christian names but there is more, much more.

Nimrod built the kingdom of Babylon, a kingdom of false worship, worshiping the sun, the root was actually worshipping Satan. That is why it is so serious and God is warning His people to come out of Mystery Babylon before He judges her. God's word tells us that Satan will deceive the whole world and you will see he truly has.

In Genesis 11:9 the worship of the sun was spread everywhere and in many languages. This is one reason the sun god had many names.

- "Therefore is the name of it called Babel; because the LORD did there confound the language of all the earth: and from thence did the LORD scatter them abroad upon the face of all the earth." (Gen 11:9)

---

[25] http://remnantofgod.org/whoreofbabylon.htm

Other Names For "Nimrod"

ARES	MARS	ODIN
BACCHUS or	CUPID	WODAN,
DIONYSUS	VULCAN	OSIRIS
EROS	MERCURY	TAMMUZ
Hephaestus	PLUTO	EL-BAR meaning
HERMES	NEPTUNE	"God the Son"
PLUTO	JUPITER	MOLECH
(HADES)	SATURN	BAAL, BEL
POSEIDON	LUPERCUS	or BELUS --
ZEUS	MARDUK	meaning "Lord"
KRONOS	NEBO	ATLAS
ABIR	CRONUS	St. VALENTINE
SHAMASH		DAGON --
		the fish-god

The sun god, called Nimrod, Tammuz, Molok, Mithras, Apollo, Zeus, **Baal** and more, are all actually names for worship of one being, *Satan*.

Notice in the list of names for the sun god, Nimrod, that he is called is Baal. The two oldest religions in the world are that of El and Bel (**aka Baal**). [God and Satan]

Bel and Baal are short for Beelzeboul or Baal zebuwb, a name for Satan.

BAAL ZEBUWB OR BEELZEBOUL

#1176 **(Hebrew) Baal Zebuwb,** bah'al zeb-oob; from 1168 and 2070; Baal of (the) fly; Baal-zebub, a special deity of the Ekronites: Baal-Zebub. [27]

Remember when the Pharisees called Yahushua the Messiah Beelzebub (Mat. 10:25) and claimed that He cast out the demons by the prince of demons (Mat. 12:24, 27; Mk. 3:22; Lk. 11:15, 18, 19). [27]

#954 **(Greek) Beelzeboul,** beh-el-zeb-ool'; of Chald. Or. [by parody upon 1176]; dung-god; Beelzebul, **a name of Satan: Beelzebub.** [27]

Notice that Baal and Beel are interchangeable: Beelzebul and Baal Zebuwb, **both are a name for Satan**, and shortened to Bel or Baal, it is still a name for Satan (the devil). Baal from the Hebrew and Bel from the Greek. Notice in the names for **the sun god, Nimrod,** Baal, was listed as one of his names. There it says that Baal, Bel means Lord but Baal or Bel is actually another name for Satan, Lucifer. Lucifer means light bearer or morning star. Our sun is a star. Sun worship is actually worshiping the morning star, Lucifer. The two oldest religions in the world are that of El and Bel (**aka Baal**). [God and Satan]

Lucifer ... according to the KJV-based Strong's Concordance means **"shining one, light-bearer"**...The word *Lucifer* is taken from the Latin Vulgate ... meaning "**the morning star**... Later Christian tradition came to use the Latin word for "morning star", *lucifer*, as a proper name ("Lucifer") for the devil; as he was before his fall. [28]

As I said, Nimrod built the kingdom of Babylon, a kingdom of false worship, the root was actually worshipping Satan. Nimrod was worshipped as a god, the father, reincarnated as Tammuz, the son. Nimrod was not just a mythical god but he was a real person. Nimrod is listed in the genealogy of Noah. He was Noah's great grandson. Nimrod was the son of Cush. Cush was the son Ham and Ham was the son of Noah.

"1) Now these *are* the generations of the **sons of Noah**, Shem, **Ham,** and Japheth: and unto them were sons born after the flood. 6) And the **sons of Ham; Cush**, and Mizraim, and Phut, and Canaan. 8) **And Cush begat Nimrod**: he began to be a mighty one in the earth." **(Gen 10:1,6,8)**

---

[26] https://worldtruth.tv/mystery-babylon-exposed-2/
[27] http://yahushua.net/baalgad.htm
[28] https://en.wikipedia.org/wiki/Lucifer

Shem, one of Noah's sons, was so angered at the rebellion of Nimrod, that he got 70 men together, that still believed in the one true God of the scriptures. Nimrod was killed and his body cut into pieces and took those pieces to all the cities to bring fear to them that they would not commit this rebellion. After Nimrod's death, Nimrod's wife, Semiramis, did not want to lose the power she had shared with Nimrod, and being pregnant made up a story that Nimrod was not dead but ascended and was the sun god and that she was pregnant by Nimrod through the rays of the sun and that her baby, named Tammuz, was the reincarnation of Nimrod. Nimrod's wife, Semiramis, mother of the sun god Tammuz, was worshipped as the Queen of heaven. Shown later, you will see that this was an abomination to God.

Jump ahead to the Roman Empire, it was a world government. The Roman Emperor Constantine I, reigned 306-337AD, a short 300 years after Christ's death. It is said that Constantine professed Christianity. Constantine wanted one united religion for his kingdom. In order to bring the pagans into the Roman Catholic Church, he brought in many of their pagan, Babylonian traditions (sun worship) into the Church, giving them Christian names. Over time all the doctrines of Babylon were adopted into the Catholic Church. **This was a secret. In order to keep the people in the dark, the Vatican even made it against the law for people to have the Bible in their own language.** Many were burned at the stake for having the scriptures or for distributing them in their laungage (shown later in this chapter).

Decree of the Council of Toulouse (1229 C.E.): "We prohibit also that the laity should be permitted to have the books of the Old or New Testament; but we most strictly forbid their having any translation of these books." [29]
Ruling of the Council of Tarragona of 1234 C.E.: "No one may possess the books of the Old and New Testaments in the Romance language, and if anyone possesses them he must turn them over to the local bishop within eight days after promulgation of this decree, so that they may be burned..." [29]
Proclamations at the Ecumenical Council of Constance in 1415 C.E.: Oxford professor, and theologian John Wycliffe, was the first (1380 C.E.) to translate the New Testament into English to "...helpeth Christian men to study the Gospel in that tongue in which they know best Christ's sentence." For this "heresy" Wycliffe was posthumously condemned by Arundel, the archbishop of Canterbury. By the Council's decree "Wycliffe's bones were exhumed and publicly burned and the ashes were thrown into the Swift River." [29]
Fate of William Tyndale in 1536 C.E.: William Tyndale was burned at the stake for translating the Bible into English. According to Tyndale, the Church forbid owning or reading the Bible to control and restrict the teachings and to enhance their own power and importance. [29]

The Vatican did not want people to read the word of God for themselves, otherwise they would see all the unscriptural traditions brought into the Church. Through the dark ages, people either accepted the Roman Catholic doctrines or were tortured and killed (See Foxes book of Martyrs, it tells of millions of deaths, giving extreme details, if you can bear them). With the passing of time and those that stood for scriptural truth, being dead, the pagan traditions of worship, were not only accepted into the Roman Catholic Church but became the bedrock, the foundation of the Catholic Church, the foundation of Christianity itself. Martin Luther, who nailed the 95 Theses on the door of Castle Church in 1517, triggered the Protestant Reformation. [30] At the reformation, when the people left the Roman Catholic Church, starting new Churches, they *unknowingly* took many of the Mother Churches', the Roman Catholic Churches' (Babylonian) doctrines with them, which God hates.

See God's strong word against heathen (Babylonian) worship in Deu 12:2-4 and Jer 10:2-4

- "2) Ye shall utterly destroy all the places, wherein the nations which ye shall possess served their gods, upon the high mountains, and upon the hills, and under every green tree: 3) And ye shall overthrow their altars, and break their pillars, and burn their groves with fire; and ye shall hew down the graven

---

[29] Bernard Starr, author of Jesus Uncensored: Restoring the Authentic Jew
http://www.huffingtonpost.com/bernard-starr/why-christians-were-denied-access-to-their-bible-for-1000-years_b_3303545.html
[30] https://2017.lutheranworld.org/content/martin-luther-131

images of their gods, and destroy the names of them out of that place. 4) **Ye shall not do so unto the LORD your God.**" (Deu 12:2-4)

- "2) **Thus saith the LORD, Learn not the way of the heathen,** and be not dismayed at the signs of heaven; for the heathen are dismayed at them. 3) For the customs of the people *are* vain: for *one* cutteth a tree out of the forest, the work of the hands of the workman, with the axe. 4) They deck it with silver and with gold; they fasten it with nails and with hammers, that it move not." (Jer 10:2-4)

One of the many Babylonian doctrines was tree worship which we just read in Jer 10:3. In Jer. 10:2 God said, "Learn not the way of the heathen". This cutting of the tree and fastening it that it does not move and decking it with silver and gold is talking about what we now call the Christmas tree. You will be amazed when you understand how many of our Christian practices, even Christmas and Easter are rooted in the heathen doctrines of Babylon. Babylon worshiped the sun. The Roman Empire celebrated "the Dies Natalis of Sol Invictus, the Birthday of the Unconquerable Sun, on December 25".[32] The actual date of Christ's birthday is unknown and the Roman Catholic Church chose the Dies Natalis of Sol Invictus, the Birthday of the Unconquerable Sun, December 25, to celebrate Christ's birthday (details shown later in this chapter). Over 35 doctrines of Babylon, (closer to 53), were adopted by Mystery Babylon, the Roman Catholic Church. Mystery Babylon's mixing of heathen doctrines in with worshiping God, is not ok with God. You cannot worship God and Satan at the same time. God is getting ready to judge Mystery Babylon in our generation.

In Rev. 18:4, just before God judges Mystery Babylon, God is calling His people out of Mystery Babylon that we receive not her plagues, that we receive not her judgements. It is very it is imperative that we know who Mystery Babylon is beyond a shadow of a doubt, that we may heed God's warning to come out of her, that we be not judged with her. Many are not aware that God's word (1 Pe 4:17) says that "judgment must begin at the house of God", with His people, and God is calling His people out of Mystery Babylon before He judges her, before He judges this great Church and her daughters that are also partakers of her sins, the Babylonian doctrines.

- "For the time *is come* that **judgment must begin at the house of God**: and if it first begin at us, what shall the end be of them that obey not the gospel of God?" (1Pe 4:17)
- "And I heard another voice from heaven, saying, **Come out of her, my people,** that ye be not **partakers of her sins, and that ye receive not of her plagues**." (Rev 18:4)

Quick Overview,
First a list from God's Word, Scriptures describing Mystery Babylon,
Then a condensed list of list of 33 Babylon's Doctrines Adopted by the Vatican.
Then detailed historic explanations, with pictures.

According to God's word: Mystery Babylon is:
1) **a woman** (Rev.17: 1,3,4,6,7,9,18), **a whore** (Rev. 17:1,15,16) - *God's* **people (His Church)** are always described as a woman, *__a her__*, because we are His Bride, His Wife. We are described as either a Virgin: Pure and Faithfully following Him or a Whore and a Harlot: Unfaithful, committing *Spiritual Adultery, Idolatry*. God describes this woman, this Church as a whore, one who is committing spiritual adultery.
2) The woman, (the Church) sitteth on (rules from) **seven Hills** (Rev 17:3,9). The woman is also **a great city which reigneth over the kings of the earth** (Rev. 17:18) – Rome is the great city of seven hills and the seat of authority for the Roman Catholic Head Quarters where she has reigned over kings.
3) The woman (the Church) sits on waters, - peoples, and multitudes, and nations, and tongues (Rev 17:1,15)**. This woman (this Church) has influence over the World** – The Roman Catholic Church has influence over the world through her Head Quarters in Rome, the Vatican.
4) **Mystery Babylon, Babylon the GREAT** (Rev. 17:5)**.** You will see in this chapter how this woman (this Church), the Roman Catholic Church, adopted over 35 Babylonian sun worship doctrines, so that God calls her

Babylon the Great. She spread the Babylonian doctrines over the earth fulfilling Rev 19:2 ***the great whore (Church), which did corrupt the earth with her fornication*** (spiritual fornication-idolatry).

5) According to the word of God, this woman (this Church) is **The Mother of harlots** (Rev.17:5) – The Roman Catholic Church is the only Mother Church. God calls Mystery Babylon the great whore in Rev. 17:1 and calls her daughters harlots because they have the mother's Babylonians doctrines, that they took with them at the reformation.

6) The woman (the Church) is arrayed in Purple and Scarlet (Rev 17:4) – The Roman Catholic Cardinals wear scarlet (red) and the Bishops wear purple.

7) The woman (the Church) is drunken with the blood of the saints, and with the blood of the martyrs of Jesus (Rev 17:6) – The Roman Catholic Church has killed over 60 Million Christians (saints- those cleansed by the blood of the Lamb).

One of the first websites I saw when I started studying this subject was http://www.remnantofgod.org/whoreofbabylon.htm. They list 53 doctrines that the Vatican (The Roman Catholic Church) adopted from Babylon. This list of Babylonian doctrines that the Roman Catholic Church adopted from Babylon is a very strong confirmation that the Roman Catholic Church truly is Mystery Babylon. I researched 33 of the doctrines from their list and the majority of what I found is in the next section, which has historic details and pictures that will help you understand. The next section has much that you need to know but first the quick over view.

This is a condensed list of the 33 Babylonian Doctrines invented for the worship of the sun god, Adopted by the Vatican that I researched. (34 and 35 are explained in the next two chapters.)

1) **Easter** - The word, Easter comes from the name of a pagan goddess; Eostre, Ostera, or Astarte and ***Ishtar, names for Semiramis of Babylon*** (the first deified queen of Babylon, goddess of the spring). ***Ishtar was pronounced as we pronounce Easter today.*** [31]
"It was at the Council of Nicaea, that the date of Easter was declared to be the first Sunday after the full moon following the spring equinox."[31] The Roman Catholic Church adopted Easter (Ishtar, a name for Semiramis) and set the date on the same day as **Resurrection of Tammuz, the son, the sun god.** Christ's resurrection was not on Easter (Ishtar) Sunday.
Easter Eggs – "According to the Jewish historian Josephus, Nimrod was punished for his rebellion by Shem, one of the sons of Noah." [32]

- (Put to death by Shem) "After Nimrods death his wife claims he did not die but was ascended into heaven and was now the sun god. She, now being the wife of the sun had to make herself a goddess. She told everyone that she had ascended into the heavens and had came back down in a giant egg and landed in the Euphrates River. She then proceeded to turn a bird into an egg laying rabbit. **She proclaimed herself as the queen of heaven.** Her egg became known as ***Ishtar's egg***, or as we call it today *"Easter egg"*."[32]
- **Coloring the Easter Egg**- "Every year the priest of Easter would impregnate virgins on the altar of Easter. The next year those infants would be 3 months old. They would kill the infants and dye eggs in their blood. To this day, certain churches will only allow their eggs to be dyed one color... blood red... This practice is clearly a rehearsal of child sacrifice."[32]

2) **Cross buns** - The history of the hot cross bun goes back to **the Babylonian queen of heaven (*Ishtar*)**... At Athens, about 1500 years before Christ, these buns or sacred bread, were used in the worship of the goddess. [33]

- "The children gather wood, and the fathers kindle the fire, and the women knead their dough, to **make cakes to the queen of heaven,** and to pour out drink offerings unto other gods, that they may provoke me to anger." (Jer 7:18)

---

[31] www.hope-of-israel.org/easter.htm

[32] www.thinknot.net/easter.htm

[33] http://www.remnantofgod.org/easter.htm

3) **Sunrise Service** – Many years after Christ's death, the Catholic church began to associate the tradition with Christ's supposed early morning resurrection in an apparent effort to compromise with their new converts' previously held religious traditions. Yet, when the ladies came to Christ's tomb early Sunday morning, *He wasn't there!* [33] The sunrise service was pagan sun worship.

- "16) ...*and they worshipped the sun...* 17) ... Is it a light thing to the house of Judah that *they commit the abominations* which they commit here?" (Ezek 8:16,17)

4) **Lent** - Tammuz...died at the age of 40 while hunting... To honor him, Semiramis started a tradition of fasting for 40 days – a day for each year of his life.[34] Fasting 40 days was a type of mourning for Tammuz.

- "...thou shalt see greater abominations that they do." (Eze 8:14) "... the LORD'S house which was toward the north; and, behold, there sat women weeping for Tammuz." (Eze 8:13)

5) **Ash Wednesday** - On Ash Wednesday, which marks the beginning of the 40 days of Lent, Catholics receive a t on their forehead. They think it represents the cross. But the top leaders of the Papal Church know that it symbolizes Tammuz.[34]

6) **Christmas** – The New Catholic Encyclopedia, "Inexplicable though it seems, the date of the [Messiah's] birth is not known. The Gospels indicate neither the day nor the month," vol. 3, p. 656. [35] ...the Latin Church, supreme in power, and infallible in judgement, placed it on the 25th of December, the very day on which the ancient Romans celebrated the feast of their goddess Bruma. Pope Julius I was the person who made this alteration" (Clarke's Commentary). [35] This fact is supported by the New International Dictionary of the Christian Church, p. 223: "December 25 was the date of the Roman pagan festival inaugurated in 274 as the birthday of the unconquered sun which at the winter solstice begins again to show an increase in light. [35]
The Catholic Encyclopedia, under Christmas, under the heading: **Natalis Invicti** states: "The well-known solar feast, however, of *Natalis Invicti*, celebrated on 25 December, has a strong claim on the responsibility for our December date." (chosen for Christ's birth) [36]
"The Romans worshiped Tammuz as the sun deity Mithras" [35] Mithras was known as the Sun Deity. His birthday, Natalis solis invicti, means "birthday of the invincible sun." [35]
The Roman Catholic Church picked solar feast of Natalis Invictus, "birthday of the invincible sun.", the sun god Tammuz's, birthday as the date to celebrate our Saviour's birthday. Shown later, Tammuz, the sun god is also called Baal, (Beelzebul and Baal Zebuwb, a name for Satan, and shortened to Bel or Baal. Baal from the Hebrew and Bel from the Greek. [27] THE RE-BIRTH OF THE SUN - DEC 25 Nimrod, Molok, Mithras, Ahura Mazda, Apollo, Zeus, Odin/Woden, and many other names have been used in various times and places. All refer to the same being; the opponent of Yahuah (God): ha shatan. (Satan) [37]
As unbelieveable as it sounds, they picked the sun god, Tammuz birthday, who is also called Baal, a name for Satan, Satan's birthday, to celebrate our Saviour's birthday! Christmas was outlawed in the Boston colony. [37]
There is so much more I have to share with you. Be sure to read all the way to the end to see what has been kept from you.

- **The Christmas Tree**: On the anniversary of his rebirth (the time of the winter solstice, December 25, Semiramis proclaimed that Nimrod would visit the evergreen tree and leave gifts under it. [35] More on this in next section

- **Gift Exchanging**: The Romans worshiped *Tammuz as the sun deity*, as Mithras in a special observance called the Saturnalia... *Tammuz, the Babylonian, counterfeit redeemer.* The Romans kept the Saturnalia in December, at the time of the winter solstice, in honor of the returning sun... "All classes exchanged gifts, the commonest being waxed tapers and clay dolls," says the Encyclopedia Britannica, Eleventh Edition. [35]

- **Saint Nick**: **Santa Claus**: "Old Nick" that was commonly used for Santa Claus has the meaning of Lucifer or Satan in old English. The World English Dictionary says: "Old Nick—a jocular name for Satan." The Cambridge Dictionary entry says: "Old Nick—the Devil—the main evil spirit in the Christian religion." [35]

---

[34] http://christianitybeliefs.org/end-times-deceptions/roman-catholic-church-is-mystery-babylon-lent-tammuz/

[35] https://yrm.org/december-25-birthday-sun/

[36] http://www.newadvent.org/cathen/03724b.htm (under the heading: Natalis Invictus)

[37] http://www.fossilizedcustoms.com/Satan.htm

- **Stockings Hung on the Chimney**: (Odin another name for Nimrod) ...children would place their boots filled with sugar, carrots or straw, near the chimney for Odin's flying horse, Sleipnir, to eat. Odin would then reward those children for their kindness by replacing Sleipnir's food with gifts or candy. [35]

7) **Semiramis of Babylon** [38] Semiramis was the queen of Babylon, and was worshipped by many names throughout the world, in the various languages of the world.

- Some of the names and titles that this 'Queen' is known under are the following: Isis (Egyptian) , Mother of God, Oaster (Easter Eastern-Star), **Ishtar (Babylonian)**, Astarte (syrian), Cybele (Roman), Ashtoreth (Isreal), Goddess of Love, Aphrodite, Venus, Goddess of Hunting and Childbirth, Artemis, Diana (Ephesus), Helena (Greek), Goddess of Crafts, War and Wisdom, Athena, Minerva, Lady of the Towers, Goddess of Growing Things, Demeter, The Holy Ghost, The Supreme Dove (Sumerian), Ceres, Gaea, Terra, Protector of Marriage and Women, the Sister and Wife of Zeus in Greece, the Wife of Jupiter in Rome, Hera, Juno, Goddess of the Hearth, Hestia, Vesta, Wife and Sister of Kronos, Sammurant (Assyrian), Rhea, Queen of Tara, Ish-Tara, the Indian deity, Sami-Rama-isi or Semi-Rama (Vedic) and **Mother Mary (Rome)** [39]

- The mother goddess, Semiramis of Babylon, was worshipped as the Queen of Heaven. The Virgin *Mary, is now worshiped by the Roman Catholic Church as the queen of heaven. In the days of the prophet Jeremiah, the Virgin Mary was not born yet,* they were worshiping Semiramis. See Jeremiah 7:18. We are never told to worship Mary in the word of God. Read all of Jeremiah 7 to see how this angers God.

- "The children gather wood, the fathers kindle the fire, and the women knead dough, to **make cakes to the queen of heaven** and pour out drink offerings to other gods, **to provoke me to anger.**" (Jeremiah 7:18)

8) **Statues of a "Madonna**-Numerous monuments of Babylon shows the Goddess mother Semiramis with her child Tammuz in her arms... [40] (**See statues in the next section**) Remember in Genesis 11:9 God changed their languages and they were scattered throughout the earth for their rebellion. They took with them the pagan worship of the divine mother and god-child with them. This explains why all nations, in one way or another worshipped a divine mother and god child. Statues of Mary (Semiramis) can be found in all Catholic churches holding baby Jesus (Tammuz) in her arm.

- 8) **Thou shalt not make thee any graven image**, or any likeness of anything that is in heaven above, or that is in the earth beneath, or that is in the waters beneath the earth: 9) Thou shalt not bow down thyself unto them, nor serve them: for I the LORD thy God am a jealous God, ... (Deu 5:8,9)

9) **Sunburst monstrance** – is the vessel used by the Roman Catholics for the Eucharistic Host. The Egyptian goddess Isis (another name for Semiramis) with her headdress showing the sun disk within the horns of an Apis bull, symbology which is virtually identical to that of the sunburst monstrance. [41] (See the pictures in next section)

10) **The Roman Catholic Eucharistic Host,** the communion wafer: "the "Wafer" itself is only another symbol of Baal, or the Sun." "There are letters on the wafer ... I. H. S. ... To a Christian these letters are represented as signifying, "*Iesus Hominum Salvator*," "Jesus the Saviour of men." But let a Roman worshipper of Isis (for in the age of the emperors there were innumerable worshippers of Isis in Rome) cast his eyes upon them, and how will he read them? He will read them, of course, according to his own well known system of idolatry: "*Isis, Horus, Seb*," that is, "The Mother, the Child, and the Father of the gods,"--in other words, "The Egyptian Trinity." Can the reader imagine that this double sense is accidental? Surely not." [42]

11) **The Halo** - The disc or circle of light surrounding the head, was found in artistic representations of the great gods and goddesses in Babylon. The disc, and particularly the circle, were well-known symbols of the Sun-divinity. [43] Now paintings of the child (Tammuz/Jesus) and mother (Semiramis/Mary) with halos or the Sun around their heads.

---

[38] http://granddesignexposed.com/indexmystery/2chap/worship.html

[39] http://missionignition.net/lynda/semiramis.php

[40] http://granddesignexposed.com/indexmystery/2chap/worship.html

[41] http://www.aloha.net/~mikesch/monstr.htm

[42] https://philologos.org/__eb-ttb/sect43.htm

[43] http://scripture-keywords.tripod.com/Babylon/07-Rome-Symbolism.html

12) **Title Pontifex Maximus** - name for chief head of the pagan Babylonian system of idolatry. [44] The title Pontifus Maximus literally the High Priest of the Babylonian Cult of Sol Invictus which was simply another incarnation of Mithraism stemming from the worship of Tammuz in Babylon. [45]

13) **The pagan high priest king** is believed to be the incarnate of the Sun god. The Pope proclaims to be Christ's Vicar (replacement of God) here on Earth. [46]

14) **Burning incense and candles** "popular among the Assyrians, Babylonians and Egyptians." [47] It angered God when His people, the Hebrews, disobeyed Him and burned incense to the queen of heaven and Baal.

- "16) ... we will not hearken unto thee. 17) But we will certainly do whatsoever thing goeth forth out of our own mouth, to *burn incense unto the queen of heaven*, and to pour out drink offerings unto her... 17) For the LORD of Hosts ... to *provoke me to anger in offering incense unto Baal*." (Jer 44:16,17)

15) **Chants and Repetitive prayers**

- "But when ye pray, *use not vain repetitions, as the heathen do:* for they think that they shall be heard for their much speaking." (Mat 6:7)

For the Roman Catholic church to proclaim to it's followers you MUST pray the Rosary is openly stating you MUST do exactly the opposite of what the Lord God Almighty has stated in His Word! [48]

16) **Infant baptism, and sprinkling of holy water** - The first essential sacrament Semiramis taught was Baptism by water, "the Priests of Nimrod would 'baptize' new-born infants", "they would become 'born-again' and become members of the Babylonian Mystery Religion." When they passed that law in 416 that every baby in the Roman Empire had to be baptized at the hands of an authorized Roman priest... OR ELSE! Those who disagreed with teaching and rejected it were soon slanderously called "ANABAPTISTS", and they were persecuted without mercy for not conforming. Historian J. M. Carroll declares, "For 30 miles on the road leading out of Rome were stakes with gory heads of ANAPTISTS...." **THE 'HOLY INQUISITION' RESULTED FROM THIS ISSUE OF BABY BAPTISM.** No wonder the Book of Revelation declared in **Revelation 17:6 that this great HARLOT false religion had become 'DRUNK with the BLOOD of the Saints'**...Historian and Bible commentator Sir Robert Anderson estimated that thru out the middle ages OVER 40 MILLION people were murdered and martyred over this one doctrine of INFANT BAPTISM [49]

17) **Human sacrifices burned by fire as offering to appease Sun god** – Children were sacrificed, burned in sacrifice to Moloch, sometimes called Molech. God made special mention of Molech and forbid his worship in II Kings 23:10 and Leviticus 18:21 Opposers of doctrines of the Roman Catholic Church were burned at the stake. [50]

18) **Gargoyles** = a pagan god of protection. Vatican as well as thousands of Catholic churches have gargoyles on their roofs for 'protection' [51]

19) **The Solar Wheel** represents the Babylonian Sun god. *St Peter's square has largest solar wheel on planet.* [51]

20) **The OBELISK**, the Egyptian obelisk was worshipped as the dwelling place of the sun god. [41] St. Peter's square, and note that around the obelisk, at the center of the huge eight-point sun wheel, is a smaller four-pointed sun wheel, the same symbol as found on the altar stone in the temple of Baal in Hatzor! [41] Finally, *this obelisk within the circle in St. Peter's Basilica was dedicated on the Satanic holiday*, April 30, 1586 [52]

---

[44] http://www.sabbathcovenant.com/creationcriesout/HowRomeSunWorship.htm

[45] http://amazingdiscoveries.org/S-deception_Pontifex_Maximus_Babylon#_

[46] http://www.remnantofgod.org/whoreofbabylon.htm

[47] https://grandislanddiaconate.wordpress.com/2012/02/22/why-is-incense-used-during-mass/

[48] http://jesus-is-savior.com/False%20Religions/Roman%20Catholicism/blasphemy.htm

[49] http://jesus-is-savior.com/False%20Doctrines/infant_baptism_exposed.htm

[50] http://come-and-hear.com/editor/br_3.html

[51] http://www.remnantofgod.org/whoreofbabylon.htm

[52] http://vaticannewworldorder.blogspot.com/2012/04/roman-catholic-sun-worship-lucifer-sun.html

21) **The Serpent** - Nimrod's victory over death through the power of the serpent. [53] Symbol of serpent on numerous Catholic Church in door handles, Papal crests, etc. [51] and [54] Serpent is another name for the Devil or Satan.

- "And the great dragon was cast out, that old serpent, called the Devil, and Satan, which deceiveth the whole world: he was cast out into the earth, and his angels were cast out with him." (Rev 12:9)
- "And he laid hold on the dragon, that old serpent, which is the Devil, and Satan, and bound him a thousand years," (Rev 20:2)

22) **Demi-gods staff with serpent** - Pope carries exact same staff (serpent crosiers). Serpent crosiers were commonly carried by bishops and high Catholic Church officials during the Middle Ages. ... it actually can be traced to the divining staff or augur of Pontifex Maximus of ancient Rome who inherited it from the priests of Babylon. [55]

23) **The three finger Trident Salute** - Hand gestures in the form of a trident found depicted in Jupiter, Buddah, Appollo, Hindu diety's, as well as "votive hands" in pagan temples [51] Actually is a Satanic hand sign. See images in the next section. (Now called the salute to the Trinity.) [51]

24) **Oanne, Babylonian fish-god (half man half fish)** was depicted by Pagan high priests by wearing a fish head mitre (head dress) ...[51] Mitres are worn by all Popes of Catholicism. Compare images in next section.

25) **Sun Worship symbols** of the "Unicorn, Peacock, and Phoenix" to signify some of their sun gods [51] [56] are used by the Roman Catholic Church.

26) **Carvings of (fauns or satyrs)** depicting a horned, hoofed-god were a common feature in all Sun Worship churches... among the most sacred items in the Vatican treasury, beneath St. Peter's Basilica. [56]

27) **The evil eye**, the "eye of Osiris" can be found all over Egyptian temples. The sun god, Nimrod was known in Egypt as Osiris, you can see *many* examples of the eye of Osiris in the Catholic Church. (See pictures in next section) [57]

28) **The Babylonian multi-level crown of the high Pagan priest** was first worn by old Babylonian gods in 1800BC, it is also the Popes crown. [51] This crown is inscribed in Latin with the words: VICARIUS FILII DEI which means in place of the Son of God. *Anti can mean in place of*. VICARIUS FILII DEI means in place of Christ, another way of saying antichrist. VICARIUS FILII DEI equals 666 (the mark of the beast) in Roman Numerals (shown in the last section of this chapter).

- "Here is wisdom. Let him that hath understanding count the number of the beast: for it is the number of a man; and his number *is* Six hundred threescore *and* six." (Rev 13:18)

29) **Quetzalcoatl's sacred heart**. Quetzalcoatl was lord of life and death in the Aztec and Toltec culture. The sacred heart was also used in pagan mysteries of *Osiris*, Vishnu, and *Bel*. [56] Osiris another name for Nimrod. Bel is another name for Satan, shown later in this chapter. The flaming hearts found on Catholic images of Mary and Jesus have no Christian origin. [56]

Mystery Babylon has put in their images of Jesus (Tammuz) and Mary (Semiramis), the sacred heart of Quetzalcoatl's, the sun god's ray glowing behind them and the three finger Trident Satanic hand sign that was brought from Babylon. Must see images in the next section.

There were a lot more but I'll mention just a few more:

30) The Midsummer festival of the Sun Worship was held on June 24 of each year (Summer Solstice), the nativity of John the Baptist is celebrated on June 24th. [51] (Remember, the Roman Catholic Church also adopted Easter (Ishtar) and set it as the same date as the resurrection of Tammuz. And set Christmas on December 25, the date the Romans worshiped Tammuz, the sun god's birthday, Natalis solis invicti, means "birthday of the invincible sun.)

[53] https://www.facebook.com/Zionians4Christ/photos/a.426638267420098.1073741825.404690029614922/912256952191558/?type=3&hc_ref=PAGES_TIMELINE

[54] http://amazingdiscoveries.org/albums?view=album&code=SerpentDragonSymbols#_

[55] http://www.markbeast.org/mark-beast-paganism.html

[56] http://www.mindserpent.com/American_History/religion/pope/rc_images.html

[57] http://vaticannewworldorder.blogspot.com/2012/03/r-eligious-symbols-religion-false.html

31) The assumption of Semiramis who became the mother goddess of all Sun Worship, The assumption of Mary is August 15th. [51] In 1950 A.D. Pope Pius XXI adopted the Pagan belief and proclaimed the assumption of Mary (Bodily ascension to Heaven without dying) to be Catholic doctrine. [135]

32) The resurrection of Tammuz at Easter and the *procession of graven images* during holy week. [51]
In ancient Babylonia, "each year, during the celebration of the great New Year Festival, the images of the city's deities were carried out through the **Ishtar Gate** and along the 'Processional Way'" [136]

33) Necromancy (Talking to the dead) [51] Mysticism (Novenas (prayers) to the dead) [51]
Necromancy, the Babylonian belief of the dead visiting the living.

- "If a person turns to mediums and necromancers, ***whoring*** after them, I will set my face against that person and will cut him off from among his people." (Leviticus 20:6)
- "And the soul that turneth after such as have familiar spirits, and after wizards, to go a ***whoring*** after them, I will even set my face against that soul, and will cut him off from among his people." (Lev 20:6)

Notice God calls this speaking to the dead, whoring. This is not physically whoring. This is spiritual whoring, spiritual adultery. God divorced Israel for this spiritual adultery in Jer 3:8. God's people are His wife and if we are fallowing the false doctrines of Mystery Babylon we are committing this whoring that God judges Mystery Babylon for.

- "And there came one of the seven angels which had the seven vials, and talked with me, saying unto me, Come hither; I will shew unto thee the judgment of ***the great whore*** that sitteth upon many waters:" (Rev 17:1)
- "And upon her forehead *was* a name written, **MYSTERY, BABYLON THE GREAT, THE MOTHER OF HARLOTS** AND ABOMINATIONS OF THE EARTH." (Rev 17:5)

It is clear, God wants us to know beyond a shadow of a doubt, who Mystery Babylon is. The Roman Catholic Church is the only one that fits all the scripture clues, the descriptions that God has given us, of Mystery Babylon in His word and the Roman Catholic Church adopted more than *35 traditions from Babylon into the Church*. She adopted so many of Babylons traditions that God calls this Church, "BABYLON THE GREAT" in Rev. 17:5. In Rev. 18:4 God is calling His people out of her, that we be not partakers of her sins, that we receive not her plagues, that we receive not her judgments. Remember God has not judged yet in Rev. 18:4. It has been the great wrath of the devil so far for he knows his time is short. Remember God's word says in 1 Pe 4:17 judgment must start at the house of God. He is starting with the house of God, the Church, named Mystery Babylon and He calling His people out of her that we receive not her plagues, her judgments. There is a specific way, we need to come out of Mystery Babylon. I'll show you precisely through God's word in the upcoming chapters.

Babylon's Doctrines of the Pagan Sun God.

Nimrod was worshiped as the Sun God and his wife, Semiramis was the Moon Goddess.
You see the rays of the sun around his head and the moon above Semiramis' head.

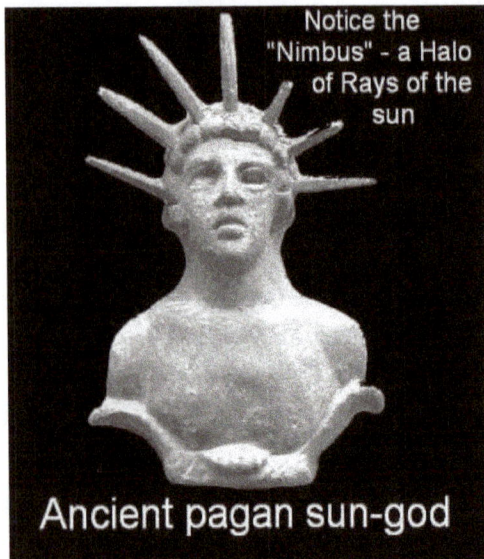

Notice the "Nimbus" - a Halo of Rays of the sun

Ancient pagan sun-god

58

59

Semiramis shared power with Nimrod and declared herself the "Queen of Heaven."
After Nimrod was killed, Semiramis claimed to have an *immaculate conception* of Nimrod's son,
(by the rays of the sun) **whom she named Tammuz, and claimed he was the reincarnation of Nimrod.** The above picture of Tammuz, (the reincarnation of the Sun god Nimrod), sits in the lap of Semiramis, These two pictures show the Babylonian Trinity: The Father, Son, and Queen of Heaven. They are known over the world by many names.

THE PAGAN SUN GOD BAAL, (NIMROD)
known by other names:
Lord of Heaven, Baal in Lebanon, El in Phoenicians, Belus in Babylon, Jupiter in Rome, Ra in Egypt, Vishnu in India, Pan-ku in China, Teotl in Mexico, Odin in Scandinavia

THE PAGAN SUN GOD BAAL, (NIMROD)
Reborn as TAMMUZ also known as:
Tammuz in Lebanon, Bacchus in Phoenicians, *Tammuz in Babylon*, Hercules in Assyria, Dionysus in Greece, Attis in Rome, Osiris, Horis in Egypt, Krishna in India, Yi in China, *Quetzalcoatl in Mexico*, Balder in Scandinavia

Semiramis, Nimrod's wife, and mother of Tammuz, was also known by many names:
Isis (Egyptian), Oaster (Easter Eastern-Star), Ishtar (Babylonian), Astarte (syrian), Cybele (Roman), Ashtoreth (Isreal), Diana (Ephesus), Helena (Greek), The Supreme Dove (Sumerian), The Sister and Wife of Zeus in Greece, The Wife of Jupiter in Rome, Sammurant (Assyrian), Rhea, Queen of Tara, Ish-Tara, the Indian deity, Sami-Rama-isi or Semi-Rama (Vedic) and Mother Mary (Rome)

---

58 https://www.pinterest.com/pin/255368241341291122/
59 http://a-voice-in-wilderness.blogspot.com/2010/04/who-is-this-woman.html

45

Now detailed explanations and historic pictures for 33 of Babylon's Doctrines Adopted by the Catholic Church:

Doctrines INVENTED FOR THE PAGAN SUN GOD BAAL

On Easter we celebrate the resurrection of Jesus (Yeshua) our Saviour but here is the origin of the word Easter and how the date to celebrate Easter was set.

- **Easter** - The word, Easter comes from the name of a pagan goddess; Eostre, Ostera, or Astarte and **Ishtar, names for Semiramis of Babylon Easter (the first deified queen of Babylon,** goddess of the spring). **Ishtar was pronounced as we pronounce Easter today.** Ralph Woodrow in Babylon Mystery Religion [31]
- **Easter (Ishtar) was called Ashtoreth by Israel.**
- GOD CALLS EASTER EVIL: "And the children of Israel did *evil* in the sight of the Lord...And they forsook the Lord, and served Baal and **Ashtaroth** [Easter]" (Judges 2:11, 13)[31]
- "...*put away* the strange gods and *Ashtaroth* from among you, and prepare your hearts unto the *Lord*, and *serve him only*...Then the children of Israel *did* put away Baalim and Ashtaroth, and *served the Lord only*" (1 Samuel 7:3-4). [31]
- Search through the Bible and you will find no evidence that either the Messiah, the apostles, or the New Testament Church ever observed Easter Sunday. Admittedly, there is one verse in the King James Version of the Bible which mentions "Easter." In that verse "Easter" is a flagrant mistranslation! The original Greek word used in Acts 12:4 is pascha meaning "Passover." Modern translations clear up this difficulty by translating the word properly. [31]
- But if the early Christians did not celebrate Easter, then what did they celebrate? Why did early translators mistakenly translate a word meaning Passover as "Easter"? Here is the answer. The Passover was a solemn holy day in ancient Israel (see Exodus 12). Israel's God "passed over" the enslaved Israelites and slew the firstborn children of their enemies -- of Pharaoh and the Egyptians. The Passover was commemorated every year in the spring on the 15th of the Hebrew month Nisan, in the evening, by eating roast lamb and herbs (see Exodus 12). This was a statute instituted for observance forever (Exodus 12: 14, 24). [31]
- In the days of the Messiah, the Jews still observed the Passover. Yeshua and his disciples observed it. This solemn holy day is mentioned by name 48 times in the Old Testament, and 28 times in the New Testament. [60]

Doctrines of Babylon Adopted by THE VATICAN

- Constantine presided over the Council of Nicaea A.D. 325 at which the "Easter question" was taken up for settlement. It was at the Council of Nicaea that the date of Easter was declared to be the first Sunday after the full moon following the spring equinox. [31]
- Semiramis was goddess of the spring. This is why they set the date the first Sunday after the full moon following the spring equinox. [60] This is not the date true of resurrection of our Lord.
- Remember (Mat 12:39-40) "there shall no sign be given to it, but **the sign of the prophet Jonas**: 40) For as Jonas was three days and three nights in the whale's belly; **so shall the Son of man be three days and three nights in the heart of the earth**."
- To be crucified on Good Friday and risen on Easter Sunday only equals two days.
- Roman Emperor Constantine had been a devoted worshipper of the sun most of his life. Pagans began to flock into the Church in droves. **They kept the same pagan days and performed the same pagan rituals, but now they did it to "Christ" instead of to Astarte or Tammuz!** [31] (Astarte another name of Ishtar, i.e. Semiramis the Babylonian Queen of Heaven)

Doctrines INVENTED FOR THE PAGAN SUN GOD BAAL

- **There was an ancient pagan custom of holding a sunrise service** in the spring to worship the risen sun-god, Baal, Tammuz, or Nimrod! ...**the false savior Tammuz was worshipped with various spring rites.**

- **The Church celebrates at <u>sunrise</u>** not realizing this is another pagan ritual of **Babylon worship to the <u>sun god</u> Tammuz** (Christ's resurrection was not actually on Easter Sunday, just as Christ's birth was not actually on Christmas day.)
- "16) **...and they worshipped the sun**... 17) ... Is it a light thing to the house of Judah that they commit the abominations which they commit here? ... 18) **Therefore will I also deal in fury: mine eye shall not spare, neither will I have pity**: *and though they cry in mine ears with a loud voice, yet will I not hear them*." **(Ezek. 8:16,17,18)**
- "Thus saith the LORD, Learn not the way of the heathen..." **(Jer 10:2)**
- **Easter Eggs -Named after the goddess of Babylon, Ishtar:** According to the Jewish historian Josephus, Nimrod was punished for his rebellion by Shem, one of the sons of Noah. He cut Nimrod's body into many pieces and sent it to the surrounding people as a warning against idolatry. Nimrod's wife Semiramis, the Queen of Babylon, collected all the parts of his body except for his penis. After Nimrods death his wife claims he did not die but was ascended into heaven and was now the sun god. She, now being the wife of the sun had to make herself a goddess. She told everyone that she had ascended in to the heavens and had come back down in a giant egg and landed in the Euphrates River. She then proceeded to turn a bird into an egg laying rabbit. She proclaimed herself as the queen of heaven. Her egg became known as Ishtar's egg, or as we call it today "Easter egg". [32]
- **Coloring the Easter Egg**- Child Sacrifice: At Babel, when the language was confused the names of the gods changed but refer to the same "gods". Every year the priest of Easter would impregnate virgins on the altar of Easter. The next year those infants would be 3 months old. They would kill the infants and dye eggs in their blood. To this day, certain churches will only allow their eggs to be dyed one color... blood red. I'm sure they have no idea why or they fabricate something about being symbolic of new birth in the blood of Jesus. This practice is clearly a rehearsal of child sacrifice. [32]
- Admits the Encyclopedia Britannica: The egg as a symbol of fertility and of renewed life goes back to the ancient Egyptians and Persians, who had also the custom of colouring and eating eggs during their spring festival (article, "Easter"). [31]
- Thus eating Easter eggs is actually a modern form of participation in ancient spring fertility rites, and the worship of the goddess of fertility, "Easter"! [31]
- The Romans called the name of this goddess of sexual fertility "Venus," and it is from this name that we derive the modern English words "venereal" and "venereal disease." [31]
- **Easter Bunny Rabbits:** This rapidly breeding and multiplying animal was another ancient symbol of fertility. [31]
- **Cross buns:** The "buns," known too by that identical name, **were used in the worship of the queen of heaven, the goddess Easter**, as early as the days of Cecrops, the founder of Athens -- **that is, 1500 years before the Christian era**. [60]
- "18)The children gather wood, and the fathers kindle the fire, and the women knead their dough, **to make cakes to the queen of heaven,** and to pour out drink offerings **unto other gods, that they may provoke me to anger.** 20) **Therefore thus saith the Lord GOD; Behold, mine anger and my fury shall be poured out** upon this place, upon man, and upon beast, and upon the trees of the field, and upon the fruit of the ground; and it shall burn, and shall not be quenched." (Jer 7:18,20)

[61] Easter Hot Cross Buns, Named after Easter, Ishtar, Semiramis the Babylonian goddess.

---

[60] http://www.bibletruth.cc/Easter.htm#Hot_Cross_Buns
[61] http://endrtimes.blogspot.it/2012/04/pagan-roots-of-easter.html

Doctrines INVENTED FOR THE PAGAN SUN GOD BAAL

- Tammuz...died at the age of 40 while hunting... To honor him, Semiramis started a tradition of fasting for 40 days – a day for each year of his life. [34]
- According to the legend, when he was slain, he went into the underworld and couldn't be brought forth unless the whole world wept for him. Through the weeping of his mother Easter, or Semiramis, he was mystically revived, his resurrection symbolized by the budding of new vegetation in the spring. Each year the pagan spring festival celebrated this resurrection story. [31]

Doctrines of Babylon Adopted by THE VATICAN

Lent came from Babylon, 40 days of fasting, one day for each of the 40 years of Tammuz life. Fasting is a way of mourning, weeping for Tammuz for 40 days.

- On Ash Wednesday, which marks the beginning of the 40 days of Lent, Catholics receive a t on their forehead. They think it represents the cross. But the top leaders of the Papal Church know that it symbolizes Tammuz. [34]
- "13) He said also unto me, *Turn thee yet again, and thou shalt see greater abominations* that they do. 14) Then he brought me to the door of the gate of the LORD'S house which was toward the north; and, behold, *there sat women weeping for Tammuz*." (Eze 8:13,14)
- So God clearly detests the worship of Tammuz of Babylon... And the observance of Lent is clearly a representation of worshiping Tammuz of Babylon. [34]

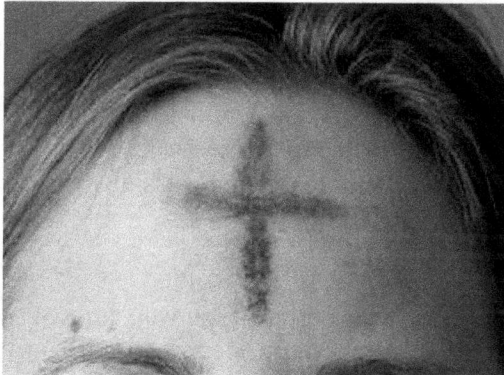

- **The Vatican adopted the Easter Traditions from Babylonian Traditions:**
  1) The name Easter came straight from the Babylonian goddess and Queen of Babylon, Ishtar. The pronunciation of Ishtar is still the same.
  2) Sun-rise Service came from Babylon to worship the Sun-god Tammuz.
  3) Ash Wednesday, Putting the t, the sign of Tammuz on their forehead.
  4) Lent came from Babylon, 40 days of fasting, one day for each of the 40 years of Tammuz life.
  5) The Easter egg coloring is a ritual straight from Babylon's child sacrifices.
  6) The Easter Bunny is another symbol for fertility from Babylon.
  7) The Cross Bun is worship of the queen of heaven, that came straight from Babylon.

  This mixing the worship of the Pagan god, Tammuz, the sun god, the first false savior, with the worship of the one true God is an abomination to the LORD.

- "and they worshipped the sun" 17) "they commit the abominations" 18) "and though they cry in mine ears with a loud voice, *yet* will I not hear them." (Ezek. 8:16,17,18)

Idolatry, i.e. **Spiritual Adultery is the reason God divorced His people.**

- "And I saw, when for all the causes whereby backsliding Israel committed adultery I had put her away, and given her a bill of divorce; yet her treacherous sister Judah feared not, but went and played the harlot also." (Jer.3:8)

Doctrines INVENTED FOR THE PAGAN SUN GOD BAAL

The reincarnation of Nimrod, **the sun god, Tammuz**, was also called Mithras. His birthday, Natalis solis invicti, **birthday of the invincible sun was December 25th.**

- The Romans worshiped Tammuz as <u>the sun deity</u> Mithras [35]
- Mithras was known as the Sun Deity. His birthday, Natalis solis invicti, means "birthday of the invincible sun." It came on December 25 [35]

Doctrines of Babylon Adopted by THE VATICAN

The birthday of Christ Jesus was unknown. The Vatican placed the birthday of our Saviour on December 25th. December 25th was the date inaugurated as <u>the birthday of the Unconquered Sun, Natalis solis invicti, the pagan feast day of Saturnalia, also called Brumalia (Bruma)</u>, sun worship that originated in Babylon, a feast of the renewal of the sun.

- Saturnalia was instituted by Romulus under the name Brumalia (Bruma) And so <u>the church established the birthday of the Savior to coincide with the heathen feast day.</u> "...the <u>Latin Church,</u> supreme in power, and infallible in judgement, <u>placed it on the 25th of December,</u> the very day on which the ancient Romans celebrated the feast of their goddess Bruma. <u>Pope Julius I was the person who made this alteration</u>" (Clarke's Commentary). [35]
- This fact is supported by the <u>New International Dictionary of the Christian Church</u>, p. 223: "<u>December 25</u> was the date of the Roman pagan festival inaugurated in 274 as <u>the birthday of the unconquered sun</u> which at the winter solstice begins again to show an increase in light. [35] "There is no historical evidence that our [Savior's] birthday was celebrated during the apostolic or early post-apostolic times," Christmas, p. 47, The New Schaff-Herzog Encyclopedia of Religious Knowledge. [35]
- The New Catholic Encyclopedia, "Inexplicable though it seems, the date of the [Messiah's] birth is not known. The Gospels indicate neither the day nor the month," vol. 3, p. 656. [35]

The nativity of the Son, Christmas Dec 25

The Catholic Encyclopedia under Christmas states: "The well-known solar feast, however, of Natalis Invicti, celebrated on 25 December, has a strong claim on the responsibility for our December date." (for Christ's birth) [62]

"In the fifth century the western church [Roman Catholic] ordered it to be celebrated on the day of the Roman Feast of the birth of Sol [the sun]. [63]

... Pope Julius I was the person who made this alteration" (Clarke's Commentary). [35]

[64]

[65]

---

[62] http://www.newadvent.org (In The Catholic Encyclopedia first under C for Christmas, then under the heading: Natalis Invictus)
[63] http://assemblyofyahweh.com/wp-content/uploads/2015/03/Is-Our-Saviors-Birth-the-Origin-of-Christmas.pdf
[64] http://www.mindserpent.com/American_History/introduction/footnotes/ft_sol_invictus_001.html
[65] http://thetruthandthetruthalone.blogspot.co.uk/2009/01/ancient-romes-pagan-religion.html

The Truth of Christmas and Easter:

- The Roman Catholic Church set Yeshua (Jesus Christ) the Son's birthday, on the birthday of the Unconquered Sun, Natalis solis invicti.
- The celebration of Passover that God commanded to be observed forever (to celebrate the Lamb of God-that God put on flesh and gave His life to save us) was mixed with the pagan Ishtar (Easter). Ishtar being the goddess of the spring, the Roman Catholic set the date the first Sunday after the full moon following the spring equinox.
- The 40 days before Easter start with a T for Tammuz put on Catholic's foreheads called Ash Wednesday, (Semiramis started the fast for each day of Tammuz life). Ishtar (Easter) a celebration of our Saviour's resurrection mixed with Nimrod the sun god reborn as Tammuz.
- All the pagan traditions of the birth of the sun and of Ishtar were kept but the names were changed to Christmas and Easter.
- These alone are a great deception that has been put on the Christian world but there is so much more that needs to be known.

Other Names For "Nimrod" [66]

ARES	MARS	ODIN
BACCHUS or	CUPID	WODAN,
DIONYSUS	VULCAN	OSIRIS
EROS	MERCURY	TAMMUZ
Hephaestus	PLUTO	EL-BAR meaning
HERMES	NEPTUNE	"God the Son"
PLUTO	JUPITER	MOLECH
(HADES)	SATURN	BAAL, BEL
POSEIDON	LUPERCUS	or BELUS --
ZEUS	MARDUK	meaning "Lord"
KRONOS	NEBO	ATLAS
ABIR	CRONUS	St. VALENTINE
SHAMASH		DAGON --
		the fish-god

This is so important to be understood, that I must repeat it:

The sun god is called by many names: Nimrod, Tammuz, Molok, Mithras, Apollo, Zeus, **Baal** and more. They are all actually names for worship of one being, *Satan*.

Notice in the names listed for the sun god Nimrod is Baal.
The two oldest religions in the world are that of El and Bel (**aka Baal**). [God and Satan]

BAAL ZEBUWB OR BEELZEBOUL

#1176 **(Hebrew)** <u>Baal Zebuwb</u>, bah'al zeb-oob; from 1168 and 2070; Baal of (the) fly; Baal-zebub, a special deity of the Ekronites: Baal-Zebub. [27]
Remember when the Pharisees called Yahushua the Messiah Beelzebub (Mat. 10:25) and claimed that He cast out the demons by the prince of demons (Mat. 12:24, 27; Mk. 3:22; Lk. 11:15, 18, 19).
#954 **(Greek)** <u>Beelzeboul</u>, beh-el-zeb-ool'; of Chald. Or. [by parody upon 1176]; dung-god; Beelzebul, <u>a name of Satan</u>: Beelzebub. [27]

Notice that Baal and Beel are interchangeable: Beelzebul and Baal Zebuwb, **a name for Satan**, and shortened to Bel or Baal, it is still a name for Satan (the devil). Baal from the Hebrew and Bel from the Greek. Notice in the names for **the sun god, Nimrod,** Baal, was listed as one of his names. It says that Baal, Bel means Lord

---

[66] https://worldtruth.tv/mystery-babylon-exposed-2/

but Baal or Bel, is actually another name for Satan, Lucifer. Lucifer means light bearer or morning star. Our sun is a star. Sun worship is actually worshiping the morning star, Lucifer. The two oldest religions in the world are that of El and Bel (**aka Baal**). [God and Satan]

The Roman Catholic Church picked the **solar feast of Natalis Invictus, "birthday of the invincible sun,"** i.e. the sun god, Nimrod's birthday, who is also called **Baal**, a name for Satan. i.e. they chose Satan's birthday, to celebrate our Saviour's birth.

"The day was not one of the early feasts of the Christian church. In fact the observance of birthdays was condemned as a heathen custom repugnant to Christians," The American Book of Days, by George W. Douglas. [35]

Another reference tells us: Christmas was outlawed in the Boston colony [37]:

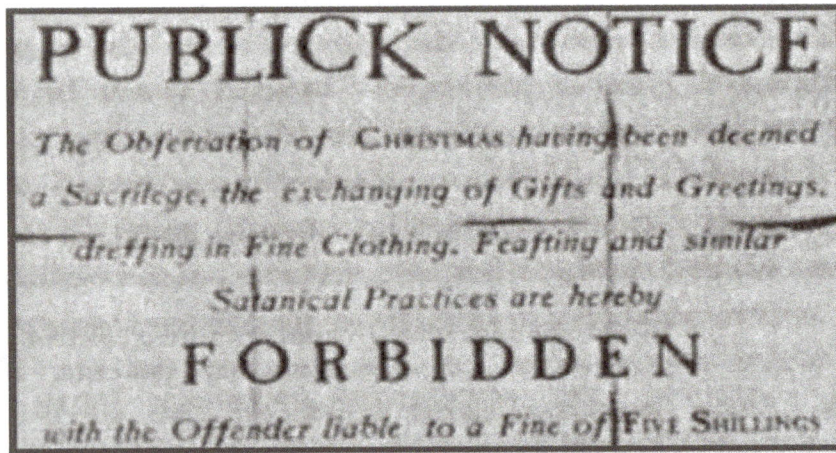

PUBLICK NOTICE

The Obfervation of Christmas having been deemed a Sacrilege, the exchanging of Gifts and Greetings, dreffing in Fine Clothing, Feafting and similar Satanical Practices are hereby

FORBIDDEN

with the Offender liable to a Fine of Five Shillings

17th CENTURY PURITAN PUBLIC NOTICE
CHRISTMAS
A SATANIC PRACTICE
TORAH INSTITUTE   TORAHZONE.NET

[37] This reference explains: In the year 525, Dionysus Exiguus (Dennis the Little) came to Rome from Scythia. He was a "monk" ... Coming upon the time of the Solstice festival celebrating the birthday of the sun, he witnessed all Rome in revelry. Reasoning that it was to be impossible to stand in the way of the frenzied fervor, he sought to "revise" the meaning for it by claiming it to be the celebration of the birth of the Messiah, not the Pagan sun idol, Mithras (Satan) -- thus justifying it by adopting this satanic ceremony into "Christianity" (violating Deut. 12:30,31). [37]

- **Syncretism** is the combining of different, often contradictory beliefs, while blending practices of various schools of thought. Syncretism involves the merger and analogizing of several originally discrete traditions, especially in the theology and mythology of religion, thus asserting an underlying unity and allowing for an inclusive approach to other faiths... [67]
- The **Syncretism**, combining of the worship of the sun, Tammuz the sun god, by God's people, in His house is an abomination to the LORD, so serious that God will not have pity and will not hear His people's cry. (See Eze 8:14-18 below)
- "14) Then he brought me to **the door of the gate of the LORD'S house** which was toward the north; and, behold, **there sat women weeping for Tammuz**. 15) Then said he unto me, Hast thou seen this, O son of man? turn thee yet again, *and thou shalt see greater abominations than these.* 16) And he brought me into the inner court of the LORD'S house, and, behold, at the door of the temple of the LORD, between the porch and the altar, were about five and twenty men, with their backs toward the temple of the LORD, and their faces toward the east; **and they worshipped the sun toward the east.** 17) Then he said unto me, Hast thou seen this, O son of man? *Is it a light thing to the house of Judah that they commit the abominations which they commit here?* for they have filled the land with violence, and have returned to provoke me to anger:... 18) *Therefore will I also deal in fury: mine eye shall not spare, neither will I have pity: and though they cry in mine ears with a loud voice, yet will I not hear them.*" (Eze 8:14-18)

[67] https://en.wikipedia.org/wiki/Syncretism

Doctrines INVENTED FOR THE PAGAN SUN GOD BAAL

The Christmas Tree: Fir trees were always green, symbolic of life… They were often set on fire to portray and beckon back the sun, hence the modern practice of stringing trees with Christmas lights and round bulbs and balls. Ultimately, the Christmas evergreen springs from that old Babylonian, Nimrod. It represents the resurrected and reincarnated man-deity. "Now the Yule Log is the dead stock of Nimrod, deified as the sun god, but cut down by his enemies; the Christmas tree is Nimrod redivivus – the slain god come to life again," *The Two Babylons*. p. 98. He was reborn as his son Tammuz. [35]

On the anniversary of his rebirth (the time of the winter solstice, December 25), Semiramis proclaimed that Nimrod would visit the evergreen tree and leave gifts under it. [35]

The "green tree" is mentioned 13 times in Scripture and in every instance it is linked with idolatry! [35]

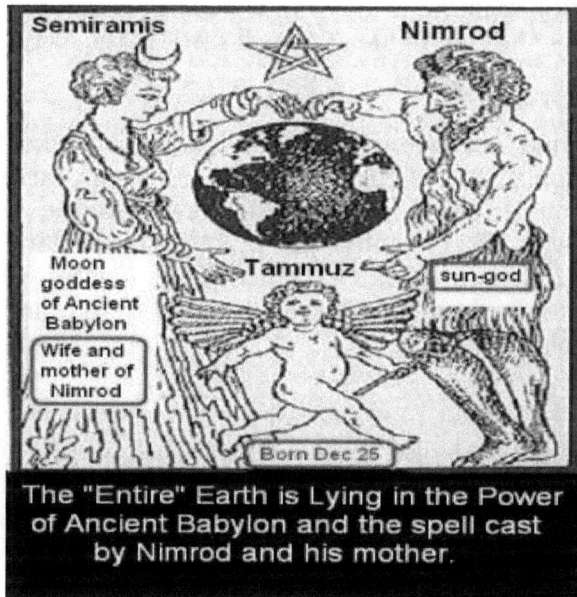

The "Entire" Earth is Lying in the Power of Ancient Babylon and the spell cast by Nimrod and his mother.

[66]

Nimrod married his mother Semiramis, and together, they built the Babylonian Empire which combined their pagan religion with their form of government. They worshiped the stars, sun, and the moon, and they sacrificed their babies to Molech. Noah's son Shem was so angry about this, that he had Nimrod killed and his body parts were delivered to different provinces within Babylon as a warning to those who worshiped Molech *aka Satan.* [66]

Nimrod's wife/mother wanted to keep this false pagan religion alive in order to keep the money coming in. **She consulted her astrologers who told her that on December 22nd the sun is the furthest away from the earth, but on December 25th, the sun is "born again." This is known as the "winter solstice" in paganism. Semiramis became pregnant on March 25th (Easter/Ishtar),** which is called *the spring equinox in paganism.* She told the Babylonian people that Nimrod was the god of the sun, and that he impregnated her, with the rays of the sun. [66]

Exactly 9 months later on December 25th, she gave birth to a son and named him Tammuz. She told the Babylonians that Tammuz was a reincarnation of Nimrod the "sun god" **born on December 25th** and that **she was the "goddess of the moon" or the "Queen of Heaven."** *Today the Roman Catholic Church officially named "Mary/Miriam"* (the mother of Jesus/Yeshua) **"Queen of Heaven"** after this pagan fertility goddess. [66]

Semiramis ordered the Babylonians to go into the forest and cut down a tree and decorate it with little balls (which were meant to be Nimrod's testicles) **to commemorate Nimrod who was "cut down" like a tree.** Elohim (God) hates this practice which is why he warned the children of Israel not to learn this custom from the pagans. [66]

- "1) Hear ye the word which YHWH (the LORD) speaketh unto you, O house of Israel: 2) Thus saith YHWH (the LORD), **Learn not the way of the heathen,** and be not dismayed at the signs of heaven; (astrology) for the heathen are dismayed at them. 3) For the customs of the people are vain: **for one cutteth a tree out of the forest, the work of the hands of the workman, with the axe.** 4) **They deck it with silver and with gold; they fasten it with nails and with hammers that it move not**." (Jeremiah 10:1-4) [66]

52

And today, Christ Mass trees are erected supposedly in the name of Jesus, but this practice was started long before Yeshua (Jesus) ever came to earth. Did YHWH (the LORD) change his mind now? No, he still hates it and he says *"learn NOT the ways of the heathen..."* [66]

- **Gift Exchanging:** The Romans worshiped Tammuz as the sun deity Mithras in a special observance called the Saturnalia. The Saturnalia was named for Saturn, otherwise known as Cronus. Cronus is **an alias for Tammuz**. His wife and mother was Rhea (Semiramis). *The Saturnalia, therefore, was just another observance for Tammuz, the Babylonian, counterfeit redeemer.* The Romans kept the Saturnalia in December, at the time of the winter solstice, in honor of the returning sun. The festival lasted seven days. **"All classes exchanged gifts, the commonest being waxed tapers and clay dolls," says the Encyclopedia Britannica, Eleventh Edition.** [35]

- **Saint Nick – Santa Claus:** "Old Nick" that was commonly used for Santa Claus has the meaning of Lucifer or Satan in old English. The World English Dictionary says: "Old Nick—a jocular name for Satan." The Cambridge Dictionary entry says: "Old Nick—the Devil—the main evil spirit in the Christian religion." [35]

- **Stockings Hung on the Chimney:** (Odin another name for Nimrod) According to Phyllis Siefker the author of Santa Claus, Last of the Wild Men, children would place their boots filled with sugar, carrots or straw, near the chimney for Odin's flying horse, Sleipnir, to eat. Odin would then reward those children for their kindness by replacing Sleipnir's food with gifts or candy. This practice survived in Germany, Belgium, and the Netherlands after the adoption of Christianity and became associated with Saint Nicholas as a result of the process of Christianization and can be still seen in the modern practice of the hanging of stockings at the chimney in some homes. [35]

The Romans worshiped Tammuz as the sun deity Mithras in a special observance called the Saturnalia. The Roman Emperor Constantine was a sun worshipper. He wanted one united religion for his world government. He professed Christianity but in order to bring the pagans into the Church, kept the pagan traditions. The pagan traditions were given Christian names. The Vatican, specifically, Pope Julius I, set the date to celebrate our Saviour birth, the Son's birthday on the day to celebrate the birth of the sun. When we truly open our eyes, we can see that the date set to celebrate Christmas and Christmas celebrations, (Christmas traditions), were adopted from Babylon. Besides Easter and Christmas, there are many, many more traditions that were adopted from Babylon and there were some were very, very, important things changed that you need to know so please don't stop reading till you get to the end.

This mixing the worship of the pagan god, Tammuz, the sun god, the first false savior, with the worship of the one true God is an abomination to the LORD.

- "16) ...and they worshipped the sun... 17) ... Is it a light thing to the house of Judah that they commit the abominations which they commit here? ... 18) Therefore will I also deal in fury: mine eye shall not spare, neither will I have pity: and though they cry in mine ears with a loud voice, yet will I not hear them." (Ezek. 8:16-18)
- "Thus saith the LORD, Learn not the way of the heathen..." (Jer 10:2)

Idol worship, Idolatry, Spiritual Adultery, is the reason God divorced His people.

- "And I saw, when for all the causes whereby backsliding Israel committed adultery I had put her away, and given her a bill of divorce; yet her treacherous sister Judah feared not, but went and played the harlot also." (Jer.3:8)

Doctrines INVENTED FOR THE PAGAN SUN GOD BAAL
Semiramis of Babylon (the first deified queen of Babylon)
The mother goddess was worshipped as the Queen of Heaven ...

- After Nimrods death, Semiramis becomes pregnant, she says by the rays of the sun. Her son was born on December 25. His name was Tammuz. He automatically became a god due to his conception being through the rays of the sun. His mother became known as the mother of god and mother child worship begins. Tammuz and his mother become not only mother and son but husband and wife. They rule the kingdom of Babylon together as gods· 32

- Semiramis was initially included in the pagan Babylonian trinity as the holy spirit or seed of the divine son in his mother's womb. With time, however, the father Nimrod was practically overlooked and worshiped only as the god-incarnate son in his mother's arms. In other words, the father became invisible and was no longer worshiped, whereas, the mother with the god-incarnate son in her arms became the grand object of worship. **Numerous Babylonian monuments show the goddess-mother Semiramis with her son in her arms. This worship of mother and child spread throughout the known world, and was given different names in the various languages of the world.** [68]

- Under her title, "mother of the gods," the goddess queen of Babylon became an object of universal worship. The mother of the gods was worshiped by the Persians, the Syrians, and with the most profound religious veneration by all the kings of Europe and Asia. When Caesar invaded Britain, he discovered the Druid priests worshiping the "mother of god" as Virgo-Patitura. In Egypt, as the **"queen of heaven"** she was the greatest and most worshiped of all the divinities. During Egyptian bondage, the Israelites repeatedly departed from the one true invisible Elohim and worshiped the pagan mother. When the Israelites fell into apostasy under King Solomon, they worshiped this mother goddess as Ashtaroth (Asherah), a name by which the pagan Babylonian goddess was known to the Israelites: [68]

[69]

The children gather wood, the fathers kindle the fire, and the women knead dough, to **make cakes to the queen of heaven** and pour out drink offerings to other gods, **to provoke me to anger. (Jeremiah 7:18)**

The LORD (YHWH) rebuked the children of Israel for worshiping this Queen of Heaven. In the days of the prophet Jeremiah, the Virgin Mary was not born yet. They were worshiping, Semiramis, goddess of Babylon. [69]

"15) Then all the men which knew that their wives had burned incense unto other gods, and all the women that stood by, a great multitude, even all the people that dwelt in the land of Egypt, in Pathros, answered Jeremiah, saying, 16) *As for* the word that thou hast spoken unto us in the name of the LORD, we will not hearken unto thee. 17) But we will certainly do whatsoever thing goeth forth out of our own mouth, to *burn incense unto the queen of heaven, and to pour out drink offerings unto her*, ... 19) And when we burned incense to the queen of heaven, and poured out drink offerings unto her, did we *make her cakes to worship her, and pour out drink offerings unto her*, without our men? 22) So that the LORD could no longer bear, because of the evil of your doings, and because of the abominations which ye have committed; therefore is your land a desolation, and an astonishment, and a curse, without an inhabitant, as at this day.* 23) Because ye have burned incense, and because ye have sinned against the LORD, and have not obeyed the voice of the LORD, nor walked in his law, nor in his statutes, nor in his testimonies; therefore this evil is happened unto you, as at this day. ... 29) And this *shall be*

---

[68] http://aletheia.consultronix.com/7.html

[69] http://ministeriomisionerodepoderenjesus.blogspot.com.br/2010/11/semiramis-priests-nimrod-tammuz-and-his.html

a sign unto you, saith the LORD, that I will punish you in this place, that ye may know that my words shall surely stand against you for evil:" **(Jer 44:15-17, 19, 22, 23, 29)**

In Jer 44:15-30 we see that it is an abomination unto God to worship the Queen of Heaven, Semiramis, goddess of Babylon. She is known under many names including the Mother Mary, Queen of Heaven. God judged His people for this abomination. In Rev. 18:4 God is warning His people to come out of Mystery Babylon (who also worships the Queen of heaven, Semiramis and have many of the other adulterous doctrines of Babylon), warning us to come out of Mystery Babylon before He judges her.

Doctrines of Babylon Adopted by THE VATICAN-
The Virgin Mary worshipped as the Queen of Heaven.

- Ancient cultures had a habit of changing a 'goddesses' name when they adopted her into their own culture. **Some of the names and titles that this 'Queen' is known under are the following**: Isis (Egyptian) , Mother of God, Oaster (Easter Eastern-Star), Ishtar(Babylonian), Astarte (Syrian), Cybele (Roman), Ashtoreth (Israel), Goddess of Love, Aphrodite, Venus, Goddess of Hunting and Childbirth, Artemis, Diana (Ephesus), Helena (Greek), Goddess of Crafts, War and Wisdom, Athena, Minerva, Lady of the Towers, Goddess of Growing Things, Demeter, The Holy Ghost, The Supreme Dove (Sumerian), Ceres, Gaea, Terra, Protector of Marriage and Women, the Sister and Wife of Zeus in Greece, the Wife of Jupiter in Rome, Hera, Juno, Goddess of the Hearth, Hestia, Vesta, Wife and Sister of Kronos, Sammurant (Assyrian), Rhea, Queen of Tara, Ish-Tara, the Indian deity, Sami-Rama-isi or Semi-Rama (Vedic**) and Mother Mary (Rome)** [39]
- Pius XII affirmed strongly the queenship of Mary, **inserting in the calendar for May 31**, a new feast of Mary Queen. New Catholic Encyclopedia. Vol. 9. p. 386 [70]
- Pius XII consecrated the world to the Immaculate Heart of Mary. **Mother and Queen, October 31, 1942, as a public recognition of her queenship.** New Catholic Encyclopedia. Vol. 9. p. 386 [70]

Nimrod
Semiramis
Semiramis - Queen of Heaven
Semiramis - Mother of god

71

72

[70] https://www.slideshare.net/kaondeandrew/the-secret-behind-the-wine-of-babylon-1-recovered

[71] http://doubleportioninheritance.blogspot.com/2012/02/queen-of-heaven-why-does-church.html

[72] http://www.pathofmary.com/daily-act-of-consecration-of-marys-own/

Doctrines INVENTED FOR THE PAGAN SUN GOD BAAL

Below is Assyrian Cylinder Seal. Notice the sun resting on a crescent-shaped monstrance. [24]

Below is Assyrian-style relief of King Bar-Raqqah from Syria, 8th Century B.C. [24]

Egyptian goddess Isis with her headdress showing the sun disk within the horns of an Apis bull, symbology which is virtually identical to that of the sunburst monstrance. [41]
[41]

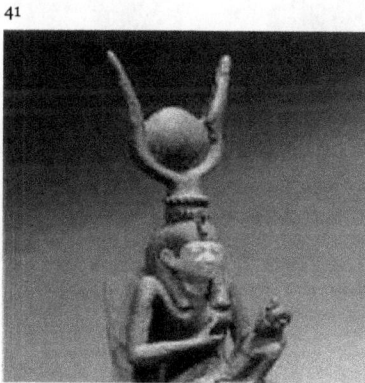

Below, A photo of a stele from Ur of the Chaldees, with the symbol of the Babylonian sun god Shamash within the crescent of the moon goddess Nanna. [41]
[41]

Doctrines of Babylon Adopted by THE VATICAN

[41]

- A close-up of a monstrance, and inside the glass enclosure is a crescent (moon), upon which the round wafer god host is placed, a virtual duplication of the symbology of the Canaanite and Chaldean stele shown above. Many monstrances use this crescent, which is officially called a "lunette" or "luna" (moon), to hold the round wafer host. The sun disk in the crescent moon is a quite common symbol for pagan religions, to include Babylon, Syria, and India. [41]
- One of many examples of the sun worship of Babylon adopted by the Roman Catholic Church.

- **The "Communion Wafer" itself is only another symbol of Baal, or the Sun**. There are letters on the wafer ... I. H. S. ... To a Christian these letters are represented as signifying, "*Iesus Hominum Salvator*," "Jesus the Saviour of men." But let a Roman worshipper of Isis (for in the age of the emperors there were innumerable worshippers of Isis in Rome) cast his eyes upon them, and how will he read them? He will read them, of course, according to his own well known system of idolatry: "*Isis, Horus, Seb,*" that is, "**The Mother, the Child, and the Father of the gods,**"--in other words, "**The Egyptian Trinity**." Can the reader imagine that this double sense is accidental? Surely not. The very same spirit that converted the festival of the Pagan Oannes into the feast of the Christian Joannes, retaining at the same time all its ancient Paganism, has skilfully planned the initials I. H. S. to pay the *semblance* of a tribute to Christianity, while Paganism in reality has all the *substance* of the homage bestowed upon it. The Two Babylons Alexander Hislop Chapter IV Section III The Sacrifice of the Mass [42]

The round disk "sun" wafer IHS symbol of Isis, Horus & Seb, eaten as food for the soul. Some wafers also had a large "+" sign engraved on them as well to symbolize Baal. [25]

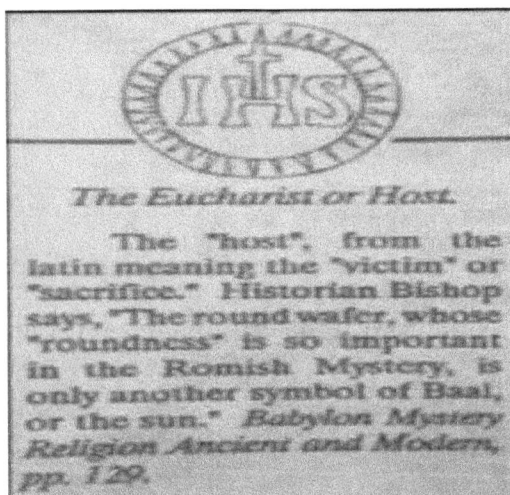

The Eucharist or Host.

The "host", from the latin meaning the "victim" or "sacrifice." Historian Bishop says, "The round wafer, whose "roundness" is so important in the Romish Mystery, is only another symbol of Baal, or the sun." *Babylon Mystery Religion Ancient and Modern, pp. 129.*

[41]

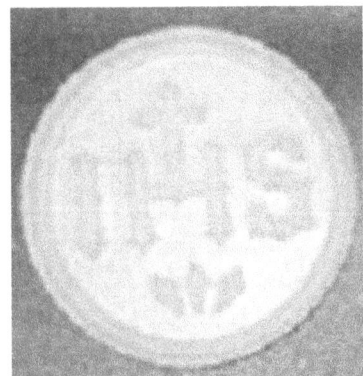

Communion Wafers/Breads [73]

"IHS" stands for "Isis, Horus, Set" - the Egyptian trinity.
ISIS, HORUS, SEB
The Real Trinity, originating in Babylon.

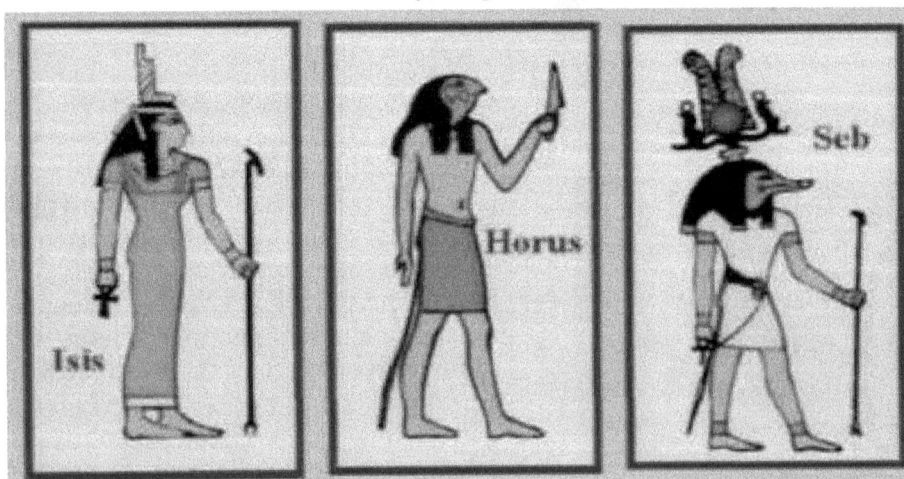

[74]

---

[73] https://www.michiganchurchsupply.com/products/2-1-2-white-altar-bread-lm45?variant=39783022412
[74] http://whale.to/c/isishorusseth.html

Note these 100 Lire coins issued by the Vatican for nearly 10 years. [41]

Pope Pius the 12th - 1958

Pope John the 23rd - 1959

Pope Paul the 6th – 1963

[41]

Incredibly enough, the woman representing the Catholic Church on the reverse side of the coins holds up a cup in her right hand, ***in which you see pagan sunburst wafer god***, which recalls these verses in Revelation: 17:4 [41]

- "And the woman was arrayed in purple and scarlet colour, and decked with gold and precious stones and pearls, having **a golden cup in her hand full of abominations and filthiness of her fornication**:" (Rev 17:4) [41]

The cup of wine of the apostate woman (church) represents spiritual and doctrinal fornication, a mixing of truth and error, Christianity and paganism, which she has taught to the world (made the nations drink). [41]

Doctrines INVENTED FOR THE PAGAN SUN GOD BAAL

- **Painting of the child (Tammuz) and mother (Semiramis) with the glory of the Sun around their heads** *A halo* (from Greek ἅλως, halōs;[1] *also known as a nimbus*, aureole, glory, or gloriole) *is a ring of light that surrounds a person in art.* They have been used in the iconography of many religions to indicate holy or sacred figures, and have at various periods also been used in images of rulers or heroes. In the sacred art of Ancient Greece, Ancient Rome, Hinduism, Buddhism, Islam and Christianity, among other religions, … [75]

---

[75] https://en.wikipedia.org/wiki/Halo_(religious_iconography)

- The disc or circle of light surrounding the head, was found in artistic representations of the great gods and goddesses in Babylon. The disc, and particularly the circle, were well-known symbols of the Sun-divinity. [76]

Ra with solar disc, before 1235 BC [75]

- Ra, with the Halo above his head, representing the Sun, Ra, another name for the Sun god Nimrod, also known as Tammuz.

Buddha with a Halo [75]

[76] http://scripture-keywords.tripod.com/Babylon/07-Rome-Symbolism.html

Doctrines of Babylon Adopted by THE VATICAN

- **Paintings of the child (Jesus) and mother (Mary) with halos or of the Sun around their heads**

77

78

79

---

[77] http://www.wisegeek.org/what-is-christmas.htm

[78] http://www.oracionesparapeticiones.com/2013/07/oracion-la-virgen-de-la-medalla.html

[79] http://new.exchristian.net/2012/06/great-virgin-isis-ancient-mythology-is.html

Doctrines INVENTED FOR THE PAGAN SUN GOD BAAL
- **Statues of a "Madonna" found in all Pagan cults as well as Egyptian Madonna Isis with her son Horus (Names for Semiramis and Nimrod or Tammuz)**

- ... there can be no doubt that the myths of Isis had a direct bearing upon the elevation of Mary, the mother of Jesus, to her celestial position in the Roman Catholic theology... In her aspect as the mother of Horus, Isis was represented in tens of thousands of statues and paintings, holding the divine child in her arms; and when Christianity triumphed these paintings and figures became those of the Madonna and Child without any break in continuity: no archaeologist, in fact, can now tell whether some of these objects represent the one or the other." [80]

80

Buddha also had virgin birth...

80   137   138

In his Latin novel of the second century ce, The Golden Ass (XI.2), Lucius Apuleius describes Isis's introduction of herself to the "hapless quadruped" as follows: "I am she that is the natural mother of all things, mistress and governess of all the elements, the initial progeny of worlds, chief of the powers divine, **_queen of heaven_**, the principal of the gods celestial, the light of the goddesses. At my will the planets of the air, the wholesome winds of the seas and the silences of hell are disposed. **_My name, my divinity, is adored throughout the world,_** in divers manners, in variable customs and **_in many names_**, for the Phrygians call me the mother of

---

[80] http://www.truthbeknown.com/mary.html
[137] http://www.ebay.com/itm/251793030692
[138] https://www.buddhagroove.com/kuan-yin-and-infant-statue-19-5-inches-tall/

the gods; the Athenians, Minerva; the Cyprians, Venus; the Candians, Diana; the Sicilians, Proserpina; the Eleusinians, Ceres; some Juno, others Bellona, others Hecate; and principally the Ethiopians who dwell in the Orient, and the ***Egyptians...do call me Queen Isis***." (Siculus, 31fn) As can be seen, Isis was fervently revered as the epitome of Divinity, long before Mary achieved that rank. [80]

Doctrines of Babylon Adopted by THE VATICAN

- **Statues of the Queen of Heaven (Egyptian Madonna Isis with her son Horus) or (Mary and her Son Jesus) can be found in all Catholic Churches**

71   81   82

Statue of Mary (or Semiramis) in the Vatican

82

Catholic Priest worshiping at the Roman mother of God Statue

Breaking God's third commandment:
- "8) Thou shalt not make thee any graven image, or any likeness of anything that is in heaven above, or that is in the earth beneath, or that is in the waters beneath the earth: 9) Thou shalt not bow down thyself unto them, nor serve them: for I the LORD thy God am a jealous God, visiting the iniquity of the fathers upon the children unto the third and fourth generation of them that hate me." (Deu 5:8,9)

[81] http://www.romeofthewest.com/2007/03/photos-of-immaculate-conception-church.html
[82] https://biggestcults.wordpress.com/category/roman-catholicism/

Doctrines INVENTED FOR THE PAGAN SUN GOD BAAL
Pontifex Maximus is the name for chief head of the pagan Babylonian system of idolatry

- When Attalus, the Pontiff and King of Pergamos died, in B.C. 133, he bequeathed the headship of the "Babylonian Priesthood" to Rome. When the Etruscans came to Italy from Lydia, (the region of Pergamos), they brought with them the Babylonian religion and rites. They set up a Pontiff who was head of the priesthood. Later the Romans accepted this Pontiff as their civil ruler. *Julius Caesar was made Pontiff of the Etruscan Order in B.C. 74. In B.C. 63, he was made "Supreme Pontiff" of the "Babylonian Order,"* thus becoming heir to the rights and title of Attalus, Pontiff of Pergamos, who made Rome his heir by will. ***Thus the first Roman Emperor became the head of the "Babylonian Priesthood," and Rome the successor of Babylon.*** Each successor to Emperor from that point forward held the title **Pontifus Maximus literally The High Priest of the Babylonian Cult of Sol Invictus which was simply another incarnation of Mithraism stemming from the worship of Tammuz in Babylon. The Pope of Rome now carries forward that High Priesthood as Pontiff.** [44]

Doctrines of Babylon Adopted by THE VATICAN
Pontifex Maximus one of the first names for the office of Pope

- The last pontiff king of Pergamum was Attalus III, who bequeathed his title to the emperor of Rome in 133 BC. In the fourth century AD, Christian emperor Gratian refused the title, and in the year 431 AD, the title was taken over by Damascus, bishop of Rome. The present-day college of cardinals with the Pope at the head is identical to the college of pontiffs with the Pontifex Maximus at the head. A statement about the Pope's position is found in William Barry's The Papal Monarchy: ...**The Emperor is no more...but the Pontifex Maximus abides; he is now the Vicar of Christ,** offering the old civilization to the tribes of the North. **He converts them to his creed, and they serve him as Father and Judge supreme** (emphases added). [45]

45

Doctrines INVENTED FOR THE PAGAN SUN GOD BAAL

- **The pagan high priest king** is believed to be the incarnate of the Sun god. [25]
- Dr. Gilbert Murray, M.A., D.Litt., LLD, FBA, Professor of Greek at Oxford University, who certainly had no ax to grind concerning Christian thought on the Sabbath question. He wrote: "Now since Mithras was the sun, the Unconquered, and the sun was the Royal Star, the religion looked for a king whom it could serve as a representative of Mithras upon earth. The Roman Emperor seemed to be clearly indicated as the true king. In sharp contrast to Christianity, Mithraism recognized Caesar as the bearer of divine grace. [83]

---

[83] https://www.sabbathtruth.com/sabbath-history/how-the-sabbath-was-changed

Doctrines of Babylon Adopted by THE VATICAN

- **Pontifex Maximus abides; he is now the Vicar of Christ**
- The Pope proclaims to be Christ's Vicar (replacement) here on Earth. It is also recorded in numerous documents that the pope believes he is god on earth. [25]
- Pope Leo XIII, *Praeclara Gratulationis Publicae (The Reunion of Christendom), June 20, 1894:* **We hold upon this earth the place of God Almighty.** [84]
- *"Pope," Ferraris' Ecclesiastic Dictionary: The Pope is of so great dignity and so exalted that he is not a mere man, but as it were God, and the vicar of God.* [84]
- *Our Sunday Visitor (April 18, 1915): 3: The letters inscribed in the Pope's miter are these:* **VICARIUS FILLII DEI, which is the Latin for, "Vicar of the Son of God."** [84]
- ***Vicar of the Son of God means in place of Christ.***
- The words **VICARIUS FILII DEI**, was inscribed in the crown or his mitre which is worn by the POPE, this was clarified and proven to us by this *Catholic Newspaper.* This crown is known as the *Papal Tiara,* or *Tri-Crown,* because it was literally three crowns placed on top of each. [85]
- The Pope claims to be High Priest, Vicar of Christ, God Almighty, but scriptures say Jesus (Yeshua) is God, the Son of God, our true High Priest and we are to hold to this profession.
- Wherefore, holy brethren, partakers of the heavenly calling, consider the Apostle and High Priest of our profession, Christ Jesus; (Heb 3:1)
- Seeing then that we have a great high priest, that is passed into the heavens, Jesus the Son of God, let us hold fast *our* profession. (Heb 4:14)
- For *there is* one God, and one mediator between God and men, the man Christ Jesus; (1Ti 2:5)

Doctrines INVENTED FOR THE PAGAN SUN GOD BAAL

Burning incense and candles

- "Herodotus, the Greek historian, recorded that it was popular among the Assyrians, Babylonians and Egyptians." [47]
- "16) As for the word that thou hast spoken unto us in the name of the LORD, we will not hearken unto 17) But we will certainly do whatsoever thing goeth forth out of our own mouth, to **burn incense unto the queen of heaven**, and to pour out drink offerings unto her, as we have done, we, and our fathers, our kings, and our princes, in the cities of Judah, and in the streets of Jerusalem: for then had we plenty of victuals, and were well, and saw no evil." (Jer 44:16,17)
- "For the LORD of hosts, that planted thee, hath pronounced evil against thee, for the evil of the house of Israel and of the house of Judah, which they have done against themselves to **provoke me to anger in offering incense unto Baal**." (Jer 11:17)

Doctrines of Babylon Adopted by THE VATICAN

- **The burning of incense and candles**

86

---

[84] http://amazingdiscoveries.org/S-deception-Sabbath_Sunday_Catholic_Church
[85] http://torch-of-salvation.blogspot.com/2011/07/man-with-number-666-that-is-mentioned.html
[86] http://josiehagenministries.blogspot.com/2013/05/you-shall-offer-no-strange-incense-fire.html

Doctrines INVENTED FOR THE PAGAN SUN GOD BAAL
- ### Chants and Repetitive prayers
  > But when ye pray, use not vain repetitions, as the heathen do: for they think that they shall be heard for their much speaking. (Mat 6:7)

Doctrines of Babylon Adopted by THE VATICAN
- ### Gregorian chants and the Rosary
- ### Here is some of the Rosary
  #6 On each bead that separates the preceding ten, the 'our Father' is repeated.

  #7 Again, the 'Hail Mary' is prayed/repeated for the next ten beads. Then the 'Glory be' is repeated

  #8 Again on this bead the 'our Father' is repeated

  #9 Again, the 'Hail Mary' is prayed/repeated for the next ten beads. Then the 'Glory be' is repeated

  #10 Again on this bead the 'our Father' is repeated

  #11 Again, the 'Hail Mary' is prayed/repeated for the next ten beads. Then the 'Glory be' is repeated

  #12 Again on this bead the 'our Father' is repeated

  #13 Again, the 'Hail Mary' is prayed/repeated for the next ten beads. Then the 'Glory be' is repeated

  #14 The end of the Rosary (for this dedication) is reached. Now the Catholic is taught to pray the 'Hail Holy Queen.' for the "first" time.

  #15 The Catholic is taught to then repeat all of the above for the next two dedications if in fact he or she is going to do an ENTIRE rosary. And as of just a few weeks back, Pope John Paul II added yet ANOTHER so called "mystery" to the rosary bringing the total to FOUR mysteries that must now be repeated, if the Catholics seek to do an entire rosary. When I was a Catholic it took me 45 minutes to recite all three sets of mysteries, (Joyful, Sorrowful, and Glorious) Since the Pope has added the mystery of "Light." "And no marvel; for Satan himself is transformed into an angel of light." [-2 Corinthians 11:14] *I am sure it would take at least an hour to repeat all four now.* [48] For the Roman Catholic church to proclaim to it's followers you MUST pray the Rosary is openly stating you MUST do exactly the opposite of what the Lord God Almighty has stated in His Word! (Mat 6:7) "use not vain repetitions"

Doctrines INVENTED FOR THE PAGAN SUN GOD BAAL
- ### Infant baptism, and sprinkling of holy water NIMROD, and his wife SEMIRAMIS, started the great pagan BABYLON MYSTERY RELIGION... The first essential sacrament Semiramis taught was Baptism by water. The Priests of Nimrod would 'baptize' new-born infants the fathers chose to keep, and they would become 'born-again' and become members of the Babylonian Mystery Religion." (Hislop,Two Babylons, p134) The Priest first must 'exorcise' evil spirits from the infant by anointing the baby's head with OIL. With the oil the priest puts the occult mark of Tammuz on the child's head by marking a "T" with the oil. (later to become the 'Sign of the Cross) The Priest then put SALT and SPITTLE on the baby's tongue to preserve it from future influence of evil spirits. "HOLY WATER" is now sprinkled or poured over the baby's head, and the baby is said to be cleansed from any original sin and is now "born-again" and a member of the Babylonian Religion. **This process was known as INFANT CHRISTENING and was practiced hundreds of years before Christ**, (Hislop,pl38) and is found NOWHERE in the Bible! There is not a single example of a baby being 'baptized' or 'christened' in the Bible! **This was called 'Baal Worship' in the Old Testament, and God called it an abomination!** [49]

- ### Doctrines of Babylon Adopted by THE VATICAN
  Infant baptism, and sprinkling of holy water When Emperor Constantine made 'Christianity' the official 'STATE RELIGION of Rome, **one of the FIRST LAWS passed was the law decreeing infant baptism as the law of the land in 416 A.D.** That simply meant that

everybody within a certain age limit had to conform to it. When they passed that law in 416 that **every baby in the Roman Empire had to be baptized** at the hands of an authorized **Roman priest... OR ELSE!** "Bible Believing Christians were labeled slanderously as 'ANABAPTISTS' because they rejected this idea of baptizing babies as pagan and not Scriptural. They would 'RE-BAPTIZE these infants when they got older and trusted Christ as Savior! Thus the term, ANABAPTISTS...which meant "*RE-BAPTIZERS*"! It was later shortened to 'Baptists'." "they were persecuted without mercy for not conforming. Historian J.M. Carroll declares, **"For 30 miles on the road leading out of Rome were stakes with gory heads of ANABAPTISTS...."**"
Armitage's History (p71-73) tells us that in the 6th century, Emperor Justin issued an edict commanding ALL UNBAPTIZED PARENTS to present themselves and their children for baptism at once. Leo III issued, another edict in A.D. 723 demanding the forcible baptism of the Jews and Montanists (anabaptists). Toward the close of the 6th century the baptism of infants was turned to gain in the shape of FEES ($$$) paid for its administration; but, the charges soon became so enormous that the poor could not pay them. And yet lest their children should DIE unsaved, the frightened parents strained every nerve to get them baptized." (Armitage's history, p71) He continues, "Suppose you owned a section of land with an oil well on it; you had a baby born into your home and you went to the priest to get the baby baptized. The priest would say I want the title to that section of land. When the thing was over, the priest would get the title to the land and the BABY would get a few drops of water on its head. **He says this is how the Mother Church of Rome come to own Czechoslovakia, Mexico, etc.** [49]

- **THE 'HOLY INQUISITION' RESULTED FROM THIS ISSUE OF BABY BAPTISM**
No wonder the Book of Revelation declared in Revelation 17:6 that this great HARLOT false religion had become 'DRUNK with the BLOOD of the Saints'...Historian and Bible commentator Sir Robert Anderson estimated that thru out the middle ages OVER 40 MILLION people were murdered and martyred over this one doctrine of INFANT BAPTISM! To illustrate this great number of those anabaptists slain, Anderson said **if you lined 40 million people in a line, four abreast and four feet apart, and they marched by at normal marching pace, it would take 4 years and 4 months for this number of people to march by!!!** [49]

- **OVER 40 Million knew the truth and wouldn't change, Murdered for their stand for truth.**

God's word on Baptism:
- "One Lord, one faith, *one baptism*." (Eph. 4:5)
- "He that ***BELIEVETH AND IS BAPTIZED shall be SAVED***; but he that believeth not shall be damned." (Mark 16:16) (This is Jesus speaking. Babies cannot believe and be baptized)
- "To give knowledge of *salvation unto his people by the remission of their sins*," (Luk 1:77)
- "38) Then Peter said unto them, **Repent, and *be baptized every one of you in the name of Jesus Christ for the remission of sins,*** and ye shall receive the gift of the Holy Ghost. 39) For the promise is unto you, and to your children, and to all that are afar off, even as many as the Lord our God shall call." (Act 2:38,39) (God's word says: Salvation is through remission of sins, through Baptism in Jesus name)
- "Neither is there salvation in any other: for there is *none other name under heaven given among men, whereby we must be saved*." (Act 4:12)
- Above we read: God's word says there is one baptism and according to Jesus it is for salvation. Jesus said in Mark 16:16 "He that believeth and is baptized shall be saved". Luke 1:77 tells us that salvation is through remission of sins. Acts tells us Baptism in Jesus name is for the remission of sins (salvation) and there is salvation in no other name.

When you understand the Mystery of God, the above will all make perfect since. Chapter 4 **The Mystery of God Revealed,** gives concrete understanding through the scriptures but first the rest of the revelation of Mystery Babylon!

Doctrines INVENTED FOR THE PAGAN SUN GOD BAAL
Human sacrifices burned by fire as offering to appease Sun god

- "Moloch (sometimes spelled "Molech") was an Old Testament god whom the Hebrews worshipped from time to time, and to whom they sacrificed (burned in the fires of Moloch) their children.
- They were so devoted (to the Babylonian religion that had deceived them) that they sacrificed their own children. What will people do who are so devoted (to the deceptions that came from Babylon) in these end days?

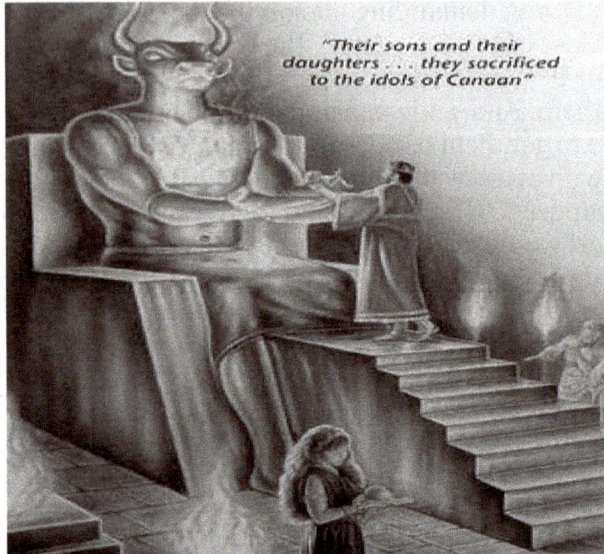

"Their sons and their daughters . . . they sacrificed to the idols of Canaan"

87

Doctrines of Babylon Adopted by THE VATICAN

- <u>Opposers of doctrines of the Roman Catholic church burned at the stake</u> [88]

1126 - Peter of Bruis - Burned at the Stake - Rejected Rome's traditions

1155 - Arnold of Brescia - Bible Preacher - Hanged and Burned

1211 - 80 Waldensians - burned at the stake

1315 - Waldensian Bishop Neumunster - Burned at the stake in Hamburg, Germany

1315 - 50 Women and children burned at the stake in Schweidnitz in Silesia

1400 - William Sawtree - Wycliffe follower - Burned at the stake

1408 - John Resby - Heresy - Burned at Perth, Scotland

1415 - John Huss - Burned for preaching the Gospel and rejecting Rome's views

1416 - 300 burned at the stake in Saxony

1417 - Sir John Oldcastle - Helped distribute Wycliffe Bible - Martyred for his faith by being roasted over fire

1481/2 - 2,000 people burned alive in Spanish Inquisition in Seville and Castile

1511 - James Brewster - Burned at the stake - Having a book of Scripture

1528 - Patrick Hamilton - Burned at the Stake in Scotland for declaring that it is the right of any person to read God's Word

1529 - Louis Berquin - Burned at the Stake in France for printing and distributing Bible tracts in French

1530 - John Tewksbury - Burned at the stake for Bible distribution - England

1531 - Richard Bayfield - Burned at the stake for Scripture distribution

1533 - Henry Forrest - Benedictine Monk who became saved - Burned at the stake in St. Andrews, Scotland

1536 - William Tyndale - Burned at the Stake for Translating the Bible into English - His translation became the groundwork for the King James Version

[87] http://www.new2torah.com/wp-content/uploads/2013/01/molech_sacrifice.jpg
[88] http://www.scionofzion.com/mcr.htm

1540 - Thomas Garrett - Friend of Tyndale - Burned at the stake - England
1546 - Stephen Polliot - Burned at the Stake for bringing Scriptures into France - His tongue was cut out so he could not witness to those around him at his execution.
1553 - Nicholas Nayle - Burned at the stake in Paris because he brought gospel books for believers.
1560 - Julian Hernandez - Burned at the stake in Spain for Bible Distribution

- The innocent were burned, sacrificed to the sun god Moloch. The Catholic Church adopted this sun god doctrine of burning the innocent, sacrificing by fire, those who disagreed with them. There were many, more, on this list that were killed for their rejection of the Catholic Doctrine that are not included here. For an extremely detailed look, see Foxe's Book of Martyrs.

Doctrines INVENTED FOR THE PAGAN SUN GOD BAAL

- In the 4th Century B.C., Plato spoke of certain teachers of his day who believed in purgatory. Buddhism, Stoicism, and the Muslim fathers also believed in a place of purification where souls must go before they can attain Heaven. These beliefs have their root in Babylon. The most probable source is that of the worship of Molech. Many pagan nations felt that fire was necessary to cleanse from sin. This is probably because they were worshippers of the sun god, and his power on earth was represented by fire. This was evidenced in the worship of Molech, as young infants were made human sacrifices and burned in the arms of the idol. God made special mention of Molech and forbid his worship in II Kings 23:10 and Leviticus 18:21. In fact, **Molech is simply another name for Nimrod**. (Tammuz, the reincarnation of the Sun god, Nimrod) The name Tammuz sheds light on this as well. **"Tam" means "perfect"; "Muz" means "by burning"**. (15) This shows that the idea of purification by fire has its roots in the Babylonian worship of Nimrod. [89]
- **Purgatory** is an intermediate state after physical death in which some of those ultimately destined for heaven must first "**undergo purification, so as to achieve the holiness** ... place or condition of suffering or torment, especially one that is temporary. [90]

Doctrines of Babylon Adopted by THE VATICAN

- The first real evidence of this doctrine in Catholicism occurred when Pope Gregory the Great claimed the existence of a third state, one different than Heaven and Hell. The idea was not officially adopted into Catholic dogma until the Council of Florence in 1459. From that point on, the Catholic Church has freely taught the concept of purgatory as a purification place for souls. [89]

There is no place called purgatory in the scriptures, no place called purgatory in God's word. Today is the day of salvation. We make our decision where we will spend eternity today, while we are alive, either to everlasting punishment or righteous into life eternal.

- "And these shall go away into everlasting punishment: but the righteous into life eternal." (Mat 25:46)
- "(For he saith, I have heard thee in a time accepted, and in the day of salvation have I succoured thee: **behold, now is the accepted time; behold, now is the day of salvation**.)" (2Co 6:2)

Doctrines INVENTED FOR THE PAGAN SUN GOD BAAL

- Gargoils = a pagan god of protection [25]

Doctrines of Babylon Adopted by THE VATICAN

- Vatican as well as thousands of Catholic churches have gargoils on their roofs for 'protection' [25]
- Gargoyles and the Catholic Church: The primary use of the gargoyle was to illustrate evil through the form of the gargoyle. In the 12th century St. Bernard of Clairvaux was famous for speaking out against gargoyles: What are these fantastic monsters doing in the cloisters before the eyes of the brothers as

---

[89] http://www.angelfire.com/la2/prophet1/maryolotry02.html
[90] https://en.wikipedia.org/wiki/Purgatory

they read? What is the meaning of these unclean monkeys, these strange savage lions, and monsters? To what purpose are here placed these creatures, half beast, half man, or these spotted tigers? I see several bodies with one head and several heads with one body. Here is a quadruped with a serpent's head, there a fish with a quadruped's head, then again an animal half horse, half goat... Surely if we do not blush for such absurdities, we should at least regret what we have spent on them.[9] [91]

Doctrines INVENTED FOR THE PAGAN SUN GOD BAAL

- **The Solar wheel is a symbol for Baal worship, Sun worship** which can be found carved into ancient as well as modern Buddhist temples, carved into ancient ornament ***representing Osiris*** [25] *(Nimrod)*

[92]

Doctrines of Babylon Adopted by THE VATICAN

St Peter's square has largest solar wheel on planet.
ALL Catholic churches have numerous solar wheels in stain glass windows as well as many other areas of the church. ...Numerous paintings, statues, ornaments, and letterheads of all Catholic churches have one or more "solar wheels" depicted upon them. [25]

Image on right ...an old photo of the center of St. Peter's square... (in the Vatican City, in Rome)

[92]

---

[91] https://en.wikipedia.org/wiki/Gargoyle
[92] http://www.aloha.net/~mikesch/wheel.htm

- *And this ONE WORLD CHURCH that started on 06-26-2000 <u>uses the solar wheel as its official logo</u>.* [93] (When you get to Chapter 5 you will see that the one world church has a constitution and confesses the Catholic Church.)

- Pope John Paul II, at World Youth Day 2000, was wearing a crimson and gold stole, which bears the symbols of Baal / Shamash within an *eight-pointed star of Ishtar*. Pope Pius XII wearing the same stole. [92]
- St Peter's, Rome, has *the largest solar wheel on the planet*, (eight pointed star) that represents Osiris (Nimrod)- a **symbol for Baal- sun worship**, Popes wear it and it is the One World Churches official logo. Later proof will show the one world Church is the Catholic Church.

---

[93] http://catholicreformation.yuku.com/topic/3123/Solar-Wheel-Mystery-Babylon-Vatican-and-One-World-Religion#.WRx6s4WcFqw

Doctrines INVENTED FOR THE PAGAN SUN GOD BAAL

- **The OBELISK**. Of the several functions of **the PILLAR** among early peoples, the Egyptian obelisk was *worshipped as **the dwelling place of the sun-god***. [92]

Doctrines of Babylon Adopted by THE VATICAN

[92]

Here is an old photo of the center of St. Peter's square, and note that around the obelisk, *at the center of the huge eight-point sun wheel, is a smaller four-pointed sun wheel, the same symbol as found on the altar stone in the temple of Baal in Hatzor!* [92]

- The reverse side of a coin celebrating the pontificate of John Paul II, and on it is the obelisk and sun wheel of St. Peter's piazza, and a very distinct sunburst emanating from the Basilica itself. The correlation of the symbology is striking.
- The pagan association of the obelisk was something well understood by the church. The Jesuit scholar, Athanasius Kircher in his book Obeliscus Pamphilius, published in 1650, gives an account of the ancient views of the obelisk as the *digitus solis, or "finger of the sun"*. [92]
- Pope Sixtus V (1585 - 1590) had the Egyptian obelisks erected all over Rome, as Counter-Reformation monuments. [92]
- ***Finally, this obelisk within the circle in St. Peter's Basilica was dedicated on the Satanic holiday,*** April 30, 1586 -- a day known to the Pagans either as Walpurgis Night or May Eve, the eve before Beltaine. ["The Magic of Obelisks", by Peter Tompkins, p. 26] [92]

- The obelisk was dedicated on the Satanic holiday. The root of sun worship is the worship of Satan. The 2nd to last section of this chapter has web addresses where you can see videos of the Roman Catholic Church in Rome worshipping Satan. St Peter's square has largest solar wheel on planet with an obelisk in the center of it, which are clearly symbols of sun worship, idolatry. God hates idols. *God divorced Israel for idolatry, spiritual adultery.* He calls Mystery Babylon a whore and her daughters, harlots, for the idolatry, the doctrines of Babylon.
- "And I saw, when for all the causes whereby backsliding **Israel committed adultery** I had put her away, and **given her a bill of divorce**; yet her treacherous sister **Judah** feared not, but went and **played the harlot also**." (Jer 3:8) (Spiritual adultery and spiritual harlotry)
- **The word matstsebah** in Hebrew **means standing images or obelisk** and it can be found in many places of the Bible. Here is Strong's definition of the Hebrew word matstsebah-H4676. matstsebah, mats-tsay-baw'; fem. (causat.) part. of H5324; something stationed, **i.e. a column or (memorial stone); by anal. an idol**:--garrison, (standing) *image, pillar.*
- In the following verses **matstsebah** has been translated as **image(s):**

- "Thou shalt not bow down to their gods, nor serve them, nor do after their works: but thou shalt utterly overthrow them, and quite break down their images." (Exo 23:24)
- "But ye shall destroy their altars, break their images, and cut down their groves:" (Exo 34:13)
- "Ye shall make you no idols nor graven image, neither rear you up a standing image, neither shall ye set up any image of stone in your land, to bow down unto it: for I am the LORD your God" (Lev 26:1)
- "But thus shall ye deal with them; ye shall destroy their altars, and break down their images, and cut down their groves, and burn their graven images with fire." (Deu 7:5)
- "And ye shall overthrow their altars, and break their pillars, and burn their groves with fire; and ye shall hew down the graven images of their gods, and destroy the names of them out of that place." (Deu 12:3)
- "He shall break also the images of Bethshemesh, that is in the land of Egypt; and the houses of the gods of the Egyptians shall he burn with fire." (Jer 43:13)
- "Thy graven images also will I cut off, and thy standing images out of the midst of thee; and thou shalt no more worship the work of thine hands." (Micah 5:13)

Doctrines INVENTED FOR THE PAGAN SUN GOD BAAL
- **Nimrod's victory over death through the power of the serpent**
- As the "god of nature," Nimrod was symbolized by a Great Tree until his death. There is nothing in Scripture regarding how he died, but legend teaches that he was hacked to death by his grandfather Ham for his rebellion against Yahweh Elohiym (Jehovah God) at the Tower of Babel.[3] After this Great Tree was cut down and killed in his prime, he was symbolized as a branchless tree stump, called the *Yule Log*. [94] (Note: my other resource said, Noah's son Shem, instead of Ham, killed him but Nimrod was a real person, listed in the Bible and was worshiped as a god, and the legend is that he was brought back to life, rebirth, by the serpent.)
- One very ancient legend tells how *Aesculapius* (the great serpent), a Babylonian symbol of life restored, came and wrapped iitself around Nimrod (the stump). Miraculously, a new tree appeared at the side of the stump symbolizing Nimrod's rebirth. This mystery was later engraved on an ancient Ephesian coin, which portrays Nimrod's victory over death[5] through the power of the serpent rather than the power of Yahweh. [94]

Doctrines of Babylon Adopted by THE VATICAN
Symbol of serpent on numerous Catholic Church door handles, Papal crests, etc. [25]

Serpent door handle, new St. Mary's Cathedral in San Francisco, California [54]

94
https://www.facebook.com/Zionians4Christ/photos/a.426638267420098.1073741825.404690029614922/912256952191558/?type=3&hc_ref=PAGES_TIMELINE

Doctrines INVENTED FOR THE PAGAN SUN GOD BAAL
- **Demi-gods staff with serpent**

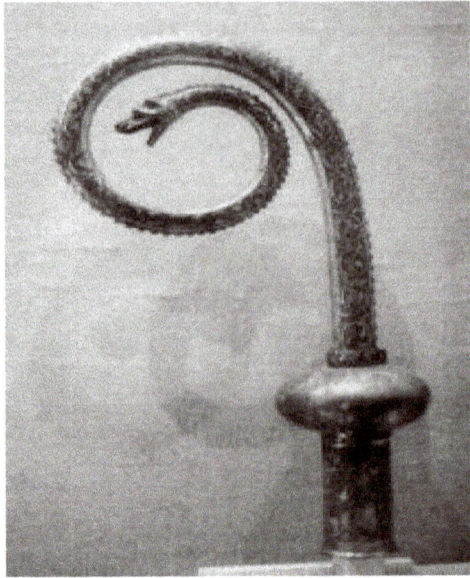

24

Doctrines of Babylon Adopted by THE VATICAN
- **Pope carries exact same staff (serpent crosiers)**

Serpent crosiers were commonly carried by bishops and high Catholic Church officials during the Middle Ages. Although it is claimed that the crosier represents the shepherd's crook, it actually can be traced to the divining staff or augur of Pontifex Maximus of ancient Rome who inherited it from the priests of Babylon. [95]

- **Crosier:** A crosier (crozier, pastoral staff, paterissa, pósokh) is the stylized staff of office (pastoral staff) carried by high-ranking Catholic, Eastern Orthodox, Anglican, and some Lutheran, United Methodist and Pentecostal prelates. ... [96]

96

Western crosier of Archbishop
Heinrich of Finstingen, 1260–1286

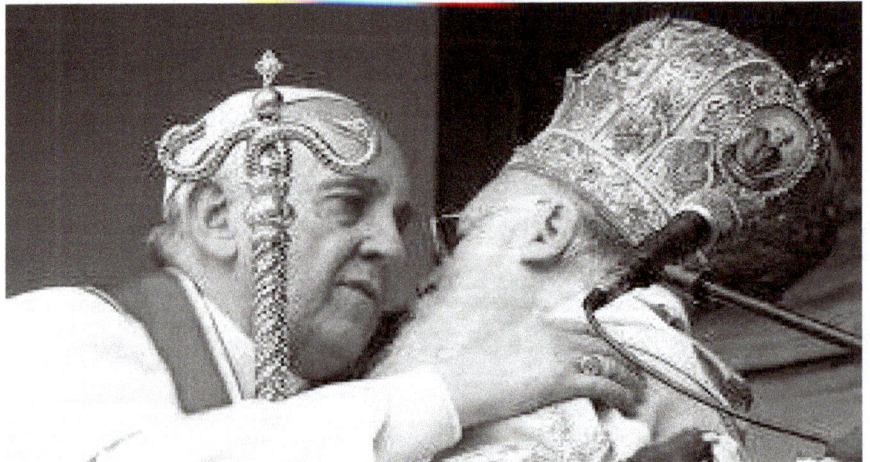

97

---

[95] http://www.markbeast.org/mark-beast-paganism.html

[96] https://en.wikipedia.org/wiki/Crosier

[97] https://awarenessdeconstructingconsciousness.files.wordpress.com/2014/12/pope-serpent.jpg

Doctrines INVENTED FOR THE PAGAN SUN GOD BAAL

- **Oanne, Babylonian fish-god (half man half fish) was depicted by Pagan high priests by wearing a fish head mitre (head dress)** upon a mans head to symbolize man and fish joining when "sun god" set into the ocean. (Neptune = case in point. Half man half fish) One particular Biblical diety = "Dagon" Dag=fish On=sun [25]

- Oannes, Babylonian fish-god, was an allegory in the mysteries of the return of Nimrod from the world of the dead. He is depicted as half-fish. Notice the fish's head over the human head. [56]
Pagan priests as half-fish, sprinkling holy water. Stone relief on temple laver from Assyria, in the Peragmum Museum, East Berlin. [56]

[56]

[56]

Each priest is depicted wearing a fish-head mitre. One of the names of this god in Babylon and Philistia was **Dagon (dag=fish, on=sun)**. One of the most common ways of depicting Dagon is described by the archaeologist, Layard: "The head of the fish formed a mitre above that of a man, while its scaly, fin-like tail fell as a cloak behind, leaving the human limbs and feet exposed. Layard's Babylon & Ninevah, p. 343. [56]

Doctrines of Babylon Adopted by THE VATICAN

- **Mitres are worn by all Popes of Catholicism**

[56]

[98]

The Pope often displays his mitre publicly. It is one of the most visible evidences that sun worship has continued under the name of Christianity. [56]

---

[98] http://nebraskaepiscopalian.org/wp-content/uploads/2013/08/cope.jpg

74

Doctrines INVENTED FOR THE PAGAN SUN GOD BAAL
The multi-level crown of the high Pagan priest was first worn by old Babylonian gods in 1800BC. The horned tiara was carved atop Assyrian winged-bull cherubims as well. The Jewish Kabbalistic solar deity wore this very same tiara, as did Krishna. [51]

Doctrines of Babylon Adopted by THE VATICAN

"The … crown or his mitre which is worn by the POPE, this was clarified and proven to us by this *Catholic Newspaper*. This crown is known as the *Papal Tiara*…" [85]

Doctrines INVENTED FOR THE PAGAN SUN GOD BAAL
Sun Worship used the symbols of the "*Unicorn, Peacock, and Phoenix*" to signify some of their sun gods. [51]

Doctrines of Babylon Adopted by THE VATICAN
Golden door in the chapel of St. Ignatius in San Francisco, California, uses several symbols identifying the wafer god. The *Unicorn, Peacock, and Phoenix* are all well known symbols in the occult for the sun, Lucifer, or Satan. [56]

56

Doctrines INVENTED FOR THE PAGAN SUN GOD BAAL
Carvings of "nature spirits" (fauns or satyrs) depicting a horned, hoofed-god were a common feature in all Sun Worship churches

Fauns or Satyrs

**Doctrines
of Babylon
Adopted by
THE
VATICAN**

56

56

This hideous horned nature spirit is found on a sacred reliquary, among the most sacred items in the Vatican treasury, beneath St. Peter's Basilica... In Roman paganism, they were called fauns; in Greek, they were known as satyrs. They are reflections of the horned, hoofed-god, traceable to the sun-god of Babylon. [56]

76

Doctrines INVENTED FOR THE PAGAN SUN GOD BAAL
The "eye of Osiris" can be found all over Egyptian temple. It was commonly used as protection against evil magic.[51] The sun god, Nimrod was known in Egypt as Osiris.

Doctrines of Babylon Adopted by THE VATICAN
Notice the eye of Osiris in the ring the two angels are holding. You can see *many* examples of the eye of Osiris in the Catholic Church. This one is in the Vatican. I have enlarged the picture so you can see it.
[52]

The eye of Osiris in a sexigesimal triangle on a Roman Catholic confessional in Milano, Italy.[99]

Piazza del Popolo in Rome [100]

[99] https://amazingdiscoveries.org/albums?view=album&code=SymbolsofGods#_
[100] http://whale.to/c/churches_ill.html#All_seeing_eye_

Doctrines INVENTED FOR THE PAGAN SUN GOD BAAL

- **Hand gestures in the form of a trident found depicted in Jupiter, Buddah, Appollo, Hindu diety's, as well as "votive hands" in pagan temples**

56

Doctrines of Babylon Adopted by THE VATICAN

Statue of St. Peter (*Actually **the old Jupiter statue of Rome** shown below on the left, enlarged next to it*) as well as millions of other statues, paintings, photos, and videos of everyone from Jesus and Mary to priests, cardinals, bishops, all the Popes, Vatican guards and even lay people in the Catholic Church seen holding up the three finger trident salute of pagan Rome. (Now called the salute to the Trinity) [51]

Another name for Jupiter is Zeus. Another name for Zeus is Enlil, which is another name for the Devil. This satanic sign, three finger trident was adopted into the Roman Catholic Church.

Continue through this whole book to see how all the puzzle pieces fit together.

56   56   101   102

---

[101] http://worldtruth.tv/wp-content/uploads/2012/03/21kjedz1.jpg
[102] https://rapsta24.wordpress.com/tag/catholic/

Doctrines INVENTED FOR THE PAGAN SUN GOD BAAL

- Quetzalcoatl, the lord of life and death in the Aztec and Toltec culture, 1000 A.D. Notice the full heart in the chest. Humans believed to possess a deified heart were sacrificed; their hearts were then offered to nourish the sun. [56] The sacred heart was also used in pagan mysteries of Osiris, Vishnu, and Bel. [56]
- Osiris is another name for the sun god, Nimrod.

56   56

Doctrines of Babylon Adopted by THE VATICAN

Catholic Sun Worship Symbols, Catholicism is actually based on paganism, and the real deity worshiped behind the scene is not Jesus Christ, but rather Osiris in whatever form he takes. [103] Remember Osiris is another name for Nimrod or his reincarnation, Tammuz, the sun-god.

Notice the sun god's glowing rays, the sacred heart of Quetzalcoatl (i.e. Osiris, Vishnu, Bel, etc.), and the satanic hand sign brought from Babylon.

104   105

- Literally hundreds of thousands of statues, paintings, posters, lithographs, etc have Jesus as well as Mary depicted in the same manner with what the Catholic church calls "The sacred heart." [56]
- The flaming hearts found on Catholic images of Mary and Jesus have no Christian origin. This heart was sacred in pagan mysteries: Osiris, Vishnu, Bel, etc., and was

[103] http://amazingdiscoveries.org/albums?view=album&code=SunWorshipSymbols
[104] http://www.catholictradition.org/Christ/precious-bloodsh1c.jpg
[105] https://www.catholicfaithstore.com/Store/Products/Cat/3bf/Sacred-Heart-Prints-and-Artwork/All.html

worn as an amulet around the necks of Roman youth. [56]

In this chapter, we have seen the Catholic Church fits God's seven scripture descriptions of Mystery Babylon and that she adopted the Babylonian sun worship doctrines, over 35 doctrines adopted into the Church is not coincidence.

I love the people in the Catholic Church. I love the people in the Catholic Church's daughter churches, (Mystery Babylon's daughter churches). I apologize for the hurt these truths bring. I had to show you these truths because God is calling His people out of Mystery Babylon that *we be not partakers of her sins* that we receive not her plagues (calling us out of her before He judges her). The roots of Babylonian sun worship is actually the worship of Satan. Later you will see that Mystery Babylon even worships Satan in the open, in a Church service, in Rome.

In the next two chapters you will see Mystery Babylon changed Two of God's Ten Commandments making them of none effect. The Catholic Church admits, and even claims they changed the first one I'm sharing with you. Please read with an open mind, remembering they claim this change is theirs, and it is another Babylonian tradition brought into the Church. God did not make these changes.

81

Mystery Babylon Admits They Changed This!

(Another Babylonian Doctrine-Tradition, Brought into the Church)

History shows that the Roman State religion was one of sun-worship (Mithraism) at first, then Constantine enforced a blended form of Christianity and Mithraism on the empire. He outlawed the true Sabbath, and enforced Sun-day worship under penalty of death. He established Catholicism (Latin meaning: Universalism) [37]

Doctrines INVENTED FOR THE PAGAN SUN GOD BAAL

- **The first day of the week kept sacred to honor the Persian sun god Mithra, "SUN"day.** *Sunday* was the day set aside in the Mithra (Roman) cult as its official day to assemble together to worship its Sun-deity. **Roman Emperor Constantine legislated Sun-day as a day of rest dedicated to the Greek and Roman Sun-god, Helios.** Constantine worshipped "Christos Helios" which means **"Christ-The-True-Sun."** [106]

Doctrines of Babylon Adopted by THE VATICAN

- **Roman Catholic Church admits the changing from God's commandment the seventh day, Saturday, to the Catholic Churches' commandment, the sixth day, "SUN" day** [107]

- The Convert's Catechism of Catholic Doctrine (1957):
  Q. Which is the Sabbath day?
  Saturday is the Sabbath day.
  Q. Why do we observe Sunday instead of Saturday?
  A. We observe Sunday instead of Saturday because the
  Catholic Church transferred the solemnity from
  Saturday to Sunday. [84]
- Cardinal James Gibbons, The Faith of Our Fathers (Ayers Publishing, 1978): 108: But you may read the Bible from Genesis to Revelation, and you will not find a single line authorizing the sanctification of Sunday. The Scriptures enforce the religious observance of Saturday, a day which we never sanctify. [84]
- Chancellor Albert Smith for Cardinal of Baltimore Archdiocese, letter dated February 10, 1920: If Protestants would follow the Bible, they should worship God on the Sabbath day by God is Saturday. In keeping the Sunday, they are following a law of the Catholic Church. [84]
- Catholic Priest T. Enright, CSSR, Kansas City, MO: It was the holy Catholic Church that changed the day of rest from Saturday to Sunday, the 1st day of the week. And it not only compelled all to keep Sunday, but at the Council of Laodicea, AD 364, anathematized those who kept the Sabbath and urged all persons to labor on the 7th day under penalty of anathema. [84] (Anathema is a formal curse or excommunicating of a person.)
- Our Sunday Visitor (February 5, 1950): ***Practically everything Protestants regard as essential or important they have received from the Catholic Church***... The Protestant mind does not seem to realize that in accepting the Bible and ***observing the Sunday, in keeping Christmas and Easter, they are accepting the authority of the spokesman for the church, the Pope.*** [84]
- Catholic Priest T. Enright, CSSR, lecture at Hartford, KS, Feb 18, 1884: I have repeatedly offered $1000 to any one who can furnish any proof from the Bible that Sunday is the day we are bound to keep...The Bible says, "Remember the Sabbath day to keep it holy," but the Catholic Church says, "No, keep the first day of the week," and the whole world bows in obedience. [84]

---

[106] http://assemblyoftrueisrael.com/Documents/Sunworship.htm
[107] https://en.wikipedia.org/wiki/Constantine_the_Great_and_Christianity

- Letter from C.F. Thomas, Chancellor of Cardinal Gibbons on October 28, 1895: **Of course the Catholic Church claims that the change was her act**...And the act is a MARK of her ecclesiastical power and authority in religious matters. [84]
- John A. O'Brien, The Faith of Millions: the Credentials of the Catholic Religion Revised Edition (Our Sunday Visitor Publishing, 1974): 400-401: But since Saturday, not Sunday, is specified in the Bible, isn't it curious that non-Catholics, who claim to take their religion directly from the Bible and not from the Church, observe Sunday instead of Saturday? Yes, of course, it is inconsistent; but **this change was made about fifteen centuries before Protestantism was born, and by that time the custom was universally observed**. They have continued the custom even though it rests upon the authority of the Catholic Church and not upon and explicit text in the Bible. *That observance remains as a reminder of the Mother Church from which the non-Catholic sects broke away—like a boy running away from home but still carrying in his pocket a picture of his mother or a lock of her hair.* [84]
- Constantine was the first so-called Christian emperor of the Roman Empire. The story of his conversion has become very well known to students of ancient history.... **Sun Worship**, you see, at that time the cult of Mithraism or sun-worship **was the official religion of the Roman Empire**. It stood as the greatest competitor to the new Christian religion. It had its own organization, temples, priesthood, robes—everything. It also had an official worship day on which special homage was given to the sun. That day was called "The Venerable Day of the Sun." It was the first day of the week, and from it we get our name Sunday. *When Constantine pressed his pagan hordes into the church they were observing the day of the sun for their adoration of the sun god. It was their special holy day.* In order to make it more convenient for them to make the change to the new religion, Constantine accepted their day of worship, Sunday, instead of the Christian Sabbath which had been observed by Jesus and His disciples. ...**the change was imposed on Christianity through a strong civil law issued by Constantine as the Emperor of Rome.** The very wording of that law, by the way, can be found in any reliable encyclopedia. After Constantine made the initial pronouncement and legal decree about the change, the Catholic Church reinforced that act in one church council after another. [108]
- **Encyclopedia Britannica** under the article, Sunday. Notice: "It was Constantine who first made a law for the proper observance of Sunday and who appointed that it should be regularly celebrated throughout the Roman empire." [108]
- **Catholic Encyclopedia**, Vol. 4, p. 153. "**The church** after changing the day of rest from the Jewish Sabbath or seventh-day of the week to the first, **made the third commandment refer to Sunday** as the day to be kept holy as the Lord's day." [108]
- On March 7, 321, **Sunday, the Day of the Sun**, was declared an official day of rest **in honor of the Roman Sun God Sol Invictus**. [107]

God's Commandment, the only one of the ten commandments of God with specific instructions to: *Remember it*.
- "8) **Remember the sabbath day**, to keep it holy. 9) Six days shalt thou labour, and do all thy work: 10) **But the seventh day is the sabbath of the LORD** thy God: in it thou shalt not do any work, thou, nor thy son, nor thy daughter, thy manservant, nor thy maidservant, nor thy cattle, nor thy stranger that is within thy gates: 11) **For in six days the LORD made heaven and earth, the sea, and all that in them is, and rested the seventh day:** *wherefore* **the LORD blessed the sabbath day, and hallowed it**." (Exo 20:8-11)
- "Wherefore the children of Israel shall keep the sabbath, to **observe the sabbath throughout their generations, for a perpetual covenant**." (Exo 31:16) (perpetual=never ending, forever)

As Christians, we are grafted into the vine, grafted into Jesus (Yeshua), a Jew. We are God's people as Israel is. Jesus (Yeshua) was Jewish and kept the Sabbath. Jews today still keep the Sabbath. Messianic Jews keep the Sabbath. The Sabbath is to be kept throughout the generations, a perpetual covenant, to be remembered, to be kept forever, not changed. Exo. 20:11 gives us understanding that remembering, honoring this commandment

---

[108] http://www.sabbathtruth.com/sabbath-history/how-the-sabbath-was-changed

is the way we acknowledge that God is the creator. We rest on the seventh day as He rested on the seventh day after he created the heavens and the earth.

- "For in six days the LORD made heaven and earth, the sea, and all that in them is, and rested ***the seventh day***: ***wherefore*** the LORD blessed the sabbath day, and hallowed it." (Exo. 20:11)

God's people are still keeping His commandments in the book of Revelations in chapter 14.

- "Here is the patience of the saints: here are ***they that keep the commandments of God***, **and the faith of Jesus.**" (Rev 14:12)
- Definition of Saints: Ones made holy, righteous, by the blood of the Lamb, by Jesus (Yeshua's) death on the cross. He paid for all of our sins and makes us righteous. [(Rom 6:23) For the wages of sin *is* death; but the gift of God *is* eternal life through Jesus Christ our Lord. (Rom 3:25) Whom God hath set forth *to be* a propitiation *through faith in his blood, to declare his righteousness* for the remission of sins that are past, through the forbearance of God; (Rom 4:5) But to him that worketh not, but believeth on him that justifieth the ungodly, his faith is counted for righteousness.]
- So the ones who have been cleansed from their sins, through faith in the blood of the Lamb, Jesus (Yeshua) *are still keeping the commandments of God.* They are not keeping the commandments in order to make themselves clean but because God has cleansed them of their sins. Because He has saved them from their sins, they show their love to Him by keeping His commandments. They are still keeping *all* of His commandments in the last book of the Bible.

Jesus rebuked the Jewish elders for following traditions of men instead of following God's commandments in Mar 7:9,13

- "9) And he said unto them, Full well ye reject the commandment of God, that ye may keep your own tradition. 13) Making the word of God of none effect through your tradition, which ye have delivered: and many such like things do ye." (Mar 7:9, 13)
- The Catholic Church did the same thing, (***made God's commandment to remember the Sabbath of none effect***), when they adopted Sunday as the official day of worship, <u>Sunday, in honor of the Roman Sun God Sol Invictus</u>, when Constantine made it a law to rest on Sunday, and the Roman Catholic Church reinforced it in counsel after counsel and is admitted to in **Catholic Encyclopedia**, Vol. 4, p. 153. "**The church** after changing the day of rest from the Jewish Sabbath or seventh-day of the week to the first, **made the third commandment refer to Sunday** as the day to be kept holy as the Lord's day." [108]

God does not take it lightly when we forget His commandments. In Hos 4:6 He says: "**... *seeing thou hast forgotten the law of thy God, I will also forget thy children.*"**

Now for the other Commandment of God, made of none effect through the traditions of Babylon.

Another, Babylonian Doctrine of the Sun God, Brought into the Church

The second of the two of God's Ten commandments that Mystery Babylon changed.

We've seen clearly in the last chapter, that Mystery Babylon claims she changed the day of rest, to Sunday and says that "the act is a MARK of her ecclesiastical power and authority in religious matters" but Jesus tells us that we must worship God in spirit and in truth in John 4:24 (i.e. according to His word, not according to Mystery Babylon's word).

- "God *is* a Spirit: and they that worship him **must worship** *him* **in spirit and in truth**." (Joh 4:24)

To "keep the Sabbath holy" is the only commandment God gave with the instructions to "remember" it and the first commandment has a special instruction too, to **hear** it. God commands His people to **hear**.

In the very first of God's Ten Commandments, He commands His people to Hear, ***Hear that He is one***... God gave this commandment in the Old Testament and Yeshua (Jesus) repeated it in the New Testament. (Deu 6:4,5 Mark 12:29,30)

- "4) ***Hear,*** O Israel: ***The LORD our God is one LORD***: 5) And thou shalt love the LORD thy God with all thine heart, and with all thy soul, and with all thy might." (Deu 6:4,5)
- "29) And Jesus answered him, ***The first of all the commandments is, Hear***, O Israel; ***The Lord our God is one Lord***: 30) And thou shalt love the Lord thy God with all thy heart, and with all thy soul, and with all thy mind, and with all thy strength: this *is* the first commandment." (Mar 12:29,30)

Yeshua's disciples understood that Yeshua is the one Lord God of the first commandment manifest in the flesh.

As God's children we are to understand that Yeshua is the one LORD God of the first commandment that was manifest in the flesh. We are to understand the Godhead and the mystery of God. God's word says we are to: Understand (Rom 1:20), Acknowledge (Col 2:2) and Be Established (Rom 16:25, 26) according to the revelation of the mystery. God commanded, the revelation be made known to all nations (Rom 16:25), to be made manifest (made known) by the scriptures (Rom 16:26), understood by the things that are made, even his ...Godhead (Rom 1:20) and says those that keep it from you are without excuse. (Rom 1:20) [109]

- "**Beware** lest any man spoil you through philosophy and vain deceit, after the *tradition of men*, after the rudiments of the world, and not after Christ. (Col 2:9) For in him dwelleth all the fulness of the Godhead bodily." (Col 2:8)

God's word says we are to: Understand (Ro 1:20), Acknowledge (Col 2:2) and Be Established (Ro16:25, 26) *according to the revelation of the mystery*, and says those that keep it from you are without excuse. (Ro 1:20) [109]

The mystery of God and the Godhead are explained completely in the Bible study: Be Not Faithless But Believing, Jesus Subtitle: The Mystery of God Revealed by Cheryl Alvarado, and a large portion of her Bible study is in this book: Sound the Alarm in Chapter 4: The Mystery of God Revealed. [109]

---

[109] Be Not Faithless But Believing, Jesus Subtitle: The Mystery of God Revealed by Cheryl Alvarado www.themysteryrevealed.info

She explains that, understanding God's name is the first step in understanding the mystery of God and the Godhead. Where ever you see the word: LORD, all in capital letters in the Old Testament, that is where God's name was taken out of His word and replaced with the word, LORD.

- "And God said moreover unto Moses, Thus shalt thou say unto the children of Israel, The LORD [H3068 **YHWH**] God of your fathers, the God of Abraham, the God of Isaac, and the God of Jacob, hath sent me unto you: **this is my name for ever, and this is my memorial unto all generations**." (Exo 3:15)

In Exo 3:15 God says His name is YHWH forever. There are two ways thought on how to pronounce YHWH: Yahweh or Jehovah. The four letters of God's name "are usually **transliterated from Hebrew** as **IHVH in Latin, JHWH in German, French, and Dutch**, and **YHWH in English.** This was variously rendered as **"Yahweh" or "Jehovah"**, since in Latin there was no distinct lettering to distinguish 'Y' from 'J', or 'W' from 'V', and the Hebrew does not clearly indicate the omitted vowels." [109:5]

Below is God's first commandment. It is easy to see that YHWH is commanding His people to hear that the LORD [**YHWH**] our God is one LORD [**YHWH**]. The disciples understood the first commandment, that **YHWH God is one YHWH.** They understood that Yahweh God is one Yahweh. They understood that (Jesus) Yeshua was the one YHWH God of the first commandment manifest in the flesh.

- "4) Hear, O Israel: The LORD [**YHWH**] our God *is one LORD [**YHWH**]*: 5) And thou shalt love the LORD [**YHWH**] thy God with all thine heart, and with all thy soul, and with all thy might." (Deu 6:4,5)

I know this is very hard to hear but the Roman Catholic Church fits God's description of Mystery Babylon to a tee and she adopted all the Babylonian traditions into the Roman Catholic Church, including the doctrine of the trinity. God's first commandment, commands His people to hear that God is one **LORD [YHWH]** God, one Yahweh God, the Roman Catholic Church (Mystery Babylon) teaches that God is a trinity, three separate persons or three separate Gods in one.

God describes the Roman Catholic Church with the name *Mystery* Babylon the Great. It was a Great Mystery. *It was completely hidden*, from the people of the Church that they were following the pagan gods and the many traditions of Babylon. God's people didn't know what had been changed because the Church kept them from reading the Bible for about a 1000 years, they had made it against the law at the Council of Toulouse to have the Bible in their native tongue. Unknowingly the traditions of Babylon became rooted deeply in God's peoples' hearts and still are today.

It is important to know that, all the *organized* churches of today are the churches that were formed coming out of the Catholic Church at the reformation and took her teachings of men, the traditions of Babylon with them. Mystery Babylon calls these Churches her daughters. God calls them harlots because they follow Mystery Babylon's Babylonian gods and doctrines instead of Him.

The traditions of men (traditions of Babylon) have made God's first commandment: *Hear, O Israel: The LORD [YHWH] our God is one LORD [YHWH]*, of non-effect, just as Yeshua warned not to do in Mar 7:13. And God's word warns us not to be deceived specifically mentioning the Godhead in Col 2:8.

- "***Beware*** lest any man spoil you through philosophy and vain deceit, after ***the tradition of men***, after the rudiments of the world, and not after Christ. (Col 2:9) ***For in him dwelleth all the fulness of the Godhead bodily***." (Col 2:8)

The Catholic Encyclopedia explains specifically, Tertullian of the Roman Catholic Church was the first to use the Latin word: trinitas.

- **New Catholic Encyclopedia** Volume 13 1977 Page 1021 Call# UKIKCB32664428 As far as is known, the first use of the Latin word *trinitas* with reference to God is found in Tertullian's *Adversus Praxean* and *De pudicitia*. **He was the first to use the term persona in a Trinitarian** and Christological context, asserting that the Logos is distinct from the Father as person and not as substance and the Holy Spirit is the "third person" in the Trinity (*Adv. Praxean* 12). (I apologize I lost my source)

The doctrine of the trinity did not exists till 325 A.D. The doctrine of the trinity came from the Catholic's Nicene Council (Mystery Babylon's council), not the word of God.

This is when the Babylonian Trinity concept entered the New Testament age. "...the Roman Council of Nicene many of the bishops in attendance practiced paganism and eastern mysticism in their own states,..." [110]

Over 1500 years ago, Constantine brought into the Catholic Church the Babylonian traditions of the sun god, changed our Jewish Saviour's name (shown shortly) Yeshua to the pagan sun god Hesus, (Iesous) which later became Jesus, changed the day of rest from Saturday to Sunday to honor the sun god, and made the first commandment to hear that the one LORD [YHWH] God is one LORD [YHWH] of none effect *with the Babylonian doctrine of three deities.*

Ancient Babylonian Triad, Truine, Trinity [110]
Babylon is the place of origin of all False Doctrine and the Trinity

THE THREE MAIN GODS		
First Person	**Second Person**	**Third Person**
Father, King	Son, Prince	Queen, Mother
Triad of Babylon		
Nimrod	Tammuz	Simerimas
Shamash	Sin	Ishtar
Triad of Backsliden Israel		
Baal	Tammuz	Ashoreth
Triad of Egypt		
Osiris	**Horus**	**Isis**
Triad of Greece		
Zeus	Apollo	Athena
Triad of India		
Brahama	Vishnu	Shiva
Triad of Rome		
Jupiter	Mars	Venus
Triad of Catholicism		
Father	Son	Holy Spirit
Jehovah	Jesus	Dove

[110] https://www.scribd.com/document/176705397/Origin-of-the-Trinity-Ancient-Babylonian-Triad-Triune-Trinity-Chart

26

The picture of the IHS monogram, is on top of the main altar of the Gesù Church, Rome, Italy. It is the Mother Church for Jesuits.[26]

The very same Babylonian religion that originated at the Tower of Babel, and was carried over into other cultures under different names. ***In Egypt* the Queen of heaven was known as Isis**, **Tammuz was known as Horus**. **Nimrod was known as Seb.** The Egyptian priests placed these initials I H S of the pagan trinity (Isis, Horus & Seb) on a round wafer to commemorate the sun god and they ate it each year on December 25th believing that the sun god was being reincarnated in them as they ate this wafer god. They re-enacted the death of Nimrod on a "tree" on March 25th (Easter) and believed he would be reincarnated on December 25th. This re-enactment was called a "Mass" or Massacre. Today, these same initials of **I H S** appear on the Catholic Eucharist Wafer...[26]

The Babylonian trinity is the true origin of the trinity of the Roman Catholic Church (Mystery Babylon) and her daughter Churches (Christian Churches) took it with them at the reformation. And as mentioned in the previous reference, the pagan Babylonian initials of I H S also appear on the Catholic Eucharist Wafer, communion. These are not coincidences.

YHWH hates the fact that His backsliding whoring wife Israel went after her Ba'als and today He sees the Christian Church doing the identical thing ...[26]

- "And I saw, when for all the causes whereby backsliding Israel committed adultery I had put her away, and *given her a bill of divorce*; yet her treacherous sister Judah feared not, but went and played the harlot also." (Jer 3:8)

Israel was committing *spiritual adultery*, going after the gods (Baals) of Babylon. Judah did the same thing. God called Judah a harlot and calls the daughter Churches of Mystery Babylon, harlots. See below how YHWH God refers to Mystery Babylon and her daughters because they are going after the gods of Babylon.

- "... I will shew unto thee the judgment of the **great whore** that sitteth upon many waters:" (Rev 17:1)
- "And upon her forehead *was* a name written, MYSTERY, **BABYLON THE GREAT**, **THE MOTHER OF HARLOTS** AND ABOMINATIONS OF THE EARTH." (Rev 17:5)
- "For true and righteous *are* his judgments: for he hath judged the **great whore**, which did corrupt the earth with her fornication, and hath avenged the blood of his servants at her hand." (Rev 19:2)

You still might say: "But God is the Father and the Son and the Holy Ghost." And I would respond: "Yes, Yes, Yes, He is, I agree. 1 Cor 2:7 says, It was a mystery, hidden wisdom. But Rom 16:25,26 says, the revelation of the mystery is now made known by the scriptures according to the commandment of God."

- "But we speak the wisdom of God in **a mystery**, even the **hidden wisdom**, which God ordained before the world unto our glory: (1Co 2:8) Which none of the princes of this world knew: **for had they known it, they would not have crucified the Lord of glory**." (1 Cor. 2:7)

- "25) Now to him that is of power to stablish you according to my gospel, and the preaching of Jesus Christ, according to ***the revelation of the mystery***, which was kept secret since the world began, 26) But ***now is made manifest (known), and by the scriptures*** of the prophets, ***according to the commandment of the everlasting God***, made known to all nations for the obedience of faith:" (Rom 16:25,26)

It had been hidden, a mystery, so that Yeshua - Jesus (the Lord of glory, God) could put on flesh and die on the cross, be crucified to pay our sin debt, death, otherwise they would not have put Him to death. (If we had to pay our own sin debt- death, it would mean eternal death – eternal separation from God in Hell.) Now that He had fulfilled what He came to do, to give His life, paying our sin debt to reconcile us to Himself, it was no longer to be hidden that He was the Lord of glory, God. [109] **Chapter 4 explains the mystery of God in detail**.

As God's name was replaced in the Old Testament with the word LORD, His name was also replaced in the New Testament. Jesus is not our Saviour's birth name. His birth name, His Hebrew name is Yeshua. Yeshua is a shortened form of Yehoshua. Yehoshua means YHWH is Salvation. Our Saviour's Hebrew name tells us who He is. That He is YHWH, (Pronounced Yahweh or Jehovah). Next is the story of how our Hebrew Saviour's name Yeshua was replaced with Jesus.

It is very understandable and shocking at the same time what happened. Some people have heard Jesus called Jesus H. Christ before, probably in a swearing manor. Please bear with me and read the whole thing as this is going to sound far-fetched again, at first, but when everything is put together it will make since. There are several parts to this story too.

Shown previously, the Emperor and High priest Constantine brought the Babylonian traditions into the Church. My next resource explains how at the Council of Nicaea, Constantine made the decision to consolidate the pagan gods into one god.

[111] At the Council of Nicaea, Constantine gathered together all the "presbyters" (pagan priests) of his day and all their gods and saviors and had them debate together in an attempt to create one composite "god" they all would agree to worship. This new "god" would be given all the combined attributes and basic life stories of their gods rolled into one.

It was in this "context" that the "god" Jesus H. Christ was created. The long list was narrowed down to the main gods of the Roman Aristocracy (Zeus and the son of Zeus, Apollo) and the gods worshipped by the bulk of the common people (Julius Caesar and the sun god Mithra) along with the Eastern god Krishna.
Up until the First Council of Nicaea, the Roman aristocracy primarily worshiped two Greek gods, Apollo and Zeus, but the great bulk of common people idolized either Julius Caesar or Mithras (the Romanized version of the Persian deity Mithra who was an ***incarnation of the Babylonian Tammuz***). Caesar was deified by the Roman Senate after his death (15 March 44 BC)... The word "Saviour" was affixed to his name, its literal meaning being "one who sows the seed", ... making him Julius Christ.

Constantine had a political problem that required a religious solution, it is that simple. He never had a "conversion" to serve YHVH through Yahusha (Jesus) as we were led to believe. This "political problem" required he create a "god" that those who worshipped Julius would accept, that would be acceptable to the factions in the Eastern and Orient who worshipped Krishna. (Krishna is Sanskrit for Christ)
All of these gods: Jove, Jupiter, Salenus, Baal, Thor, Gade, Apollo, Juno, Aries, Taurus, Minerva, Rhets, Mithra, Theo, Fragapatti, Atys, Durga, Indra, Neptune, Vulcan, Kriste, Agni, Croesus, Pelides, Huit, Hermes, Thulis,

[111] http://www.sabbathcovenant.com/christianitythegreatdeception/CouncilofNicea.htm

Thammus, Eguptus, Iao, Aph, Saturn, Gitchens, Minos, Maximo, Hecla and Phernes and many more were narrowed down from literally hundreds down to 53 then after much debate down to only 5 through balloting: Caesar, Krishna, Mithra, Horus and Zeus (Historia Ecclesiastica, Eusebius, c. 325). So we were given the god Jesus H. Christ literally by a group of pagan priests who cast their "vote" for their pagan god by ballot!

To make a very long and detailed story short, the council could not come to a decision on just one god they all could accept, so **Constantine exercised his authority as Emperor and High Priest** to consolidate the 3 primary gods that would effectively represent the Greek masses and the Eastern and the Oriental religions of the Roman Empire. **Every one of these so called "gods" are nothing more than later incarnations of the Babylonian Religion whose saviour was Tammuz** the second member of the Babylonian Trinity and son/sun of "God". So, Constantine chose the following "gods" to unite his empire:

- To placate the powerful British factions he chose the great *Druid god* which was the *sun god* **Hesus**
- To placate the faction from Egypt he chose the *Assyrian sun god* **Horus**
- To placate the Eastern/Oriental factions he chose the *Eastern Saviour-god*, **Krishna** (Christ) (*Krishna is Sanskrit for Christ*) [111]

IMPORTANT NOTE*: Krishna, which is Sanshrit for Christ, is not our Hebrew Messiah, Yeshua (Jesus).* Krishna is the reincarnation of Vishnu. Vishnu is the second god of the Hindu trinity. The other two gods are Brahma and Shiva. Shiva is Satan, who is also called Zeus, Nimrod and Tammuz. Krishna (*Krishna, Sanskrit for Christ*) is the reincarnation of the second member of the Babylonian trinity, Tammuz.
Vishnu is the second god in the Hindu triumvirate (or Trimurti)... **The other two gods are Brahma and Shiva**. [112] **Krishna is one of the most powerful incarnations of Vishnu**, the Godhead of the Hindu Trinity of deities. [113]
Satan is Shiva? The most ancient religion that predates Abrahamic religions by thousands of years Sanatana Dharma [Hinduism] ancient head God and Creator is Sanat Kumara...

The Yezidi's in Iraq state they came from ancient India and... brought this God with them. But **they call him Satan which is a spelling of Sanat.... Sanat is also a title of Shiva**, who carries the trident [pitch fork], is adorned with serpents and animal skins, is the God of nature and the wilds, secret knowledge and has the crescent moon in the image of horns on His head. And is sometimes shown as red in color the symbol of the rising sun of the reborn soul. The scholar and doctorate, Alian Danielou proved Shiva is the European God Dionysus who is also known as Zeus the archetypical God of Indo-Europeans. Dionysus is shown in the same way of Shiva from riding on the bull or panther, the serpents, trident, spear, wearing of animal skins to even being depicted as red in color, sometimes with horns. The folkish image of Satan...[114]
End of IMPORTANT NOTE.
---

[111] So, Constantine chose the following "gods" to unite his empire:

- To placate the powerful British factions he chose the great *Druid god* which was the *sun god* **Hesus**
- To placate the faction from Egypt he chose the *Assyrian sun god* **Horus**
- To placate the Eastern/Oriental factions he chose the *Eastern Saviour-god*, **Krishna** (Christ) (*Krishna is Sanskrit for Christ*)

---

[112] http://www.bbc.co.uk/religion/religions/hinduism/deities/vishnu.shtml
[113] https://www.thoughtco.com/who-is-krishna-1770452
[114] https://mythoughtsbornfromfire.wordpress.com/2013/10/17/shiva-bel-satan-set-and-typhon/

These three main sun god/saviors were then united into one composite deity **called Hesus Horus Krishna** which *later became known in its English derived name as Jesus H. Christ*. Satisfying the Julius, Esu, Horus, and Krishna faithful who made up the vast majority of his empire. *Constantine now had a "god" for his new religion which was not new at all but the rebirth of Babylonian sun worship.* A "god" easily acceptable by all throughout his realm (except true followers of Yahusha). [111]

Hesus is a later derivate of the name Esus pronounced "eh-soos". **This is identically to the latin name Iesous where we get the English word "Jesus".**
Strong's #2424: Iesous (pronounced ee-ay-sooce'). **Hesus** [115]

When we simply take a step back and admit to ourselves what happened at the Council of Nicaea the similarities between Hesus and "Jesus" can easily be understood. They are one in the same as Hesus became "J"esus when the letter "J" was introduced into the vocabulary centuries later. We'll get more into the "meaning" of the name Jesus later. Hesus was the second member of a Trinity. [115]

Constantine's Babylonian trinity of *Hesus Horus Krishna* became the New God: Jesus H. Christ

This is a picture of "Jesus" as Hesus, Teutates, and Taranis.

[115]

Below is the triune god worshipped by the Vikings,
another version of this triple diety of Hesus, Teutates, and Taranis.

Trinity. Norway,
14 Century, CE

[115]

SUN GODS: Isis, Horus, & Seb

[115]

Horus too was the second member of a Trinity. This is the very Trinity of the Catholic/Christian Church of **Isis, Horus, and Seb** or I.H.S. the monogram of Jesus H. Christ with the cross of Tammuz all in the middle of the invincible sun god. [115] (The cross of Tammuz, actually a T standing for Tammuz.)

---

[115] http://sabbathcovenant.com/christianitythegreatdeception/newgodcreated.htm

91

Krishna was the second member of the Hindu Trinity just like Horus and Tammuz and (Hesus) Jesus are all second members of their respective pagan trinities. [115] Krishna was the Hindu incarnation of the Babylonian Tammuz in their language and culture. (Sanskrit is the ancient Hindu language.) [115]

The word "Krishna" is **Sanskrit for Christ** and over time the word evolved from Krishna to Krischto to Chresto to Christ. It means "the anointed one" and the meaning is very different from the Hebrew word "messiah".

We see "Jesus" and Krishna portrayed in paintings and the similarities are striking. These images are complete with the solar deity traits of the cross of The Zodiac in front of the blazing sun:

[115]

The people in the Middle Ages didn't know that they were following or worshiping pagan gods, that had been given names of saints because they were not allowed to read the Bible for themselves in their own language. They believed what they were taught, the pagan traditions, as the Church's traditions, not knowing what they were following. Those who did know and refused to accept the pagan doctrines were put to death by the Papacy. They knew that to follow another god other than the one true God is spiritual adultery (idolatry). This is the great deception that Mystery Babylon, (who God calls the great whore), has put on the world, idolatry, spiritual adultery, the one thing God divorced His people for.

- "And I saw, when for all the causes whereby backsliding Israel committed adultery I had put her away, and given her a bill of divorce; yet her treacherous sister Judah feared not, but went and played the harlot also." (Jer 3:8)

God's word says, the devil deceives the whole world. He didn't just start deceiving the world recently. He started in Babylon and the devil used Mystery Babylon to deceive the whole world.

- "And the great dragon was cast out, that old serpent, called the *Devil, and Satan, which deceiveth the whole world:* he was cast out into the earth, and his angels were cast out with him." (Rev 12:9)
- The Bible was forbidden so the doctrine of the trinity, God being three, was taken as truth, causing God's people to commit spiritual adultery. Making the first commandment of none effect through Babylonian traditions. God's first commandment that commands us to: Hear O Israel the LORD [YHWH] God is one LORD [YHWH]... (Deut 6:4 and Mark 12:29) Yahweh is one Yahweh.
- Chapter 4 explains how Yeshua (Jesus) is the one YHWH God manifest in the flesh, through scriptures.

- "God *is* a Spirit: and **they that worship him must worship *him* in spirit and in truth**." (Joh 4:24)

Now that we have the Bible and the internet, we can search out the truth. The truth is, the leaders of the Catholic Church brought over 35 Babylonian traditions, (closer to 53 Babylonian traditions) into the Church including the Babylonian tradition of the trinity. God's first commandment says: YHWH God is one YHWH. (The LORD God is one LORD).

God divorced His people, Israel, because they went after the Babylonian gods. God is getting ready to judge Mystery Babylon, who has taught God's people to follow the same Babylonian traditions. God calls Mystery Babylon the great whore. I know it is hard but I pray Catholics and Christians will heed God's word to come out of Mystery Babylon, out of the Babylonian sun god traditions. God does not want His people to receive her judgments and He is calling us, His people out of Mystery Babylon. He is giving us warning that judgment is coming. Israel did not heed God's warnings and He judged them. He divorced them. They suffered greatly, they suffered the holocaust and were scattered from their promise land. Because they rejected Him and refused to hear His warnings, their eyes have been blind for 2000 years, they have not known their Messiah Yeshua (Jesus). We must open our eyes and heed His warning in Rev. 18:4. **Come out of her *my people***, that ye be not partakers of her sins, that ye receive not her plagues (That we receive not Mystery Babylon's Judgments).

- "And I heard another voice from heaven, saying, **Come out of her, my people**, that ye be not partakers of her sins, and **that ye receive not of her plagues**." (Rev 18:4)

I have shared so much with you but there is still more. The papacy brought in a long list of pagan doctrines from Babylon into the Church including changing the commandment: Remember the Sabbath (The 7th day of the week that commemorates the day God rested after His six days of creation) to the 1st day of the week to honor the Babylonian Sun god and brought in the trinity from Babylon, changing God's first commandment that says, YHWH is one YHWH, to God is three in one.

The next revelations are so extremely big but they can be revealed now after understanding the other extreme deceptions that have taken place. **Again this one is extreme so read the whole thing.**

I mentioned earlier that in the Bible, God's name was replaced with LORD.
Baal (The Babylonian Sun God) in English, became Lord.
So now, Bibles that are in English, where God's name, YWWH, was taken out
it was replaced with the Babylonian sun god name Baal, LORD in English.

Gad (Fortune, a Babylonian Deity: that troop.) became God.
"The astrologers of Babel called Jupiter (**Zeus**) by the name "**Gad.**"
#1408 Gad, gad; a var. of 1409; Fortune, a Babylonian Deity: that troop. [27]

So when, in ignorance, we have said: Jesus is **LORD God**,
it is really calling Jesus, the Babylonian sun god **Baal Zeus**
But this is not all!

This is what the Bible says:
"And in all that I have said to you take heed, and make no mention of the name of other mighty ones, let it not be heard from your mouth," Ex. 23:13. [27]
"...And make no mention of the name of their mighty ones, nor swear by them, nor serve them, nor bow down to them," Josh. 23:7. [27]

Satan has deceived the world into calling Him God. Hold on to your hat, this is unbelievable but true, "Babylon worshipped, Baal, *the Sun-god under the name BEL.*

I mentioned this earlier but I give more information here, that helps to bring understanding of how Satan has deceived the world into calling him god.

93

The two oldest religions in the world are that of El and Bel (aka Baal). (God and Satan)
Beelzebub, Baʿal Zebub (Hebrew זבוב בעל) occurs in 2 Kings 1:2–6 as the name of the Philistine god of Ekron. **Beelzebub, also Beelzebul, is also identified in the New Testament as Satan, the "prince of the demons".**[n 15][n 16] In Arabic the name is retained as Baʿal dhubaab / zubaab (ال ذب اب ب عل), literally "Lord of the Flies".[citation needed] Biblical scholar Thomas Kelly Cheyne suggested that it might be a derogatory corruption of Baʿal Zəbûl, "Lord of the High Place" (i.e., Heaven) or "High Lord".[60] **The word Beelzebub in rabbinical texts is a mockery of the Baʿal religion, which ancient Hebrews considered to be idol (or, false god) worship.**[61]

The Babylonians worshiped the Sun-god Baal as Bel (short for Belzubub), which is another name for Satan, Lucifer.

#1167 ba'al, bah'al; from 1166; a **_master_**; hence a **_husband_**, or (fig.) **_owner_** (often used with another noun in modification of this latter sense):- + archer, + babbler, + bird, captain, chief man, + confederate, + have to do, + dreamer, those to whom it is due, + furious, those that are given to it, great, + hairy, he that hath it, have, +horseman, **husband, lord,** man, + married, master, person, + sworn, they of. 27

Now, if these were the only uses of the word baal, we really couldn't complain, could we? Why? Because even Scripture reveals that YHWH was a husband to Israel (cf. Isa. 54:5; Jer. 31:32). This in Hebrew, would be, "YHWH is baal to Israel." Thus, baal is used in a good sense. But this is not the only usage of the word, as we shall show.

#1168 ba'al, bah'al; the same as 1167; **Baal, a Phoenician deity:-Baal, (plur.) Baalim.**
...Ba'al was the founder of Babel (Babylon), according to secular history. He is identified with **Zeus,** Jupiter, Ammon, Asshur, Assur, Kronos, and Bel-Marduk. Morris Jastrow, Max Müller, and W. H. Roscher all three agree: **Baal is the Babylonian sun deity.** 27

This reference says, Baal is the Babylonian sun deity. It gets bigger!
BAAL ZEBUWB OR BEELZEBOUL
#1176 (Hebrew) Baal Zebuwb, bah'al zeb-oob; from 1168 and 2070; Baal of (the) fly; Baal-zebub, a special deity of the Ekronites: Baal-Zebub.
Remember when the Pharisees called Yahushua the Messiah Beelzebub (Mat. 10:25) and claimed that He cast out the demons by the prince of demons (Mat. 12:24, 27; Mk. 3:22; Lk. 11:15, 18, 19). 27
Well, now go to Strong's Greek #954 and be ready for a shock!
#954 (Greek) Beelzeboul, beh-el-zeb-ool'; of Chald. Or. [by parody upon 1176]; dung-god; Beelzebul, **a name of Satan:** Beelzebub. 27
- Notice above that **Baal and Beel are interchangeable**: Beelzebul and Baal Zebuwb, **the name for Satan, and shortened to Baal, in English Lord.**
- **Here's the bomb shell:**
  In Exodus 3:15 God tells us His name is YHWH, and that it is His name forever.
  But in our English Bibles, God's name, YHWH, was replaced with: LORD. Lord which came from Baal. _Remember baal can mean_ master; hence a husband, or (fig.) owner, or _lord_ **but baal is also short for the name: Baal= Baal Zebuwb (in Hebrew), Bel=Beelzeboul (in Greek),** Beelzebub (in English, See Luk 11:15). Beelzebub, Baal Zebuwb (Baal for short) is another name for Satan, the Devil. The devil put his name: Baal (LORD in English) in place of God's name, YHWH.
- "And God said moreover unto Moses, Thus shalt thou say unto the children of Israel, The **LORD [YHWH]** God of your fathers, the God of Abraham, the God of Isaac, and the God of Jacob, hath sent me unto you: **this _is_ my name for ever**, and this _is_ my memorial unto all generations." (Exo 3:15)
- "How long shall this be in the heart of the prophets that prophesy lies? yes, they are prophets of the deceit of their own heart; Which think to **cause my people to forget my name** by their dreams which they tell every man to his neighbor, **as their fathers have forgotten my name for Baal.**" **(Jeremiah 23:26-27)**

How many of God's people these days know God's name, YHWH, Yahweh?

And there is still a lot more you need to know. Those who we think are serving God, are openly serving Satan. God says in 2 Cor. 11:13 false apostles turn themselves into apostles of Christ.

- "13) For such are **false apostles**, deceitful workers, **transforming themselves into the apostles of Christ.** 14) And no marvel; for Satan himself is transformed into an angel of light. 15) Therefore it is no great thing if his ministers also be transformed as the ministers of righteousness; whose end shall be according to their works." (2 Co 11:13-15)

POPE VISITS HOLY SITE OF SERMON ON THE MOUNT

CNN LIVE

"This cross is not broken, but turned upside down. It indicates the rejection of Jesus Christ and contempt for the gospel of salvation. Inverted symbols are typical of the opposite values pursued by Satanists. People who are sometimes sacrificed to Satan on Black Sabbath are crucified upside down in accordance with this tradition." [116]

And on the next page the Roman Catholic Church openly worship Satan in Rome. See the video with the upside down cross at: You Tube Popes Inverted cross! Video PROOF! [117]

As unbelievable as it seems, the translators of the Bible actually put the abbreviation for Satan's name, Baal, (LORD in English), in the place of the name of God YHWH in the Bible and

Mystery Babylon actually worships Satan in the open as Babylon Did (Seen on Video)

The Vatican actually worships Satan in Rome! In a recent live televised Roman Catholic worship service, Pope Francis stood on an elevated stage, as the church worshiped Lucifer.

There are three different videos listed here.

The first video resource 118 is longer. It starts with an interview of Father Malachi Martin and then about two minutes into the video it shows the actual worship of Satan in the service, in the Vatican on Easter (Istar). It shows the same thing in the two other videos but with a different person leading the worship in each one.

---

[116] http://www.jesus-is-savior.com/False%20Religions/Roman%20Catholicism/satanism_in_the_vatican.htm
[117]

https://www.youtube.com/watch?v=x-y8jF25scU

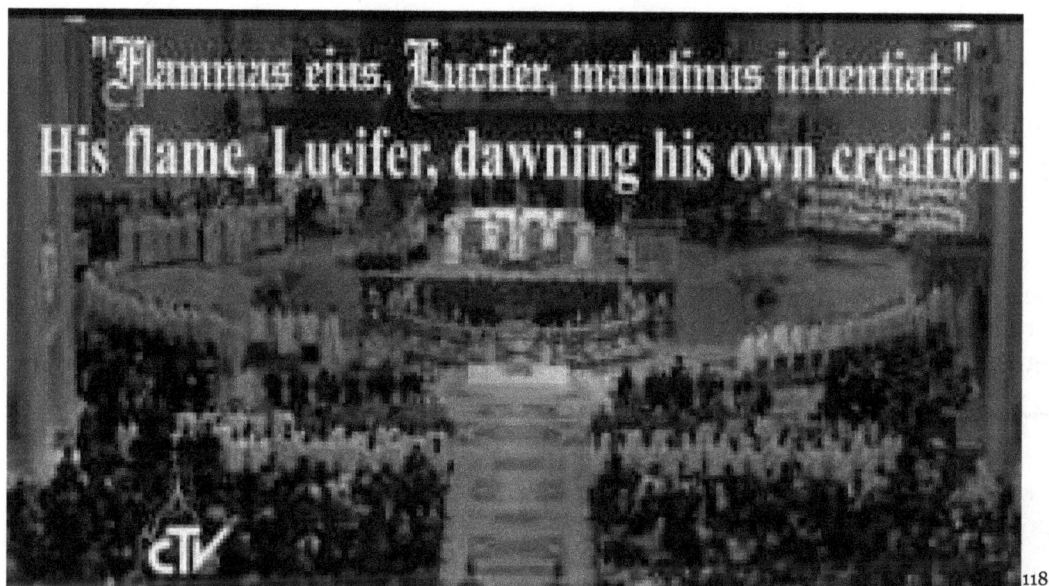

"Flammas eius, Lucifer, matutinus inbeniat:"
His flame, Lucifer, dawning his own creation:

CTV [118]

At resource [119] shown below, at this website, the first video, it is with Pope Francis.

At resource [118] You tube: Full Blown Lucifer Worship At The Catholic Vatican
Approximately two minutes into the video its hows the worship of Lucifer and shows the words being said:
"Flaming Lucifer finds mankind, I say: Oh Lucifer who will never be defeated CHRIST IS YOUR SON (!!!!)
Who came back from hell shed his peaceful light and is alive and reigns in the world without end."
In Latin he sings:
"Flammas eius Lucifer matutinus inveniat: ille, inquam Lucifer qui nescit occasum Christus Filius tuus, (!!!!)
Qui regressus ab inferis, humano generi serenus illuxit, et vivit et regnat in saecula saeculorum."
Then
Flammas eius Flaming Lucifer
Lucifer matutinus inveniat Lucifer finds mankind
ille, inquam Lucifer qui nescit occasum Christus Filius tuus, (!!!!)
I say: Oh Lucifer who will never be defeated CHRIST IS YOUR SON (!!!!)
The second time it is repeated, the people respond: Amen [118]

Here is the third video, THE VATICAN WORSHIPS LUCIFER/SATAN: [120]
This video translates the words they are singing as:
"His flame, Lucifer, dawning his own creation: May, I say, O Lucifer, who knows no setting. Christ your son who came back from the dead and shed his peaceful light to the human race, and is alive and reigns forever and ever."

The Babylonians worshipped the Sun god, Baal, Bel, Beelzebub, (names for Satan, names for Lucifer) so does Mystery Babylon, the Catholic Church. They have worshiped Baal (Satan) in secret, with the doctrines of Baal worship and now in public! The shocking truth is the Catholic Church has all the Babylonian doctrines, made two of God's commandments of none effect with Babylonian traditions, and is seen in the Vatican worshiping, Satan, Lucifer, the Sun-god Baal.

---

[118] https://www.youtube.com/watch?v=sUN-XEU6HUc
[119] https://reptiliandimension.wordpress.com/2014/12/08/devil-worship-at-vatican-was-pope-francis-declared-son-of-lucifer-at-a-televised-roman-catholic-luciferian-worship-service/
[120]

https://www.bing.com/videos/search?q=you+tube%3a+full+blown+lucifer+worship+at+the+catholic+vatican&view=detail&mid=DA29D82D9EC66E0639D5DA29D82D9EC66E0639D5&FORM=VIRE

Babylon worshipped Baal, Baal is (the devil) Satan. Baal worship is Satan worship.
Zeus the Greek god, holds the symbol of the thunder, a lightning bolt.
His position of chief god and holder of the thunder originated Mesopotamia.
He is called Marduk in Babylon, **Baal** in Canaan, Adad in Assyria, Jupiter in Rome, and **Enlil** the hoofed, horned, **lord of demons** (from which we get the symbolic figure of **the devil**) in Sumaria. [24]

Look at the similarities!
Zeus also called Enlil, another name for the devil.
The devil's stomach has a serpent staff and the Pope also has a serpent staff.
The Pope giving the same sign as the devil.

Zeus (Baal) Thunder Bolt	The Devil Triode Staff	Roman Catholicism Staff with a serpent
Another name for **Zeus** is Enlil **(the devil)**.	**Notice the Pope's staff**, *The serpent staff is also on the devil's stomach.*	**Notice The Pope giving the same hand sign as the devil.**

Mystery Babylon, the Roman Catholic Church, under Constantine, put all the pagan gods (of Babylon) into one religion, and gave this god the name: **Hesus Horus Krishna**, which became Jesus H. Christ. Hesus was the great Druid god which was the sun god (an incarnation of Nimrod/Tammuz), who the Greeks called Zeus. Zeus is Enlil, another name for Satan. And the Roman Catholic Church openly worships Satan in Rome (See videos given earlier).

The Roman Catholic Church, the Vatican, fits God's description of Mystery Babylon, the great mother Church, who adopted over 35 traditions of Babylon into the Church, doctrines of Baal (the devil), and the next chapter tells exactly how the mark of the beast, 666, is on the leader of mystery Babylon's crown and what it means.

Mystery Babylon's Leader, The Antichrist
And 666 The Mark of the Beast Match Perfectly

This may be different than you've ever heard but I encourage you read the whole thing and you will see it fits perfectly. In Rev. 13 God gives us the description of the beast and tell us the number of the beast is 666.

In Revelation 14 God is warning, whoever takes the mark of the beast, the smoke of their torment will ascend up forever and ever. And in this 14th chapter God is warning if any man receive the mark of the beast they shall drink of the wrath of God.

Then four chapters from the end of the Bible, **in Revelation 18:4 God is calling His people** to come out of Mystery Babylon that we receive not her plagues (that we receive not her judgements). God's people (Catholics and Christians) are still here, (the rapture has not taken place yet- explained in chapter 2 or God would not be calling us, His people out of Mystery Babylon that we receive not Mystery Babylon's plagues (her judgments).

- "9) And the third angel followed them, saying with a loud voice, *If any man worship the beast and his image, and receive his mark in his forehead, or in his hand, 10) The same shall drink of the wine of the wrath of God,* which is poured out without mixture into the cup of his indignation; and he shall be tormented with fire and brimstone in the presence of the holy angels, and in the presence of the Lamb: 11) *And the smoke of their torment ascendeth up for ever and ever: and they have no rest day nor night, who worship the beast and his image, and whosoever receiveth the mark of his name.*" (Rev 14:9-11)
- "16) And he causeth all, both small and great, rich and poor, free and bond, **to receive a mark in their right hand, or in their foreheads**:17) And that no man might buy or sell, save he that had the mark, or the name of the beast, or the number of his name. 18) Here is wisdom. Let him that hath understanding count **the number of the beast**: for **it is the number of a man; and his number is Six hundred threescore and six.**" (Rev 13:16-18)
- In the King James Plus Version of the Bible, next to Six hundred threescore and six, it has the number **G 5516** and says it is the Greek: **chi xi stigma**
- **When you look up, Stigma,** in the Intralinear Greek-English New Testament it is **G4742** **and says:** *a mark* (to stick, that is, *prick*) incised or punched (*for recognition of ownership*)
- So 666 is a stick or prick, like from a needle, that is for recognition of ownership.
- "And they worshipped **the dragon which gave power unto the beast**: and they worshipped the beast, saying, Who is like unto the beast? who is able to make war with him?" (Rev 13:4)
- "And **the great *dragon*** was cast out, that old serpent, ***called the Devil, and Satan,*** which deceiveth the whole world: he was cast out into the earth, and his angels were cast out with him." (Rev 12:9)

Take note in Revelation 13:4, it is the dragon that gave the beast its power. Rev. 12:9 tells us the dragon is Satan. Satan is the one behind the one world government- the beast, Mystery Babylon and its leader. This is why we cannot take the mark of the beast. The mark of the beast is actually the mark of Satan. A mark incised or punched *for recognition of ownership*, giving Satan ownership of those who take this mark. This is why God's word says: whoever takes the mark of the beast, the smoke of their torment will rise forever (Rev. 14:11), because they will be in hell forever with their owner, Satan. Remember Mystery Babylon, the Catholic Church adopted over 35 traditions of Baal worship. Baal worship is actually worshiping Satan (the devil).

God's word tells us that the man of sin, the antichrist, will sit in the Temple of God in Jerusalem claiming to be God. There have been two temples of God (in Jerusalem). One was destroyed in 587 BCE and the other was destroyed in 70 AD. Scriptures show us there will be another temple built, the third temple of God, in Jerusalem. God told John to measure the temple of God in Revelation 11:1 but not to measure the outer court **because it is given to the Gentiles for 42 months, three and a half years, the time of the great tribulation.**

- "1) And there was given me a reed like unto a rod: and the angel stood, saying, Rise, and **measure the temple of God,** and the altar, and them that worship therein. 2) But the court which is without the temple leave out, and measure it not; for it is given unto the Gentiles: and *the holy city* shall they tread **under foot forty and two months.**" (Rev 11:1,2)

We can see from Rev. 11:1,2 and 2 Th 2:3,4 that the Jewish temple will be built again in the holy city, Jerusalem. At the time of the writing of: Sound the Alarm, there is no temple of God, in Jerusalem, although everything is ready for it to be erected. Israel has everything ready so that they will start sacrifices, according to the Old Testament scripture, as soon as it is built. It will be built immediately after the peace agreement with Israel and Palestine and the United Nations. The antichrist will confirm the peace agreement. The temple will be built prefab so it won't take long to put it up. Then the antichrist will sit (rule) in the temple of God, as God, **the abomination of desolation Jesus foretold** in Matthew 24:15, **that starts the great tribulation** in Matt 24:21.

- "1) Now we beseech you, brethren, *by the coming of our Lord Jesus Christ, and by our gathering together unto him,* 2) That ye be not soon shaken in mind, or be troubled, neither by spirit, nor by word, nor by letter as from us, as that the day of Christ is at hand. 3) <u>Let no man deceive you by any means: for *that day shall not come,* except there come a falling away first, and that man of sin be revealed</u>, the son of perdition; 4) Who opposeth and exalteth himself above all that is called God, or that is worshipped; so that **he as God sitteth in the temple of God, <u>shewing himself that he is God.</u>**"(2Th 2:1-4)
- "When **ye therefore shall see the abomination of desolation**, spoken of by Daniel the prophet, stand in the holy place, (whoso readeth, let him understand:)" (Mat 24:15)
- "For **then shall be great tribulation,** such as was not since the beginning of the world to this time, no, nor ever shall be." (Mat 24:21)

In 2 Thess. Chapter 2, God's word is talking about the abomination of desolation, the man of sin, the antichrist, sitting in the temple of God as God. The man of sin, the antichrist is revealed when he sits (rules) in the temple of God. 2 Th 2: 1-4 tell us, do not to let anyone deceive you, the coming of our Lord Jesus (our Messiah Yeshua) and our gathering together unto Him (the rapture), **shall not take place until the man of sin be revealed, who sits in the temple calling himself God.**

In other words, the gathering together unto Christ (the rapture) will not come till the man of sin, the antichrist sits (rules) in the temple of God as God so Christians will see the abomination of desolation, the antichrist sitting in the temple of God. The same one that confirms the peace agreement, will stand in the Temple, in Jerusalem, calling himself God and will stop the sacrifices, the oblation, just as Daniel 9:27 said he would do.

- "And he shall confirm the covenant with many for one week: and in the midst of the week **he shall cause the sacrifice and the oblation to cease,** and for the overspreading of abominations he shall make it desolate, even until the consummation, and that determined shall be poured upon the desolate." (Dan 9:27)

God's word foretells what will happen. Watch who sits (rules) in the temple of God in Jerusalem and stops the daily sacrifices.

Straight from the Scriptures

- "And he doeth great wonders, so that he maketh fire come down from heaven on the earth in the sight of men, Rev 13:14 And *deceiveth them that dwell on the earth by the means of those miracles which he had power to do in the sight of the beast*; …" (Rev 13:13)

Rev. 13:13 warns us not to be deceived by any great wonders or miracles. Remember the strong possibility of a hologram in the sky (*even with sound*), perhaps of a false rapture or more likely of a false alien attack that will appear very, very real. (See references 16 through 20 in Chapter 2 and watch their videos)
Jesus warns us in Matt. 24:24

- "For there shall arise false Christs, and *false prophets, and shall shew great signs and wonders; insomuch that, if it were possible, they shall deceive the very elect*." (Mat 24:24) (The words elect and chosen are both G1588)
- "But **ye *are* a chosen** generation, a royal priesthood, an holy nation, a peculiar people; that ye should shew forth the praises of him who hath called you out of darkness into his marvellous light:" (1Pe 2:9)
- "These shall make war with the Lamb, and the Lamb shall overcome them: for he is Lord of lords, and King of kings: and **they that are with him *are* called, and chosen**, and faithful." (Rev 17:14)

The word elect (G1588) in Matt 24:24 *is rendered as chosen in 1 Pe 2:9 and Rev 17:14. The elect (G1588) and chosen (G1588) are the same people.* You can tell from 1 Pe 2:29 and Rev. 17:14 that the chosen are Christians. The chosen and the elect are both Christians. Where Jesus is warning the elect not to be deceived in Mat 24:24 by false prophets and great signs and wonders, Jesus is warning a chosen generation, a royal priesthood, an holy nation, a peculiar people, Christians, He is warning us, not to be deceived by the great signs and wonders of the false Christs and false prophets because we will still be here at the time of great sign and wonders.

It will happen in neighborhoods all over the world (I pray it doesn't happen in America), people will pledge allegiance to the one world government and one world religion (Mystery Babylon) and it's leader (the antichrist), probably the same way we used to put our hand over our heart and say the pledge of allegiance to the flag of the USA, but now it will be to the one world order and I imagine people will say something like "I do." when asked a question like: Do you promise to be faithful to the one world government? They will show people getting the mark of the beast on TV, (It won't be called the mark of the beast). Nobody will be able to buy or sell anything unless they get this chip. When the mark is taken, it will mean they are the beast's people, the antichrist's people, the devil's people, a chip showing ownership (like a chip in a dog shows ownership, it shows who owns the dog).

- "Here is wisdom. Let him that hath understanding count the number of the beast: for it is the number of a man; and his number *is* Six hundred threescore *and* six." (Rev 13:18)

Here it is, the mark of the beast,
Mystery Babylon's leader, the Pope, has 666 inscribed in his crown!

The Roman Catholic Churches' Headquarters is in Rome, and *inscribed in Latin* (the language of Rome- having Roman numeric values, Roman numerals), the words inscribed in his crown, declare that he is the antichrist. He is the one you will see on TV, standing (ruling) in the temple of God (in Jerusalem) as God, the abomination of desolation that Jesus (Yeshua) foretells to start the great tribulation in Matt 24:15 and 21.
First I'll explain, then I'll show you the Pope's crown with the inscription.

The pope's crown is inscribed with:
VICARIUS FILII DEI, (which means the Vicar of Christ).
The literal meaning is: in place of the son of God.
Roman Latin numerals equivalents: [121]
I=1, (U=5, V=5), X=10, L=50, C=100, D=500, M=1000

[121] VICARIUS FILII DEI:
VICARIUS: V=5 ,I = 1, C = 100, A = 0, R = 0, I = 1,U= 5, S = 0.............................5+1+100+1+5=112
FILLI: F= 0, I= 1, L= 50, I= 1, I=1...1+50+1+1=53
DEI: D =500, E= 0, I=1 ....500+1=501
....*Totaling* 666
[121] THE LITERIAL MEANING:
VICARIUS- substituting for, or in place of
FILII – means son
DEI – means God

---

[121] http://www.aloha.net/~mikesch/666.htm

VICARIUS FILII DEI, which is the Latin for Vicar of the Son of God...” [121]
In scribed on the Popes crown is VICARIUS FILII DEI.
The Latin VICARIUS FILII DEI = 666 in Roman Numerals.
VICARIUS FILII DEI means The Vicar of Christ.
The Vicar of Christ means: **In place of Christ.**
(See 2. below) One meaning of Anti is *__in place of__*.
The first part of antichrist is anti, *__in place of__*.
Antichrist = *In place of Christ* = **VICARIUS FILII DEI** = 666

The leader of the Roman Catholic Church, the Pope, the leader of Mystery Babylon,
His crown is inscribed: VICARIUS FILII DEI which equals 666 and means in place of Christ, *antichrist*.

The definition for anti from the: Thayer's Greek Lexicon STRONGS NT 473: ἀντί
1. properly, it seems to have signified over against, opposite to, before, in a local sense (Alexander Buttmann (1873) Gram., p. 412; (cf. Curtius, § 204)). Hence,
2. indicating exchange, succession, for, instead of, *__in place of__* (something).[122]

Popes have literally crowned themselves **VICARIUS FILII DEI, *in place of Christ, antichrist***, having it inscribed on their crown and declaring it through their quotes:

- Pope Leo XIII, *Praeclara Gratulationis Publicae (The Reunion of Christendom)*, June 20, 1894:
  We hold upon this earth the place of God Almighty. [84]
- “Pope,” *Ferraris' Ecclesiastic Dictionary: The Pope is of so great dignity and so exalted that he is not a mere man, but as it were **God, and the vicar of God**.* [84]

The words **VICARIUS FILII DEI**, was inscribed in the crown or his mitre which is worn by the POPE, this was clarified and proven to us by this *Catholic Newspaper*. This crown is known as the *Papal Tiara*, or *Tri-Crown*, because it was literally three crowns placed on top of each. [85]

Lucifer, Satan, the devil has used Mystery Babylon the Great to deceive the world!
Lucifer said in his heart he would be like the Most High and this is what he has done through Mystery Babylon. He is being worshiped as God and Mystery Babylon's leader: the Pope, the antichrist possessed **by Lucifer, will sit on the mount of the congregation (in God's temple in Jerusalem) as God (The abomination of desolation).**

- "How art thou fallen from heaven, O **Lucifer**, son of the morning! *how* art thou cut down to the ground, which didst weaken the nations! (Isa 14:12**) For thou hast said in thine heart**, I will ascend into heaven, I will exalt my throne above the stars of God: **I will sit also upon the mount of the congregation,** in the sides of the north: (Isa 14:13) I will ascend above the heights of the clouds; **I will be like the most High.**" (Isa 14:14)

We have seen clearly through all the puzzle pieces that Mystery Babylon is the Roman Catholic Church. Who is the Roman Catholic's leader? The Pope. The Pope is the leader of Mystery Babylon and has antichrist (VICARIUS FILII DEI) inscribed on his crown which equals 666 (the mark of the beast) in Roman numerals. Pope Francis stands on an elevated stage worshiping Satan in the Catholic service in Rome on video. (See videos, Resource #'s 118, 119, 120)

Rev 14:9-11 says those who take the mark of the beast... the smoke of their torment ascendeth up for ever and ever: and they have no rest day nor night...
- "9) And the third angel followed them, saying with a loud voice, **If any man worship the beast and his image, and receive his mark in his forehead, or in his hand,** 10) **The same shall drink of the wine of the wrath of God**, which is poured out without mixture into the cup of his indignation; and he shall be tormented with fire and brimstone in the presence of the holy angels, and in the presence of the Lamb: 11) **And the smoke of their torment ascendeth up for ever and ever: and they have no rest day nor night, who worship the beast and his image, and whosoever receiveth the mark of his name.**" (Rev 14:9-11)

The reason taking the mark of the beast brings this damnation is because it is making covenant with the antichrist, it is pledging to the beast, to Satan. (IT IS SPIRITUAL ADULTERY, God divorced Israel for spiritual adultery). Antichrist means in place of Christ, in God's place. Satan has put himself in the place of God as he said in Isa. 14:13 and 14 ...**I will sit also upon the mount of the congregation...**13)...**I will be like the most High.**"14)

Many others have been aware of the identity of the antichrist. It is not a coincidence that many left the Catholic Church and started new Churches at the time of the reformation. Listen to what Martin Luther said.
- The Lutheran Church called the pope the antichrist. This is what Martin Luther said, "We here are of the conviction that the papacy is the seat of the true and real antichrist... personally I declare that I owe the Pope no other obedience than that to antichrist." Taken from The Prophetic Faith of Our Fathers, Vol.2, pg 121 by Froom. (Aug. 18,1520) [123]
- The Baptist Church called the pope the antichrist. 1689 London Baptist Confession: "The Lord Jesus Christ is the Head of the church... neither can the pope of Rome in any sense head thereof but is that antichrist, that man of sin, the son of perdition that exalteth himself in the church against Christ, and all that is called God, whom the Lord shall destroy with the brightness of His coming." (Colossians 1:18, Matthew 28:18-20, Ephesians 4:11,12, 2 Thessalonians 2:2-9) Chapter 26 Of the Church [123]

---

[123] https://www.bing.com/videos/search?q=you+tube+lutheran+church+called+pope+antichrist&view=
detail&mid=BE64507256B25AB7DE2DBE64507256B25AB7DE2D&FORM=VIRE

I know the people in the Catholic Church love God and are so dedicated to God. God loves them. I love them but they have been deceived by Mystery Babylon. God doesn't want them to receive Mystery Babylon's plagues, Mystery Babylon's judgments, so He is calling His people out of Mystery Babylon before He judges her. It is an extreme shock that God Almighty is calling His people out of the Roman Catholic Church, out of Mystery Babylon. It is such an extreme shock but it is true!

And what about the daughters of Mystery Babylon, they are the daughters of the Catholic Church that left at the time of the reformation, and started new denominations. Many of them are coming back to the mother Church now. They've got to come out of Mystery Babylon, that they be not partakers of her sins and receive the same judgment as the mother. God loves them. I love them. They're God's people. They love God. They're my brothers and sisters in Christ. I pray that God's people everywhere share this book around the world, sounding the alarm that God loves them and God is calling them, "Come out of her my people that ye be not partakers of her sins, that ye receive not her plagues" (Rev.18:4). They can't take the mark of the beast! Whoever takes the mark of the beast, the Bible says the smoke of their torment will ascend forever and ever! (See Rev 14:9-11)

Mystery Babylon (The Catholic Church) is getting ready to rule the world in our generation through the one world Church and the one world government. Here are a few more notes from them:

Western Watchman (A Roman Catholic publication out of St. Louis): The [Roman Catholic] church has persecuted. Only a tyro [i.e., novice] in church history will deny that...one hundred and fifty years after [Roman Emperor] Constantine, the Donatists were persecuted and sometimes put to death...Protestants were persecuted in France and Spain with the full approval of the [Roman Catholic] church authorities...***When she thinks it good to use physical force, she will use it.***" [124]

Pope Pius IX, Quanta Cura (December 8, 1864): Which false and perverse opinions [of democracy and individual freedom] are on that ground the more to be detested, because they chiefly tend to this, that that salutary influence be impeded and (even) removed, which **the Catholic Church**, according to the institution and ***command of her Divine Author, should freely exercise even to the end of the world -- not only over private individuals, but over nations, peoples, and their sovereign princes;*** ... [124]

Pope John Paul II, in his apostolic letter Ad Tuendam Fidem (May 18, 1998), made bold statements about the need for submission to the Pope on doctrinal issues. He declared that lack of submission was worthy of punishment: Whoever denies or places in doubt any truth that must be believed with divine and catholic faith, or repudiates the Christian faith as a whole, and does not come to his senses after having been legitimately warned, **is to be punished as a heretic...whoever obstinately rejects a teaching that the Roman Pontiff or the College of Bishops, exercising the authentic Magisterium, have set forth to be held definitively**, or who affirms what they have condemned as erroneous, and does not retract after having been legitimately warned, is to be punished with an appropriate penalty. [124]

Catholic Encyclopedia volume 14 (1911): 767-768: **There is no graver offense than heresy**... and ***therefore it must be rooted out with fire and sword.*** [124]

Of course, it will be called heresy to say, the truth, that the Pope is not God but is the antichrist and they will do their best to kill those who say the truth, those who do not take the mark of the beast.

- "And I saw thrones, and they sat upon them, and judgment was given unto them: and *I saw the souls of them that were beheaded for the witness of Jesus, and for the word of God, and which had not worshipped the beast, neither his image, neither had received his mark upon their foreheads, or in their hands;* and they lived and reigned with Christ a thousand years." (Rev 20:4)

---

[124] http://amazingdiscoveries.org/R-Papacy_aggressive_Pope_Catholic_Chiniquiy

Hebrews 3:1 and Hebrews 4:14 and Hebrew 9:11, confirm that Jesus is our High Priest, not the Pope.

- "Wherefore, holy brethren, partakers of the heavenly calling, consider the Apostle and **High Priest of our profession, Christ Jesus**;" (Heb 3:1)
- "Seeing then that **we have a great high priest**, that is passed into the heavens, **Jesus the Son of God, let us hold fast** *our* **profession.**" (Heb 4:14)
- "But **Christ being come an high priest** of good things to come, by a greater and more perfect tabernacle, not made with hands, that is to say, not of this building;" (Heb 9:11)

God's name, YHWH was replaced with Baal (another name for Satan) LORD in English, in the Old Testament and in the New Testament Yeshua was replaced with Hesus, who the Greeks called Zeus. Zeus is another name for Baal, another name for Satan. (Hesus later became Jesus.) So in the Old and New Testament God's name was changed to honor Baal another name for Satan. The Roman Catholic Church caused two of God's Ten Commandments to be of none effect- the first commandment to: Hear that YHWH thy God is one YHWH (not three separate Gods-persons in one) and say that changing the 4th commandment to: Remember the Sabbath, to Sunday is the MARK of her authority. Through Constantine, the Roman Catholic Church took out the Feasts of the LORD [YHWH] and replaced them with pagan sun worship doctrines, the Passover changed to Easter (Ishtar) - another name for Semiramis, over 35 of the pagan doctrines of Babylonian sun worship were adopted into the Roman Catholic Church. *The people that came out of the Roman Catholic Church at the reformation unknowingly brought with them, the Mother Church's doctrines of the sun god, Tammuz, also called Baal, i.e. the devil, the doctrines of devils, with them when they started Protestant Churches. So Christianity was no longer the true worship that God had instructed.* The leader of this sun worship, the leader of Mystery Babylon the Pope, the Vicar of Christ, which equals 666, the replacement of Christ, the antichrist, will stand in the Temple of God and call himself God (the abomination of desolation).

God's word says have no fellowship with the works of darkness. In other words it is not ok to mix the Babylonian doctrines, doctrines of devils, with worshipping Him. He judged His people, Israel for partaking in the Babylonian doctrines, He divorced them and dispersed them from their promise land. They suffered greatly, remember the Holocaust. Neither Catholicism, nor today's Christianity, is following the true worship, how the LORD [YHWH] God instructed us to in His word but instead are following the doctrines of Mystery Babylon. God is warning His people, in Revelations 18:4, come out of her, (come out of Mystery Babylon) my people, that ye be not partakers of her sins, that ye receive not her plagues, that we receive not her judgments.

- "And have no fellowship with the unfruitful works of darkness, but rather reprove them." (Eph 5:11)
- "And I heard another voice from heaven, saying, Come out of her, my people, that ye be not partakers of her sins, and that ye receive not of her plagues." (Rev 18:4)

God's word says we must Worship Him in spirit and in truth.

- "But the hour cometh, and now is, when the true worshippers shall worship the Father in spirit and in truth: for the Father seeketh such to worship him." (Joh 4:23)
- "God *is* a Spirit: and they that worship him must worship him in spirit and in truth." (Joh 4:24)

Worship in truth, means to serve God how He says to serve Him, in His name, His commandments, His Sabbaths, His Feasts, His Holy days, in other words, how He has instructed His people to do. We are not to have any fellowship with the doctrines of Babylon, the doctrines of devils.

The Church today as a whole does not seem to have the power that the early disciples had. Perhaps it is because we have not been following Him, serving Him how He commanded us too but following pagan traditions instead. *Yeshua (Jesus) in grafted us in the vine, into Him, into His covenants.* One of the things we need to understand is **the Feasts of YHWH, that they are appointed times to meet with Him, and how to observe them.** Many of His people have no clue about these appointed times, these holy days. YHWH commands them to be observed forever. I do not know a lot about these feasts yet but here are three scriptures.

- "And this day shall be unto you for a memorial; and ye shall keep it a feast to the LORD [YHWH] throughout your generations; **ye shall keep it a feast by an ordinance for ever**." (Exo 12:14)
- "And ye shall observe *the feast of* unleavened bread; for in this selfsame day have I brought your armies out of the land of Egypt: therefore shall **ye observe this day in your generations by an ordinance for ever**." (Exo 12:17)
- "And ye shall keep it a feast unto the LORD [YHWH] seven days in the year. *It shall be a statute for ever in your generations*: ye shall celebrate it in the seventh month." (Lev 23:41)

Now that you understand that Mystery Babylon, the Roman Catholic Church, adopted *into the Church* the pagan sun doctrines of Babylon, ***now you need to know some other very, very important things that were taken out of the Church such as the understanding of the mystery of God.***

The next chapter explains the Mystery of God and why it is so important to understand it. God's people have been lied too and told that they cannot understand the Godhead, the Mystery of God but this is not true. Cheryl Alvarado's Book, Be Not Faithless But Believing, Jesus Subtitle: The Mystery of God Revealed explains:

The 1ˢᵗ TRUTH: You can understand The Mystery of God and The Godhead.

God's word says, We are to: Understand (Ro 1:20), Acknowledge (Col 2:2) and Be Established (Ro16:25, 26) according to the revelation of the mystery. God commanded, the revelation be made known to all nations (Rom 16:25), made manifest (made known) by the scriptures (Rom 16:26), understood by the things that are made, even His ...Godhead (Rom 1:20) and says those that keep it from you are without excuse. (Rom 1:20)[109]

Chapter 4   The Mystery of God Revealed

Below are my extensive notes (quotes) from Cheryl Alvarado's book, <u>Be Not Faithless But Believing, Jesus Subtitle: The Mystery of God Revealed</u>. This Bible study is approximately 90% scripture. I've never seen a Bible study like it. I highly recommend getting it, even though I have put many quotes here. God's word tells us that the revelation of the mystery is made known through the scriptures and her book does just that, it reveals the mystery of God through the scriptures. The quizzes at the end of each chapter help you understand and receive truth through groups of scriptures that emphasize the same point, bringing clarity from the scriptures so that you know you are getting the truth.

This revelation of the mystery of God doesn't takes quite as long to explain as Mystery Babylon did so please stay with me to the end, even if you don't understand it at first, or even if it makes you angry at first. You see we have been rooted in the false doctrines of Babylon for so long, (not only 100's of years but almost 2000 years) that when we hear the truth, we may need to hear it several times. This revelation is very, very, important. God's word says we are to be established according to the revelation of the mystery and that this revelation is for the obedience of the faith. This revelation has been kept from God's people. God's wrath is against those that keep it from you, and His word says, they are without excuse. Since Catholics and Christians have been so entrenched in the doctrines of Babylon for close to 2000 years, the Babylonian doctrines are really set in and you may need to go over this chapter more than once or even better yet, get the book: <u>Be Not Faithless But Believing, Jesus The Mystery of God Revealed</u>, because Yeshua (Jesus) told us, continue in His word and ye shall know the truth and the truth will make you free (free from the pagan Babylonian doctrines).

- "Now to him that is of ***power to stablish you*** according to my gospel, and the preaching of Jesus Christ, according to ***the revelation of the mystery***, which was kept secret since the world began, 26) But ***now is made manifest (known), and by the scriptures*** of the prophets, according to the commandment of the everlasting God, made known to all nations ***for the obedience of faith***:" (Rom 16:25)

- "For **the wrath of God** is revealed from heaven against all ungodliness and unrighteousness of **men, who hold the truth in unrighteousness**; 20) For the invisible things of him from the creation of the world are **clearly seen**, being **understood** by the things that are made, **even his** eternal power and **Godhead; *so that they are without excuse***:" (Rom 1:18,20)

- "Then said Jesus to those Jews which believed on him, If ye **continue in my word**, then are ye my disciples indeed; 32) **And ye shall know the truth**, and the truth shall make you free." (Joh 8:31)

<u>Cheryl Alvarado explains in her book: Be Not Faithless But Believing, Jesus The Mystery of God Revealed</u> that: There are 4 very important truths that have been kept from the majority of Catholics and Christians but first I must go into more detail about God's name, because understanding God's name is the first part of understanding the mystery of God and the Godhead. I will show you something fantastic about God's name.

As shown previously,
God's name was replaced, both in the Old Testament and the New Testament. In the Old Testament, God's name YHWH was replaced with the sun god's name: Baal, (LORD in English) and in the New Testament our Hebrew Saviour's name, Yeshua, was replaced with Druid sun god's name: *Hesus*, (which was called Iesous in the Greek, eventually became the English name "Jesus").

I start quoting from <u>Be Not Faithless But Believing, Jesus The Mystery of God Revealed</u>, here:
(All reference numbers in this chapter are from her references[125])

---

[125] Chapter 4 reference list from: Be Not faithless But Believing, Jesus The Mystery of God Revealed www.themysteryrevealed.info

- "And God said moreover unto Moses, Thus shalt thou say unto the children of Israel, The **LORD [YHWH]** [H3068] God of your fathers, the God of Abraham, the God of Isaac, and the God of Jacob, hath sent me unto you: **this *is* my name for ever**, and this *is* my memorial unto all generations." (Exo 3:15)

- "I *am* the **LORD [YHWH]** [H3068]: that *is* my name: ..." (Isa 42:8)

יהוה

These four letters are usually transliterated from Hebrew as IHVH in Latin, JHWH in German, French, and Dutch, and YHWH in English. This was variously rendered as **"Yahweh" or "Jehovah"**, since in Latin there was no distinct lettering to distinguish 'Y' from 'J', or 'W' from 'V', and the Hebrew does not clearly indicate the omitted vowels. [5]

Now that we understand that God says His name is YHWH forever, let's look at our Saviour's name.
- "Now when *Jesus was born in Bethlehem of Judaea* in the days of Herod the king, behold, there came wise men from the east to Jerusalem," (Mat 2:1)
- Matt 2:1 tells us that our Saviour was born in Bethlehem of Judaea. Judah was known in Greek and Latin as Judaea [23]. Hebrews from Judah were referred to as Jews (Judahites) [23]. Our Saviour was Hebrew, a Jew. He was Jewish, not Greek. The name Jesus is not a Jewish name. The name Jesus is the English translation that came from the Greek, Iesous.

Our Saviour's real name, **His Jewish name** is Yeshua.

Mat.1:21 says: And she shall bring forth a son, and thou shalt call his name [Yeshua] Jesus: for he shall save his people from their sins.

Our Saviour's birth name, Yeshua, actually means Salvation.

Salvation H3444 **yeshuah** ... something *saved*, that is, (abstractly) *deliverance*; hence *aid, victory, prosperity*: - deliverance, health, help (-ing), salvation, save, saving (health), welfare. [3]

Wow, that is awesome but it gets better!

Here is what the NAS Exhaustive Concordance of the Bible with Hebrew-Aramaic and Greek Dictionaries says:

It said Yeshua is the same as #3091 Yehoshua, so I looked up #3091.
#3091 Yehoshua said it is from Yhvh, [Yhvh in Latin, YHWH in the English, **God's name forever Exo 3:15**] and #3091 Yehoshua means the LORD [YHWH] is salvation.
So Yeshua=Yehoshua=YHWH is Salvation.

From NAS Exhaustive Concordance of the Bible with Hebrew-Aramaic and Greek Dictionaries
#3442. יֵשׁוּעַ Yeshua (221c); the same as 3091, q.v. [6]
#3091. יְהוֹשׁוּעַ **Yehoshua** [or] יְהוֹשֻׁעַ Yehoshua (221c); **from 3068** and 3467; **"the LORD is salvation,"** Moses' successor, also the name of a number of Isr.:—NASB - Jeshua(28), Joshua(219). [10]
#3068. יהוה **Yhvh** (i.e. יְהֹוָה **Yehovah or** יַהְוֶה **Yahveh**) [217d]; from 1933b; the proper name of the God of Israel:—NASB - GOD(314), LORD(6399), LORD'S(111). [11]

***Jesus birth name, Yeshua, tells us who He is,* that He is YHWH!**
Yeshua's name tells us He is YHWH, [God's name for ever Exo 3:15] isn't that fantastic!
Continue with me in the scriptures and you will see, all the scriptures agree.

...and *all flesh shall know* that **I *the LORD [YHWH] am thy Saviour*...** (Isaiah 49:26)

Next we need to understand some important definitions: [7]
Mar—Aramaic meaning Master/Lord.
Mari means 'my Lord'.
Adon—Hebrew meaning Lord.
Adonai means 'my Lord'.
YHVH—(Yahweh) Hebrew name of God used throughout the Tanakh (Old Testament) <u>over 6500 times</u>. This is the eternal, memorial name of God.
Yah—short version of YHVH [Yahweh]
MarYah—contraction of Mar and Yah, meaning 'Master/Lord Yah'. When the Rabbis translated the Tanakh (Old Testament) to Aramaic—circa 50 BC to 50 AD—**they used MarYah in all 6500+ places where YHVH was used in the original Hebrew. MarYah is used extensively throughout the Peshitta Aramaic NT**. (YHWH is the English transliterated from Hebrew)

Here are four scripture examples out of the 30 from this above reference. **The Aramaic makes it very clear that Yeshua [Jesus] is YHVH**. [YHWH, when transliterated to English.] The King James Version is listed first, then from this reference.

- "Ye *are* my witnesses, **saith the LORD**, and my servant whom I have chosen: that ye may know and believe me, and understand that I *am* he: before me there was no God formed, neither shall there be after me. 11) I, *even* I, *am* the LORD; **and beside me *there is* no Saviour**." (Isa 43:10-11) KJV
- "You are My witnesses, **declares YHVH,** and My servant whom I have chosen, in order that you may know and believe Me, and understand that I am He. Before Me there was no God formed, and there will be none after Me. 11) **I am, YHVH, and besides Me there is no Savior.**" (Isaiah 43:10-11) [7]

- Took branches of palm trees, and went forth to meet him, and cried, Hosanna: Blessed is the King of Israel that cometh **in the name of the Lord**. (John 12:13) KJV
- (Triumphal Entry) took branches of the palm trees, and went out to meet Him, and began to cry out, "Hosanna! Blessed is the King of Israel who comes **in the name MarYah [Lord Yah=YHVH]**. (John 12:13) [7]

- "Then Peter said unto them, Repent, and be baptized every one of you **in the name of Jesus Christ [Yeshua]** for the remission of sins, and ye shall receive the gift of the Holy Ghost." (Act 2:38) KJV
- "(Peter speaking) Then Shimon (Peter) said to them, "Repent and be baptized, every one of you, **in the name MarYah Yeshua [Lord YHVH Yeshua]** for the forgiveness of sins, so that you may receive the gift of the Holy Spirit...." (Acts 2:38) [7]

- "The word which God sent unto the children of Israel, preaching peace by Jesus Christ [Yeshua]: **(he is Lord of all:)** (Act 10:36)" KJV
- "(Peter speaking) For God sent the word to the children of Israel, preaching peace and tranquility by <u>Yeshua THE Messiah, **He is MarYah [Lord Yah=YHVH] of all**</u>." (Acts 10:36) [7]

[Jesus] Yeshua truly is YHWH. Yeshua is a contraction of Yehoshua. Yehoshua means YHWH is Salvation or YHWH-Salvation. **YHWH-Salvation is a compound name describing God.**
[Jesus] Yeshua= Yehoshua= YHWH is Salvation or YHWH-Salvation
God has many compound names. One example you may recognize is Jehovah [YHWH] Jirah.

Understanding, having knowledge of God's name is the first part of understanding the mystery of God.

[Jesus] Yeshua truly is LORD [YHWH]
[Jesus] Yeshua= Yehoshua=YHWH-Salvation=YHWH

Now for the very important 4 TRUTHS that have been kept from you.

1ˢᵗ TRUTH: You can understand The Mystery of God and the Godhead.
God's word says, We are to: <u>Understand</u> (Rom 1:20), <u>Acknowledge</u> (Col 2:2) <u>and Be Established</u> (Rom16:25, 26) according to the revelation of the mystery. <u>God commanded, the revelation be made known to all nations</u> (Rom 16:25), made manifest [made known] by the scriptures (Rom 16:26), understood by the things that are made, even his ...Godhead (Rom 1:20) and says those that keep it from you are without excuse. (Rom 1:20)

2ⁿᵈ TRUTH: <u>God's first commandment is</u>:
"**Hear** O Israel the LORD [**YHWH**] our **God is one** LORD [**YHWH**] and thou shalt love the LORD [**YHWH**] thy God with all thine heart, and with all thy soul, and with all thy might."(Deu 6:4,5 Mark 12:29,30)
"I and my Father are one" (John 10:30), "These three are one" (1 John 5:7), "ONE Lord" (Eph. 4:5)

"Call his name JESUS [Yeshua]: for he shall save his people from their sins." (Mat 1:21)
Yeshua=Yehoshua=YHWH-Salvation= **YHWH** God's name forever (Exo 3:15)
YHWH shall save His people from their sins.

"know that the LORD [**YHWH**] he *is* God; *there is* none else beside him." (Deu 4:35)
"know... the LORD [**YHWH**] he *is* God ... *there is* none else." (Deu 4:39)
"know that the LORD [**YHWH**] is God, *and that there is* none else." (1 Ki8:60)
"I am the LORD [**YHWH**], and there is none else, there is no God beside me:" (Isa 45:5)
"There is none beside me. I am the LORD [**YHWH**], and there is none else." (Isa 45:6)
"I *am* the LORD [**YHWH**]; and *there is* none else." (Isa 45:18)

<u>"I, *even I, am* the LORD [YHWH]; and beside me *there is* no Saviour."</u> (Isa 43:11)
<u>"I the LORD [YHWH]? and *there is* no God else beside me; a just God and a Saviour;</u>
<u>*there is* none beside me"</u> (Isa 45:21)
<u>"As for our redeemer, the LORD [YHWH] of hosts *is* his name, the Holy One of Israel." (Isa 47:4)</u>
"I the LORD [**YHWH**] am thy Saviour" (Isa 49:26)
"I the LORD [**YHWH**] am thy Saviour" (Isa 60:16)

The Jews understood [Jesus] Yeshua was claiming to be the one YHWH God of the first commandment. "Thou, being a man, makest thyself God" (Joh 10:33). This is why they crucified Him. They did not understand that He really was the one YHWH God. **It was hidden wisdom, a Mystery so that,** The Lord of Glory, the one YHWH of the first commandment, could do it all to save us (See 1 Co 2:7, 8).

After YHWH completed His secret mission, to put on flesh and give His life, three days later, [Jesus] Yeshua=Yehoshua= YHWH-Salvation= **YHWH, God manifest in the flesh**, resurrected, and commanded: "Teach all nations" (Matt 28:19)

- "And without controversy great is the mystery of godliness: **God was manifest in the flesh**, justified in the Spirit, seen of angels, preached unto the Gentiles, believed on in the world, received up into glory." (1Ti 3:16)

Yeshua is the one YHWH of the first commandment who was manifest in the flesh and gave Himself for us: (Deu 6:4, Mark 12:29) **Hear O Israel, YHWH our God is one YHWH.**

After He completed His mission to give His life to save us, and was resurrected He gave the command in Matt 28:19 Go and Teach..., The command to teach all nations was to teach the mystery of God and of the Father and of Christ because it was no longer to be hidden that He was the Lord of glory [the one YHWH God of the first commandment]. If they knew He was the one YHWH God they would not have crucified Him. It had been kept secret so He could give His life for us on the cross.

109

- "7) But we speak the wisdom of God in a mystery, *even* the hidden *wisdom,* which God ordained before the world unto our glory: 8) Which none of the princes of this world knew: **for had they known *it,* they would not have crucified the Lord of glory**." (1 Co 2:7, 8)

Rom. 16:25, 26 says ... "**the revelation of the mystery**, which was kept secret since the world began, 26) **But now is made manifest, and by the scriptures** ..." We must remember that the mystery was hidden since the world began, it was even hidden in Genesis. Now please bear with me as we look at the scriptures, remembering before Yeshua [Jesus] was crucified, they were not supposed to understand the mystery but now we are to understand by the scriptures.

The first scripture of many that I will share, is Romans 1:20. It says we are to understand the Godhead by the things that are made.

- Rom. 1:20 says: "For the invisible things of him from the creation of the world are clearly seen**, *being understood by the things that are made, even his*** eternal power and **Godhead**; so that they are without excuse:"

Here are some examples of things that God made:
#1. The land, sea, and sky are the make up, of the earth we live on, *these 3 are 1*, 1 called earth, not 3 separate earths in 1.
#2. An egg yolk, egg white, and eggshell has the name - *egg, these 3 are 1,*1 egg, not 3 eggs in 1.
#3. Liquid, solid, and gas are the 3 roles that, the 1, water, plays.
#4. The best example is Man, we are made in God's image.

- "So ***God created man in His own image***, in the image of God created He him; male and female created He them." (Gen. 1:27)

- "For there are three that bare record in heaven, the Father, the Word, and the Holy Ghost: and ***these three are one***." (1 John 5:7)

Notice 1 John 5:7 says: "these three are one" and that it does not say they are three in one.

God's word says I am created in God's image, [i.e. in His image, I look like God].
God is a Father and is a Son and is the Holy Spirit, His word says: "these three are one".
I am a mother, a daughter and a spirit, (that lives in a body), these 3 are one, me, Cheryl.
I am made in God's image. I am one person, not 3 persons in 1. My husband says he has a wife, a lover, and a girlfriend and I don't get mad, because I know, these 3 are one, they are me, the name of all 3 of them is Cheryl.
The Father, The Son, and The Holy Spirit, ***these 3 are one***
and His name is [Jesus] Yeshua= Yehoshua=YHWH-Salvation=**YHWH, forever Exo 3:15**.

Keep reading, it will come together and you will understand the mystery of God.
God's word tells us that there is one Lord, one God.
- "**ONE Lord [YHWH]**, one faith, one baptism." (Eph. 4:5)
- "**I am the LORD [YHWH], and there is none else**, **there is no God beside me**: I girded thee, though thou hast not known me:" (Isa 45:5)
- "That they may know from the rising of the sun, and from the west, that **there is none beside me. I am the LORD [YHWH], and there is none else.**" (Isa 45:6)
- "Tell ye, and bring them near; yea, let them take counsel together: who hath declared this from ancient time? who hath told it from that time? have not **I the LORD [YHWH]**? and **there is no God else beside me; a just God and a Saviour; there is none beside me.**" (Isa 45:21)
- "For there is **ONE GOD**, and one mediator between God and men, **THE MAN Christ Jesus [Yeshua HaMasiach].**" (1 Tim. 2:5)
- *Yeshua=Yehoshua= YHWH-Salvation=YHWH, God's name for ever* (Exo. 3:15)

- In John 14:9 Yeshua (Jesus) said, "**he that hath seen me hath seen The Father**"
- And in John 10:30 He said, "**I and my Father are one**".
- "There is one body, and **one Spirit**, even as ye are called in one hope of your calling;" (Eph 4:4)
- James 2:19 *says*: "**Thou believest that there is one God; thou doest well:** the devils also believe, and tremble."

God's word says, the revelation of the mystery of God that was kept secret since the world began is now made manifest, **made known, by the scriptures.**

- "25) Now to him that is of power to stablish you according to my gospel, and the preaching of Jesus Christ, according to **the revelation of the mystery, which was kept secret since the world began, 26) But now is made manifest [known], and by the scriptures** of the prophets, according to the commandment of the everlasting God, made known to all nations for the obedience of faith:" (Rom 16:25, 26)

The Mystery of God Revealed [By the scriptures] is:

The Jews understood that Yeshua was claiming to be the one YHWH God of the first commandment.

Thou being a man, makest thyself God (Joh 10:33)

The one LORD [YHWH] God of the first commandment,
Is **A** Spirit (John 4:24) *Singular*
One Spirit (Eph 4:4)
Is Holy (Rev.4:8)
and is called The Holy Spirit

In order to reconcile us to Himself, (2 Col 5:18)
The Holy Spirit overshadowed the virgin Mary, (Luke 1:35)
and she was found with child of the Holy Spirit, (Matt 1:18)
The Holy Spirit played the role of Father

Then Christ the Lord was born, (Luke 2:11)
God was manifest in the flesh, (1 Tim 3:16)
The Holy Spirit purchased us with his own blood, (Acts 20:28)
The Holy Spirit played the role of Son

The mystery revealed through the scriptures is that the one LORD [YHWH] God, who is A Spirit, is Holy and is called the Holy Spirit, overshadowed the virgin Mary. Mary was found with child of the Holy Spirit. The one Spirit, the Holy Spirit, YHWH, played the role of Father. Christ was born. YHWH God was manifest in the flesh as the Son of God and gave His life for us.

- "For there are three that bare record in heaven, the Father, the Word, and the Holy Ghost: and **these three are one**." (1 John 5:7)

It was hidden, a mystery, that Yeshua [Jesus] was the Lord of glory, the one LORD [YHWH] God so that He could pay our sin debt, death.

- "7) But we speak the wisdom of God in a mystery, even the **hidden wisdom**, which God ordained before the world unto our glory: 8) Which none of the princes of this world knew: **for had they known it, they would not have crucified the Lord of glory**." (1 Cor. 2:7,8)

Yeshua [Jesus], being a Jew knew the first commandment. He quoted it (Mar 12:30) "Hear O Israel, Lord [YHWH] our God is one Lord [YHWH]"... and said (Joh 8:24) "I said therefore unto you, that ye shall die in your sins: for if ye believe not that I am *he,* ye shall die in your sins."

Yeshua [Jesus] was saying He is the **I AM**, the One YHWH God of the first commandment.

- "...***GOD WAS MANIFEST IN THE FLESH***..." (1 Tim. 3:16)
- *"As for* our redeemer, the LORD [**YHWH**] of hosts *is* his name, the Holy One of Israel." (Isa 47:4)
- "...and all flesh shall know that I the LORD [**YHWH**] **am thy Saviour and thy Redeemer**..." (Isa 49:26)
- "... and thou shalt know that I the LORD [**YHWH**] *am* **thy Saviour and thy Redeemer**..." (Isa 60:16)

Yeshua [Jesus] was fully God and fully man.
Yeshua [Jesus] was YHWH God and Man

**God**	_**Man**_
God was manifest	*...in the flesh (1 Tim 3:16)*
Being in the form of God	*...took upon the form of a servant and was made in likeness of men (Phil 2:6,7)*
The great God and Saviour	*...Jesus Christ [Yeshua HaMasiach] (Titus 2:13)*
There is One God	*...the man Christ Jesus [The Messiah Yeshua] (1 Tim 2:5)*
	...Son Jesus Christ [Yeshua HaMasiach]
This is the true God and eternal life	*... (1 John 5:20)*
	...a Child is born (Is. 9:6)
His name shall be called ....The Mighty God...	

3rd TRUTH: There is one Baptism.
Eph.4:5 One Lord, one faith, **one baptism**.
There are Eight very, very, strong reasons for Baptism
1) **Baptized into Christ** [Messiah] have put on Christ [Messiah] (Ga 3:27),
2) **Baptized into Jesus Christ** [Yeshua HaMasiach] are baptized into Christ's [Messiah's] death (Ro 6:3),
3) **Buried with Christ** [Messiah] in baptism (Col 2:12),
4) **Baptized into Christ's** [Messiah's] death, for the resurrection (Ro 6:3, 5),
5) **Espoused to Christ** [we, the bride, take his name] (2 Co 11:2),
6) **Baptized... in the name of Jesus Christ** for the remission of sins [salvation] (Acts 2:38),
7) **Preaching of Jesus Christ**...for the obedience of the faith (Rom 16:25,26)
8) **Confesses him as LORD [YHWH]** (Yeshua, Yehoshua, YHWH-Salvation, YHWH)
   There is no God else beside me; a just God and a Saviour; there is none beside me. (Isa 45:21),
   As for our redeemer, the LORD [YHWH] of hosts *is* his name, the Holy One of Israel. (Isa 47:4)
   I the LORD [YHWH] am thy Saviour (Isa 49:26)
Because Baptism has 8 very strong reasons to be baptized, including remission of sins [Salvation] and is part of our marriage to the Lamb of God [Yeshua], it is extremely important we understand Jesus [Yeshua's] disciples always baptized in His name. When you look up every scripture in the New Testament with the words **baptize and baptism** in them you will see, the only way they baptized in the New Testament was in Jesus [**Yeshua's**] Name. First I will show you the list of scriptures then I will show you historic proof the baptism was changed by Mystery Babylon.

THE ONLY WAY THEY BAPTIZED IN THE NEW TESTAMENT WAS IN JESUS [Yeshua's] NAME	Search the scriptures and you will see, **NOT ONE TIME, DID THEY BAPTIZE IN THE TITLES: FATHER, SON, AND HOLY GHOST IN THE NEW TESTAMENT**
"Then Peter said unto them, Repent, and be **baptized every one of you in the name of JESUS Christ** for the remission of sins, and ye shall receive the gift of the Holy Ghost." (Acts 2:38) "(For as yet he was fallen upon none of them: only they were **baptized in the name of the Lord JESUS**.)" (Acts 8:16) "And he **commanded them to be baptized in the name of the Lord**. Then prayed they him to tarry certain days." (Acts 10:48) "When they heard *this*, they were **baptized in the name of the Lord JESUS.**" (Acts 19:5) "And such were some of you: **but ye are washed**, but ye are sanctified, but ye are justified **in the name of the Lord JESUS**, and by the Spirit of our God." (1 Cor. 6:11) "Know ye not, that so many of us as **were baptized into JESUS CHRIST** were baptized into his death?" (Rom. 6:3) "For as many of you as have been **baptized into Christ** have put on Christ." (Gal. 3:27) "Neither is there salvation in any other: for **there is none other NAME** under heaven given among men, *whereby we must be saved*." (Acts 4:12) "And whatsoever ye do in word or deed, *do* **all in the name of the Lord JESUS**, giving thanks to God and the Father by him." (Col. 3:17) "Go ye therefore, and teach all nations, baptizing them **in the NAME** of the Father, and of the Son, and of the Holy Ghost:" (Matt. 28:19) "One Lord, one faith, **ONE BAPTISM**," (Eph. 4:5)	

Scripture List from Pastor Gary R. Dornbach II [8]

Note that these next three historical references also show that the disciples obeyed the word of our Lord Jesus, to baptize "in the name":
1) The New Testament knows only the baptism in the name of Jesus. **Schaff – Herzog Religious Encyclopedia**, Volume 1, page 435 [19]
2) The early church baptized in the name of the Lord Jesus until the second century. **Canney Encyclopedia of Religion,** page 53 [20]
3) Christian baptism was administered using the words, "in the name of Jesus." page 377. Baptism was always in the name of Jesus until time of Justin Martyr, page 389. **Hastings Encyclopedia of Religion,** Volume 2 [21]

Notice in the next historical references that the papacy changed the form of baptism. They changed it when they declared: "it is also obligatory to mention the separate persons of the Holy Trinity, and any ceremony that did not observe this form, invalid." Remember every baptism recorded in the New Testament is in Jesus name (in Yeshua's name).
1) **Britannica Encyclopedia**, 11th Edition, Volume 3, page 365 Baptism was changed from the name of Jesus to words Father, Son & Holy Ghost in 2nd Century. [22]

2) **The Catholic Encyclopedia**, 1913 Edition, Vol. 2, Page 263 states: "...some theologians held to, that the Apostles baptized in the name of Jesus only." [16]

3) **The same Catholic Encyclopedia**, on the same page, says, "In addition to the necessary word "baptize", or it's equivalent, **it is also obligatory to mention the separate persons of the Holy Trinity." AND "Any ceremony that did not observe this form has been declared invalid."** [16]

Jesus (Yeshua's) disciples had understanding of the mystery of God, they understood that He was the one YHWH God manifest in the flesh. It is very serious, to take the name of the one YHWH God, out of His baptism, which is for remission of our sins, for our salvation, that He put on flesh for and then paid our sin debt with His blood. It is actually denying the name of the one Lord [YHWH] God.

Jesus words show us that baptism is exceeding important, that it is a salvation issue. Jesus said in Mar 16:16 **He that believeth <u>and is baptized shall be saved</u>**; but he that believeth not shall be damned.

- **"This is the record**, that God hath given to us eternal life, and <u>this life is in his Son</u>. He that hath the Son hath life; and he that hath not the Son of God hath not life. **These things have I written unto you that believe on the name of the Son of God;** that ye may know that ye have eternal life, and that ye may **believe on the name of the Son of God**." (1 Joh 5:11-13)

Remember Yeshua (Jesus) words, when He was talking to, so called, doubting Thomas, John 20:27, 28, 29 ..."Be not faithless but believing" then after Thomas called him, My Lord and My God. Yeshua said **"Blessed are they that have not seen, and yet have believed"** then in John 20:31 it says: "But **these are written,** that ye might believe that Jesus is the Christ (Yeshua is the Messiah), the Son of God; and **that believing ye might have life through his name.**"

Genesis 1:27 So God created man in his own image... <u></u> [We look like God]
Exo 3:15 gives us God's name.
"And God said ...The LORD [YHWH] God ... this *is* my name for ever..." (Exo 3:15)
"Hear, O Israel: The LORD [YHWH] our God *is* one LORD [YHWH]:" (Deu 6:4)
Mark 12:29 says "...the Lord [YHWH] our God is one Lord [YHWH]..."

I am one and I can play more than one roll at a time, as God is One, He can play more than one role at a time. I am created in His image. *Column A shows God's roles and His name. Column B shows my roles and my name.*

Ex 3:14	Gen 1:27
A) God is (I AM THAT I AM):	**B) Me, I am:**
#1) A <u>Father</u>	**#1)** A <u>mother</u>
A <u>Son</u>	A <u>daughter</u>
A <u>Spirit</u>, Who is	A <u>spirit</u>
The Holy <u>Spirit</u> that	that lives
put on flesh, <u>a body</u>	in <u>a body</u>
#2) He told us to	**#2) Sign this check**
Baptize *in the name*	***in the name***
of the Father and of the	**of the mother and**
Son and of the Holy Spirit	**of the daughter,**
(See Matt. 28:19)	**who is a spirit [that lives in a body]**
#3) His word tells us	**#3) Sign the check**
Baptize *in the name*	***in the name***
of Jesus Christ [Mar Yah-Yeshua]	**of Cheryl**
(See Acts 2:38)	

First look at #1 in Column A and B. God is the <u>I AM THAT I AM</u>, and <u>Me, I am</u> also. Notice both are singular and I am made in His image. Then look at Column B, notice it says the same thing in # 2 and #3, to sign the check in Cheryl's name. Those who understood, knew that the mother and daughter, who is a spirit that lives in a body is one and her name is Cheryl, made in God's image- who is one YHWH. Column A, #2 and #3 say the same thing twice also, to baptize ***in the name,*** Jesus Christ [Mar Yah-Yeshua], the name of the Father and the Son and the Holy Spirit.

In John 5:43, Jesus [Yeshua] said He came in His Father's name. Yeshua is our Saviour's true name. Yeshua means salvation. Yeshua is a contraction of Yehoshua which means YHWH-Salvation.
Yeshua=Yehoshua= YHWH-Salvation=YHWH, God's name for ever Exo. 3:15

In Joh 10:30 Jesus [Yeshua] said: **I and *my* Father are one**. [One God, One YHWH, **one Spirit**, who is called the Holy Spirit.]

The Father and the Son are one God, one Spirit, The Holy Spirit, and have one name - YHWH, just like I, the mother and the daughter are one spirit [that lives in a body], and have one name – Cheryl

Matt. 28:19 and Acts 2:28 are not two different formulas for baptism. God's word simply says the same thing twice, to baptize in the name, but it says it in two different ways, as I did in column B, #2 and #3. God's word says there is one baptism, and that one baptism is ***in His name*** [see column A, #2 and #3 say the same thing twice] and Acts 2:38 tells us His name.

Matt. 28:19 does not say to baptize in the phrase: in the name of the Father and of the Son and of the Holy Spirit ***but in the name, Singular***.

If you were to sign a check, a legal document, Father or Son, it would not get cashed because that is your title, the role or roles you play, not your name. **Legal agreements require a name, not the title or role you play**. **The New Covenant** is our legal agreement, document, in Jesus Christ's (Yeshua the Messiah's) name, **the blood covenant (Luke 22:20), that is recognized in the court of heaven, by the judge of heaven,** for the right to forgiveness of sins, remission of sins (Acts 2:38), for salvation (Luke 1:77). The Holy Scriptures are actually our Wedding document. They tell us all that our Bridegroom has done for us and will do for us, and our rights as His Bride.[1] Chapter 6 gives fascinating Jewish insight to scriptures on our espousal, our wedding, to Christ.

- "And this is the record, that God hath given to us eternal life, and this life is in His Son... 13) These things I have written unto you that ye **believe on the Name** of the Son of God; that ye may know that ye have eternal life and that ye may **believe on the Name** of the Son of God." (1 John 5:11-13)

*In this one scripture, it says, twice, to believe on the **name** of the Son of God, for eternal life [for salvation, for remission of sins].*

Here is a little example of legal documents requiring a name.

Instructions:
First: Imagine the check on the next page for the imaginary million dollars is real and when you sign it, sign it, *in the name of* the father and of the son and of the spirit (***assuming you are a father and a son and a spirit*** [*a spirit that lives in a body*]) and you will receive, in full, the imaginary payment of one million dollars.
Then: Fill in today's date.
Then: Think about what you will write in the signature line, remembering the instructions to sign it *in the name* of the father and the son and the spirit [YOU]. Will you write your title, father? No, because that is not your name. Will you write your title, son? No, because that is not your name. Will you write spirit? No because that is not your name but what you are, a spirit, that lives in a body. Will you write all three: father, son and spirit since you are all three of these? No, because they are roles you play, they are your titles, not a name. The instructions were to sign in the name... legal documents require a name.

115

Now sign this check ***in the name of the father and the son and the spirit*** [your name] or for women sign the check ***in the name of the mother and the daughter and the spirit*** [your name] for the imaginary one million dollars and receive the understanding of the mystery of God and of the Father and of Christ. The understanding that YHWH God is one YHWH, *[Yeshua=Yehoshua=YHWH-Salvation=YHWH, God's name for ever Exo. 3:15]* just as His first commandment says He is.

The Mystery of God Revealed	1111
Rom 1:20, Rom 16:25,26, Col 2:2	

DATE _____

PAY TO THE
ORDER OF: the father and the son and the spirit $1,000,000.00

$ One Million Dollars and no cents--------------------------------Dollars

Memo: *Revelation of Truth*   _____

1:000000000: :000000000:   1111

John 1:12 says, "But as many as received Him, to them gave he power to become the sons of God, even to them **that believe on his *Name*.**" He, Yeshua [Jesus], gave power to become sons of God [to be born again, born of His Spirit] **that believe on his *Name*.** John 3:7 says ... ye must be born again.

God's Word says in both Matt. 28:19 and in Acts 2:38 "...***Be baptized in the name***" Father and Son are titles and Holy is a description of the one YHWH, they are not a name. Acts 4:12 says...there is none other "NAME" ...where by ye must be saved. How are we to be saved in His name? In baptism. Acts 2:38...be baptized every one of you *in the NAME of Jesus Christ* [Yeshua HaMasiach] for the remission of sins [for salvation] and ye shall receive the gift of the Holy Spirit [Born again – become a son of God through belief in His name].

"...***Behold I set before thee an open door, and no man can shut it: for thou hast a little strength, and hast kept my word, and hast not denied my Name.***" (Rev. 3:8)

Exo. 3:15 tells us that God's name is **YHWH, forever.**
YHWH =Yahweh,
Yah—short version of YHWH [Yahweh] [Example: Hallelujah means Praise Yah]
Mar means Master/ Lord
MarYah—contraction of Mar and Yah, meaning 'Master/Lord Yah'.
Yeshua is our Saviour's Hebrew name meaning Salvation.
Mar Yah Yeshua is our Saviour's true name, it is a compound name meaning
Master YHWH is Salvation.
YHWH has many compound names, at least forty compound names.
See list of YHWH's 41 compound names [139] at:
http://www.prayertoday.org/NamesofGod/Jehovah-names.htm
One you may already know is Jehovah Jirah, or Yahweh Yirah meaning YHWH is provider.

The truth is so important, the 1st commandment says, the LORD [**YHWH**] God is One LORD [**YHWH**] *but Mystery Babylon and many other denominations continue to follow the* teaching that God is three in one. God's word never says, three in one. If you are following a God that is three in one, that is the false God created by Mystery Babylon, that is not the one YHWH God of the first commandment, [Jesus] Yeshua, Yehoshua, YHWH-Salvation, YHWH, who put on flesh and died to save you. Following any other god other than the one YHWH [**Mar Yah Yeshua**] of the first commandment is Idolatry, Spiritual Adultery, it is the reason God divorced Israel. Israel was following the Baal [Lord] of Babylon.

"And I saw, when for all the causes whereby **backsliding Israel committed adultery** I had put her away, and **given her a bill of divorce**; yet her treacherous sister Judah feared not, but went and played the harlot also." (Jer 3:8)

God calls Mystery Babylon the great whore and her daughters harlots because they have went after the Babylonian gods. A god that is three in one is not the God of the Bible but is the god of Mystery Babylon.

God's word tell us **the preaching of Jesus Christ** was **according to the Revelation of the Mystery** and was **made known by the scriptures** in Rom 16:25 & 26

"25) Now to him that is of power to stablish you according to my gospel, and **the preaching of Jesus Christ, according to the revelation of the mystery,** which was kept secret since the world began, 26) But **now is made manifest, and by the scriptures** of the prophets, according to the commandment of the everlasting God, made known to all nations *for the obedience of faith*:" (Rom 16:25, 26)

Scriptures reveal the mystery: Jesus is called the Father and the Son and the Holy Ghost.

Jesus being called:

The Father:
"For unto us a **child is born**, unto us a Son is given: ...and **his Name shall be called...The everlasting Father...**" (Is.9:6)
"**I and my Father are One**." (John 10:30)

"Jesus saith unto him, Have I been so long time with you, and yet hast thou not known me, Philip? **he that hath seen me hath seen the Father;** and how sayest thou then, show us the Father?" (John 14:9)

The Son:
"The beginning of the gospel of **Jesus Christ, *the Son* of God;**" (Mar 1:1)
"...Thou art the **Christ, the Son** of the living God." (Matt. 16:16)

The Holy Spirit:
"But ye are not in the flesh but in the Spirit if so be that **The Spirit of God** dwell in you. Now if any man have not **The Spirit of Christ,** he is none of his." (Romans 8:9)
[The Spirit of Christ is the Spirit of God, the one Spirit of Eph.4:4.]
"There is one body, and **one Spirit**, even as ye are called in one hope of your calling;" (Eph 4:4)

The Holy Spirit in the role of the Son, Jesus
"Take heed therefore unto yourselves, and to all the flock, over the which **the Holy Ghost** hath made you overseers, to feed the church of God, which **he hath purchased with his own blood.**" (Acts 20:28)
[The Holy Ghost, he purchased with his own blood- Jesus, God manifest in the flesh.]

Peter preached according to the revelation of the mystery of God. He exhorted them to be baptized in the name of Jesus [Yeshua], saying: save yourselves. 3000 people were baptized, in Jesus [Yeshua's] name in one day after hearing how to save themselves. Jesus [Yeshua] is still the way to be saved.

- "Then Peter said unto them, **Repent, and be baptized every one of you in the name of Jesus Christ [Yeshua]** for the remission of sins, and ye shall receive the gift of the Holy Ghost. 39) For **the promise is** unto you, and to your children, and *to all that are afar off*, *even as many as the Lord our God shall call.* 40) And with many other words did he testify and exhort, saying, **Save yourselves** from this untoward generation. (Act 2:41) Then **they that gladly received his word were baptized**: and the same day there were added unto them about **three thousand souls.**" (Act 2:38)

We have seen Historic Proof the baptism was changed:

1) **Britannica Encyclopedia**, 11th Edition, Volume 3, page 365 Baptism was changed from the name of Jesus to words Father, Son & Holy Ghost in 2nd Century.

2) **The Catholic Encyclopedia**, 1913 Edition, Vol. 2, Page 263 states: "...some theologians held to, that the Apostles baptized in the name of Jesus only." [16]

3) **The same Catholic Encyclopedia**, on the same page, says, "In addition to the necessary word "baptize", or it's equivalent, **it is also obligatory to mention the separate persons of the Holy Trinity." AND "Any ceremony that did not observe this form has been declared invalid."** [16]

And when we search the scriptures, we find the only way Jesus [Yeshua's] Apostles baptized was in His name. Not one time in all the scriptures did they baptized in the phrase: in the name of the Father and of the Son and of the Holy Ghost. Baptism was changed from in our Saviour's name Jesus [Yeshua] when the Papacy declared: "In addition to the necessary word "baptize", or it's equivalent, it is also obligatory to mention the separate persons of the Holy Trinity." AND "Any ceremony that did not observe this form has been declared invalid."

This is extremely serious because Jesus [Yeshua] said: "he that believeth and is baptized shall be saved." Jesus was calling baptism a salvation issue. His Apostles called it a salvation issue, Peter said, in Acts 2:38 "be baptized every one of you *in the name of Jesus [Yeshua] for the remission of sins*" *then in Acts 2:40 repeated: "save yourselves" and in Acts 2:41 3000 gladly received his word to be baptized in [Jesus] Yeshua's name and were baptized.*

God's first commandment is to Hear that, "YHWH God is one YHWH" (Deu 6:4, Mark 12:29)
The first commandment has not changed, God is one YHWH, from Genesis to Revelations.
God's word says: "... the Father, the Word, and the Holy Ghost: and these three are one." (1 Joh 5:7).

God's first commandment is clear: YHWH God is one YHWH.
[Jesus] Yeshua=Yehoshua=YHWH is Salvation=YHWH
[Jesus] Yeshua is not part of the Trinity.
[Jesus] **Yeshua is YHWH** [LORD], **God manifest in the flesh**
YHWH put on flesh [Yeshua] and paid our sin debt, death.

To believe that God is three separate Gods or three separate persons in one and that [Jesus] Yeshua is only part of the Godhead is a doctrine of men, a doctrine of Mystery Babylon. Mystery Babylon brought it into the church. It is Spiritual adultery. Spiritual adultery, going after another God, other than the one YHWH, is the one thing God divorced His people, Israel, for! And in Rev. 18:4 god is calling His people [Catholics and Christians] out of Mystery Babylon that they do not receive her plagues, her judgments.

"And I saw, when for all the causes whereby **backsliding Israel committed adultery** I had put her away, and **given her a bill of divorce**; yet her treacherous sister Judah feared not, but went and played the harlot also." (Jer 3:8)

"And I heard another voice from heaven, saying, **Come out of her, my people, that ye be not partakers of her sins, and that ye receive not of her plagues.**" (Rev 18:4)

118

Come out of her. Repent and be baptized in the name of [Jesus] *Mar Yah Yeshua* for remission of sins. God's word says there is Salvation (remission of sins) is in no other name.

4ᵗʰ TRUTH: Faith [Belief] is an Action Word.

If you believe the chair will hold you, you sit down on it [the action of belief].
If you believe the air plane will fly you, where you want to go, you get on it.

If you believe the key will start the engine, you turn the key.
All the believing the key starts the engine, will not work without action.

If you believe the switch will turn on the light, you flip the switch.
If you believe the on button turns the TV on, you push the on button.

Believing gives you the faith to do the action. If you don't believe the chair will hold you, you don't sit on it, you don't take action. No belief- No action.

If you believe not that the plane will fly, you don't get on it. No belief - No action.
If you believe not that the key will start the car, you don't turn it. No belief- No action.
If you believe not that the light switch will turn the light on, you don't flip it on. You believe not- no action.
If you believe not that the on button will turn on the TV, you don't push the on button. No belief- no action.
If you do not believe, you do not take action.
Yeshua [Jesus] said ....If ye believe not [no action-no baptism in His name] that I am (He), ye shall die in your sins.

Mark 16:16 Our Saviour said: "If ye Believe and are Baptized" [*Baptism in Yeshua (Jesus) name is the action of belief in who "He" is]* **"ye shall be saved, but he that believeth not shall be damned"**, in John 8:24 he said "... for if ye believe not that I am *he*, ye shall die in your sins." Because if ye believe not, you won't obey God's word in Acts 2:38 and be baptized in Yeshua's [Jesus] name for the remission of sins (salvation) and there is salvation in no other name.

"Faith [belief], if it hath not works [actions], is dead" (Jas 2:17)
"Faith without works [actions] is dead" (Jas 2:20)
"Faith without works [actions] is dead" (Jas 2:26)
God's word states three times Faith without works [actions] is dead and in the middle of these three scriptures, stating faith without works [actions] is dead, Jas 1:19 says: **"Thou believest that *there is one God*; thou doest well: the devils also believe, and tremble."**
The devils know there is one God but do not obey.
Those who believe [have faith] there is one God, do the works, the action of faith:

Acts 19:4,5 says: "(4) ***...Believe on him*** ... that is, on Christ Jesus [Yeshua HaMasiach]. (5) **When they heard this, *they were baptized in the name of the Lord Jesus [Yeshua]*.**" [They Believed and did the action of belief]

Yeshua=Yehoshua=YHWH-Salvation=YHWH, The one YHWH God of the first commandment put on flesh, suffered and died to pay our sin debt, and rose again on the third day, to reunite us to Himself. This is the gospel, the good news.

"Call his name JESUS [**Yeshua**]: for he shall save his people from their sins." (Mat 1:21)
Yeshua=Yehoshua=YHWH-Salvation= **YHWH**, God's name forever (Exo 3:15)
YHWH shall save His people from their sins.

"know that the LORD [**YHWH**] he *is* God; *there is* none else beside him." (Deu4:35)
"know... the LORD [**YHWH**] he *is* God ... *there is* none else." (Deu 4:39)

119

"know that the LORD **[YHWH]** is God, and that there is none else." (1Ki8:60)

"I am the LORD **[YHWH]**, and there is none else, there is no God beside me" (Isa 45:5)

"There is none beside me. I am the LORD **[YHWH]**, and there is none else." (Isa 45:6)

"I am the LORD **[YHWH]**; and there is none else." (Isa 45:18)

"I, even I, am the LORD [YHWH]; and beside me there is no Saviour." (Isa 43:11)

"I the LORD [YHWH]? and there is no God else beside me; a just God and a Saviour; there is none beside me" (Isa 45:21)

"As for our redeemer, the LORD [YHWH] of hosts is his name, the Holy One of Israel." (Isa 47:4)

"I the LORD **[YHWH]** am thy Saviour" (Isa 49:26)

"I the LORD **[YHWH]** am thy Saviour" (Isa 60:16)

Get the book: <u>Be Not Faithless But Believing, Jesus Subtitle: The Mystery of God Revealed</u>, and do the quizzes at the end of each Chapter and you will understand the mystery of God.

Here are some questions from: <u>Be Not Faithless But Believing God Subtitle: The Mystery of God Revealed</u> from several of the quizzes. You can find the answers in this chapter of Sound the Alarm. Most of the answers are from in the King James Version of the Bible and can be found by the scripture address given.

From Chapter 6 The Mystery Revealed Short quiz

1) We can __ __ __ __ __ __ __ __ __ __ __ the Godhead by the thing that are __ __ __ __ Romans __:__ __.

2) We are to have full __ __ __ __ __ __ __ __ __ __ __ __ __ __ __, to the __ __ __ __ __ __ __ __ __ __ __ __ __ of the mystery of God, and of the Father, and of Christ; (This scripture is saying we are to have complete understanding and acknowledge that we have the understanding of the mystery of God, and the Father, and of Christ. (Col 2:2)

3) We are to be established according to the __ __ __ __ __ __ __ __ __ __ of the mystery (Ro 16:25)

From Chapter 4 The Replacing of God's Name Short quiz

4) In Exo.3:15 God says His name is __ __ __ __ [i.e. LORD] forever.

5) Jesus Hebrew name, Yeshua, is the short form of Yehoshua and means __ __ __ __ is Salvation or __ __ __ __- Salvation).

From Chapter 5 What Did Jesus Say About Himself? [i.e. the doctrine of Christ] Short Quiz

6) In John 12:45, Yeshua [Jesus] said: AND HE THAT SEETH ME SEETH __ __ __ THAT SENT ME.

7) In John 14:9 Yeshua [Jesus] said: ...HE THAT HATH SEEN ME HATH SEEN THE __ __ __ __ __ __ __...

8) In John 10:30 Yeshua [Jesus] said: I AND MY FATHER ARE __ __ __. [i.e. One God 1 Tim 2:5, James 2:19, One Lord Eph.4:5, Mark 12:29,30, One Spirit Eph.4:4, John 4:24]

From Chapter 6 The Mystery Revealed Short Quiz

9) 1Jn 5:7 For there are three that bear record in heaven, the Father, the Word, and the Holy Ghost: and these three are __ __ __.

10) Col.2:8, 9 says: Beware lest any man spoil you   through philosophy and vain deceit, after traditions of __ __ __, after the rudiments of the world, and not after Christ, for in him dwelleth all the fullness of the Godhead bodily. God is the Father and is the Son and is the Holy Spirit and God word say these three are one. God's word never says He is three but always says God is one. The doctrine of God being three, a Trinity came from Tertullian17. [a Catholic doctrine]. The Trinity is a doctrine, tradition of __ __ __.

11) 1 Cor. 2:7,8 explains that it had been __ __ __ __ __ __ __ __ __ __ __ __, [i.e. it had been kept a mystery] that Jesus [Yeshua] was the Lord of Glory (7) But we speak the wisdom of God in a mystery, even the <u>hidden wisdom</u>, which God ordained before the world unto our glory: (8) Which none of the princes of this world knew: **for had they known it, they would not have crucified the Lord of glory.** [YHWH= YHWH-Salvation=Yehoshua=Yeshua]

12) 1 John 5:20 also explains: And we know that the Son of God is come, AND HATH GIVEN US __ __ __ __ __ __ __ __ __ __ __ __ __ __ __, that we may know him that is true, and we are in him that is true, even in his Son Jesus Christ [Yeshua HaMasiach]. This is the true God and eternal life. [This is saying Yeshua is the true God and eternal life, Yeshua= Yehoshua=YHWH-Salvation=YHWH, God's name forever!]

13) Isa. 45:5 says: I am the LORD [__ __ __ __], and there is __ __ __ __ else, there is __ __ God beside me.

14) Isa 45:6 says: there is __ __ __ __ beside me. I am the LORD [__ __ __ __], and there is __ __ __ __ else. Isa 45:6

15) Isa 45:21 says: There is no God else beside me; a just God and a Saviour; there is __ __ __ __ beside me.

16) Isa 49:26 says: I the LORD [__ __ __ __] am thy Saviour

17) Isa 60:16 says: I the LORD [__ __ __ __] am thy Saviour

18) According to God's first commandment, how many Gods are there? __ __ __ Deu 6:4, 5 Mark12:29, 30

19) 1 John 5:7 says For there are three that bare record in heaven, the Father, the Word, and the Holy Ghost: and these three __ __ __ __ __ __ . The Father, The Son, and The Holy Spirit, these 3 are one and His name is Yeshua= Yehoshua=YHWH-Salvation=__ __ __ __ forever Exo 3:15.

From Chapter 5 What Did Jesus Say About Himself? [i.e. the doctrine of Christ] Short Quiz

20) John 20:29 Yeshua [Jesus] says: ...Blessed ARE THEY THAT HAVE NOT SEEN AND YET HAVE BELIEVED. Believed what? That He is the One ___ ___ ___ ___ and ___ ___ ___. [Of the first commandment Mark 12:29,30]

From Chapter 8 Baptized Quiz

21) Jesus [Yeshua] said, in Mark 16:16: He that Believeth and is __ __ __ __ __ __ __ __ shall be __ __ __ __ __...

22) (Act 10:43) To him give __ __ __the prophets witness, that through his __ __ __ __ whosoever believeth in him shall receive __ __ __ __ __ __ __ __ __ __ __ __ __ __ __.

23) (Acts 2:38)... Repent and Be Baptized every one of you in the name of Jesus Christ [Yeshua HaMasiach] __... [Remission means pardon, forgiveness so for the pardoning of sins, for the forgiveness of sins, i.e. for the Saving from sins, i.e. for Salvation]

24) Three verses after Peter said for everyone to be baptized in the name of Jesus Christ [Yeshua HaMasiach] on the same day, how many were baptized in his name? _____ (See Acts 2:38 and Acts 2:41)

From Chapter 9 Believe Short Quiz

25) James 2:20 says: But wilt thou know, O vain man, that faith [belief] without works [__ __ __ __ __ __ __] is dead? We are God's bride, His wife. Baptism is a part of our betrothal, espousal, marriage to God.

From Chapter 11 The Jewish wedding Short Quiz

26) (Hosea 2:19) "And ___ will betroth you to __ __forever...Then you will know the LORD [YHWH]." [Betroth, i.e. espouse] Notice God refers to Himself in the singular I and me.

27) 2 Cor.11:21 says: For I am jealous over you with godly jealousy: for I have espoused you to __ __ __ husband, that I may present you as a chaste virgin to __ __ __ __ __ __ [Messiah]. Christ [Messiah] is the Lamb of God in Rev.19:7-9. He is the One LORD [YHWH] God who betroths us to Himself forever from Hosea 2:19

So you can check your work, the quiz answers are at the back of this book.

The next chapter shows some very important details about the One World Churches' Constitution, Mystery Babylon's Constitution, that all of God's people need to be aware of.

Chapter 5   The One World Church And It's Constitution

God had revealed so much to me, step by step, by step. The revelation of who Mystery Babylon is, the understanding of the Mystery of God, and of the Father and of Christ according to the scriptures (Shown in chapter 4), the identity of the antichrist, how the first five trumpets of the book of Revelations have already occurred, the next trumpet too be blown, the sixth trumpet, is the Euphrates River War that kills one third of mankind, that we are already in, that Christians will still be here during this 6th trumpet war, during the great tribulation, and I found the Constitution for the One World Church, the World Council of Churches, 9th Assembly Feb. 2006 Called to be One. [126] It was the one world Church, Mystery Babylon's constitution. Everything fit together like a perfect puzzle.

I had never heard of a constitution for a church and this was a constitution for a world church. But it made since, the Bible foretells a one world government and a one world Church. I read and read and read, then came to the subtitle: Rules. I continued reading.

It said: A Church seeking affiliation … must agree with the basis and fulfil the criteria for membership and below under Criteria it said: Churches applying to join the World Council of Churches ("applicant churches") **are required to first *express agreement* ….** a) Theological 1. In its life and witness, *the church professes faith in the triune God…* **3. The church baptizes in the name of the one God, "Father, Son and Holy Spirit"**

Again, I was in shock. I knew how baptism had been changed… and now there is a world constitution requiring to express agreement and profess faith in a triune God. I quoted Jesus [Yeshua's] words to myself: Mark 12:29, 30 And Jesus answered him, The first of all the commandments *is,* Hear, O Israel; The Lord [**YHWH**] our God is one Lord [**YHWH**]: And thou shalt love the Lord [**YHWH**] thy God with all thy heart, and with all thy soul, and with all thy mind, and with all thy strength: this *is* the first commandment.

I continued to read: **World Council of Churches 9th Assembly Feb. 14-23 2006 Called to be One Church (as adopted)**

… II 3. **We confess one, holy, catholic, and apostolic Church** as expressed in the Nicene-Constantinopolitan Creed (381), The Churches oneness is an image of the unity of the Triune God… 9. **Our common belonging to Christ through baptism in the name of the Father and of the Son and of the Holy Spirit….We affirm there is one baptism…**

- This world church specifically confesses the Catholic Church mentioning the Triune baptism
- But scriptures say we are to confess Jesus [Yeshua] and be baptized in the name of Jesus [Yeshua].
- "That if thou shalt *confess* with thy mouth the Lord *Jesus [Yeshua],* … thou shalt be saved." (Rom 10:9)
- We are to confess Yeshua. Being baptized in Yeshua's name is confessing Him as the one LORD [YHWH] God of the first commandment. [*Yeshua=Yehoshua=YHWH-Salvation=YHWH*]
- Being baptized in the Catholic (triune- three person or three Gods in one) form is confessing the Catholic Church, being baptized in the triune form is confessing Mystery Babylon.

---

[126] https://www.oikoumene.org/en/resources/documents/assembly/2006-porto-alegre/
1-statements-documents-adopted/institutional-issues/constitution-and-rules-as-adopted

- "26) How long shall this be in the heart of the prophets that prophesy lies? yes, they are prophets of the deceit of their own heart; 27) Which think to **cause my people to forget my name** by their dreams which they tell every man to his neighbor, **as their fathers have forgotten my name for Baal.**" (Jeremiah 23:26-27)

And it is a very serious thing to take the one YHWH God's name out of his baptism. Mystery Babylon took Yeshua's name [Yeshua=Yehoshua=YHWH-Salvation=YHWH] out of the baptism (the only way Yeshua's Apostles baptized in the Bible) when they stated "In addition to the necessary word "baptize", or it's equivalent, it is also obligatory to mention the separate persons of the Holy Trinity." AND **"Any ceremony that did not observe this form has been declared invalid."** [127-16]

The Hebrew people told God that they would perform their vows to the queen of heaven (Baal worship) and God swore by his name that they would be consumed with sword and famine and would know whose words shall stand, his, or theirs.

- "25) **Thus saith the LORD [YHWH] of hosts,** the God of Israel, saying; Ye and your wives have both spoken with your mouths, and fulfilled with your hand, saying, **We will surely perform our vows that we have vowed, to burn incense to the queen of heaven,** and to pour out drink offerings unto her: ye will surely accomplish your vows, and surely perform your vows. 26) Therefore hear ye the word of the LORD [YHWH], all Judah that dwell in the land of Egypt; Behold, **I have sworn by my great name, saith the LORD [YHWH],** that my name shall no more be named in the mouth of any man of Judah in all the land of Egypt, saying, The Lord GOD liveth. 27) Behold, I will watch over them for evil, and not for good: and all the men of Judah that *are* in the land of Egypt **shall be consumed by the sword and by the famine,** until there be an end of them. 28) Yet a small number that escape the sword shall return out of the land of Egypt into the land of Judah, and all the remnant of Judah, that are gone into the land of Egypt to sojourn there, **shall know whose words shall stand, mine, or theirs.**" (Jer 44:25-28)

When God gives us clear warning, we must heed His warning. The Jews suffered a lot for their rebellion, for Baal worship, spiritual adultery and refusing to stop worshiping the queen of heaven (Semiramis). God divorced them, cast them out of their promise land to all the nations of the earth, persecuted them with sword and famine (one example: the holocaust). They ignored God's warnings. We seriously must heed God's warning to come out of Mystery Babylon, who has the same traditions of Baal worship as Babylon, that we receive not her plagues, that we receive not her judgments. 1 Pe 4:17 tells us, judgment must start at the house of God.

- "For the time *is come* that judgment must begin at the house of God: and if *it* first *begin* at us, what shall the end *be* of them that obey not the gospel of God?" (1Pe 4:17)

In Rev 17:1, God describes the Mother church, Mystery Babylon as a whore and the daughter Churches of Mystery Babylon as harlots in Rev. 17:5

- "And there came one of the seven angels which had the seven vials, and talked with me, saying unto me, Come hither; **I will shew unto thee the judgment of the great whore** that sitteth upon many waters:" (Rev 17:1)

- "And upon her forehead was a name written, **MYSTERY, BABYLON THE GREAT, THE MOTHER OF *HARLOTS* AND ABOMINATIONS OF THE EARTH.**" (Rev 17:5)

MYSTERY BABYLON THE GREAT, The great Catholic Church taught her daughter Churches to follow the adulterous Babylonian doctrine that God is three, triune, therefore they were worshiping a false god instead of the one YHWH God of the first commandment, Yeshua. [Yeshua= Yehoshua= YHWH-Salvation= YHWH]

---

127 Chapter 5 reference list from: Be Not Faithless But Believing Jesus The Mystery of God Revealed www.themysteryrevealed.info

Remember where the name Jesus came from and that our Hebrew Saviour's name is Yeshua and that Yeshua is not part of the Godhead, he is the fullness of the Godhead (Col. 2:8-9) that was manifest in the flesh. The one God, YHWH, [YHWH= YHWH-Salvation=Yehoshua= Yeshua], who did it all to save us. Worshiping any other, worshiping a Jesus [Yeshua] that is one third of the Godhead is not worshiping the one true YHWH God. It is spiritual adultery. Approximately 85%, of the Christian Churches today worship this way and are in Mystery Babylon or are in a daughter church of Mystery Babylon. God calls the mother church a great whore and the daughter churches harlots for going after other gods, other than the one YHWH God of the first commandment because they are committing idolatry, spiritual adultery. This is the one thing God divorced Israel for. We are YHWH's bride, the Lamb of God's bride. God refers to Himself as YHWH and as the Lamb of God. In Rev. 18:4 He is warning His people in Mystery Babylon to not be partakers of her whoredom, her spiritual adultery, and to come out of her.

- "And I will betroth you to me forever...Then you will know the LORD [**YHWH**]." (Hosea 2:19) (Betroth, i.e. espouse) Notice YHWH refers to Himself in the singular I and me.
- 2 Cor. 11:21 says: For I am jealous over you with godly jealousy: for I have **espoused you to one husband**, that I may present you as a chaste virgin **to Christ (Messiah).**
- "The next day John seeth Jesus coming unto him, and saith, Behold the Lamb of God, which taketh away the sin of the world." (Joh 1:29)
- Jesus is the Lamb of God. The marriage of the Lamb of God is come in Rev.19:7-9 and He is the One LORD [YHWH] God who betroths us to Himself forever from Hosea 2:19
- "And I saw, when for all the causes whereby backsliding ***Israel committed adultery*** I had put her away, and ***given her a bill of divorce***; yet her treacherous sister Judah feared not, but went and played the harlot also." (Jer 3:8)

His people refused to hear the truth and continued worshiping idols. They pushed Him out, so He was out. He warned them repeatedly and repeatedly took His protection off of them, allowing other nations to come against them many times, and Babylon and Germany (the holocaust). Their judgments came through their enemies, plagues, and the ground even opened to swallow them.

This is why the Mystery of God is so extremely important to understand now. Lest we fall into the same ditch, judgment, for idolatry, spiritual adultery as Israel did, following the doctrines of Babylon's Baal worship. God is warning His people. He is going to judge Mystery Babylon, (The Catholic Church and her daughter Churches) but God's people don't have to be judged with Mystery Babylon. God is calling His people out of Mystery Babylon that they be not partakers of her sins and receive not her plagues, that they receive not her judgments.

The first commandment is the only commandment with a direct command for God's people: to listen, *to hear*, that YHWH God is one YHWH, that Yahweh is one Yahweh. Jesus [Yeshua] was YHWH [Yahweh] in the flesh and He repeated the first commandment in Mark 12:29-30

- "29) And Jesus answered him, The first of all the commandments is, **Hear**, O Israel; The Lord [**YHWH**] **our God is one** Lord [**YHWH**]: 30) And thou shalt love the Lord [**YHWH**] thy God with all thy heart, and with all thy soul, and with all thy mind, and with all thy strength: this is the first commandment." (Mar 12:29, 30)

- "4) **Hear**, O Israel: The LORD [**YHWH**] **our God is one** LORD [**YHWH**]: 5) And thou shalt love the LORD [**YHWH**] thy God with all thine heart, and with all thy soul, and with all thy might." (Deu 6:4, 5)

The World Council of Churches, constitution, says to join them, the Church must agree with their baptism and most Churches already do. Baptism is extremely important because Jesus [Yeshua] said: "He that believeth and is baptized shall be saved;" Jesus [Yeshua] made baptism a salvation issue.
The gospel (the good news) is that the one God of the first commandment, YHWH,
[YHWH= YHWH-Salvation= Yehoshua=Yeshua (Jesus)],

the one LORD [YHWH] God, who is a Spirit, the Holy Spirit, overshadowed the virgin Mary, (Luke 1:35), and Mary was with child of the Holy Spirit (Matt. 1:18), the Holy Spirit was the Father. This is how the one Spirit, the one YHWH put on flesh, God manifest in the flesh, taking the role of the Son to die for us, to pay our sin debt and reunite us to Himself. Baptism was and is, in His name for the remission of sins, for salvation. This is the good news, the gospel, and when we hear this good news that the one YHWH God put on flesh and gave His life for us so we don't have to pay our own sin debt, believe it and are baptized in His name for the remission of sins, we receive the gift of the Holy Spirit, we are born again of His Spirit, we are saved.

Aprox. 200 years after Yeshua's death and resurrection. Aprox. 200 A.D. Tertullian (a Catholic) was the first person to introduce the doctrine of the Trinity. **312 A.D.** At the Council of Nicene, there was a vote and the Catholic Church (Mystery Babylon) established the doctrine of the Trinity. **318 A.D.** At the Council of Constantinople, the final approval of the doctrine of the Trinity was given. **From 500 A.D. to 1500 A.D. 1000 years of the Dark Ages,** They made a law no laity could have or read the Bible. People either accepted the Catholic doctrines or were killed. Read Foxes book of Martyrs. Eph. 4:5's one baptism, that is for salvation (remission of sins) was declared invalid, changed, by the Catholic Church, changed by Mystery Babylon.

Historical Proof it was changed:
1) Britannica Encyclopedia, 11th Edition, Volume 3, page 365 Baptism was changed from the name of Jesus to the words Father, Son & Holy Ghost in the 2nd Century [2nd Century = 101AD-200AD]. [127-22]
2) It was a Catholic doctrine that took our Saviour's name out of baptism:[15]
The Catholic Encyclopedia, 1913 Edition, Vol. 2, Page 263 states: "...some theologians held to, that the Apostles baptized in the name of Jesus only." [127-16]
3) The same Catholic Encyclopedia, on the same page, says, "In addition to the necessary word "baptize", or it's equivalent, **it is also obligatory to mention the separate persons of the Holy Trinity." AND "Any ceremony that did not observe this form has been declared invalid."**
[127-16]

Biblical Proof, Jesus disciples baptized every time in His name.

THE ONLY WAY THEY BAPTIZED IN THE NEW TESTAMENT WAS IN JESUS [Yeshua's] NAME	Search the scriptures and you will see, **NOT ONE TIME, DID THEY BAPTIZE IN THE TITLES FATHER, SON, AND HOLY GHOST IN THE NEW TESTMENT**
"Then Peter said unto them, Repent, and be **baptized *every one* of you in the name of JESUS Christ** for the remission of sins, and ye shall receive the gift of the Holy Ghost." (Acts 2:38) "(For as yet he was fallen upon none of them: only they were **baptized in the name of the Lord JESUS**.)" (Acts 8:16) "And he **commanded them to be baptized in the name of the Lord**. Then prayed they him to tarry certain days." (Acts 10:48) "When they heard *this*, they were **baptized in the name of the Lord JESUS**." (Acts 19:5) "And such were some of you: **but ye are washed**, but ye are sanctified, but ye are justified **in the name of the Lord JESUS**, and by the Spirit of our God." (1 Cor. 6:11) "Know ye not, that so many of us as **were baptized into JESUS CHRIST** were baptized into his death?" (Rom. 6:3) "For as many of you as have been **baptized into Christ** have put on Christ." (Gal. 3:27) "Neither is there salvation in any other: for **there is none other NAME** under heaven given among men, *whereby we must be saved*." (Acts 4:12) "And whatsoever ye do in word or deed, *do* **all in the name of the Lord JESUS**, giving thanks to God and the Father by him." (Col. 3:17) "Go ye therefore, and teach all nations, baptizing them **in the NAME** of the Father, and of the Son, and of the Holy Ghost:" (Matt. 28:19) "One Lord, one faith, **ONE BAPTISM**," (Eph. 4:5) Scripture List from Pastor Gary R. Dornbach II	

[127-8]

People who are not actually Catholic but are being baptized in the Catholics form, the World Council of Churches' baptism, the triune formula, in the phrase: in the name of the Father and of the Son and of the Holy Spirit are in the daughter churches of the Catholic Church, the daughter Churches of Mystery Babylon. They are the daughters that the Catholic Church started welcoming back in at the Vatican Council II in the early 1960s. The people that left the Catholic Church at the reformation of Church, started new churches and unknowingly took with them many of the teachings and doctrines of the Mother Church, the Babylonian traditions of Baal worship from Mystery Babylon.

These Churches, that the mother Church calls daughters, and God calls harlots in Rev 17:5, they took the Trinitarians' doctrines with them, from the mother Church, who took it from Babylon, shown in chapter 3. God is getting ready to judge Mystery Babylon, in our generation. We are in the end times now. We must heed God's warning to come out of Mystery Babylon. In Rev 18:4 God is warning us, warning His people of the plagues (His judgment) coming to Mystery Babylon (the Catholic Church and her daughter Churches) for this harlotry, this spiritual adultery, in our generation. Remember in the Old Testament God divorced His people for Baal worship, idolatry, spiritual adultery and in the New Testament the one acceptable reason God gives for divorce is adultery. Unknowingly we have followed pagan gods and doctrines of Babylon. By understanding the prophecies of the end times (explained in chapter 1 and 2) we see that God is judging Mystery Babylon for this whoredom, in our generation, and those that take the mark of the Beast (the one world government and one world religion) the smoke of their torment will ascend up forever, that's why it's so extremely important to understand these mysteries now and heed God's call to come out of her now.

And Baptism also is actually a part of our marriage ceremony to Jesus (Yeshua=Yehoshua=YHWH-Salvation=YHWH, the one God of the first commandment).
If we are not baptized in the name of the one YHWH God, who are we being espoused to when we are espoused, baptized, in the One World Church, Mystery Babylon's, the Catholic Church's Trinitarian formula?

- "**For your husband is your Maker**, whose name is the **LORD [YHWH]** of hosts" (Isaiah 54:5)

  Yeshua=Yehoshua=YHWH-Salvation=YHWH

The next chapter explains the Jewish wedding, our marriage to the Lamb of God, who is the one YHWH God.

Chapter 6   The Marriage of the Lamb

If you've read all the way up to here, you know about how God's name was taken out in the Old Testament and replaced with Baal (LORD in English) and in the New Testament how His name Yeshua was replaced with the three different names of the second person of the Babylonian trinity. The three main sun god/saviors were then united into one composite deity called *Hesus Horus Krishna* which later became known in its English derived name as *Jesus H. Christ. Hesus* was Iesous in the Greek and eventually became Jesus. And you've seen how God's name was taken out of His baptism and replaced with the phrase: The Father and the Son and the Holy Spirit. Baptism is part of our espousal, our marriage to the Lamb of God, to YHWH, and His name cannot be taken out. (Chapter 3 explains many of the changes that have taken place and chapter 4 explains God's name and the Mystery of God.)

Hopefully now that you have seen all the changes that have been made, you have decided to take the name of the one YHWH God (Mar Yah Yeshua) in baptism, for the remission of sins and to be espoused (married) to Yeshua = Yehoshua= YHWH-Salvation= YHWH, the one YHWH God (Mar Yah Yeshua) of the first commandment, who was manifest in the flesh, and gave Himself for us, as the Lamb of God. This chapter will bring wonderful understanding of how baptism and lifting up the cup of Communion are both part of our marriage ceremony to Mar Yah Yeshua and much more.

- "For I am jealous over you with godly jealousy: for I have **espoused you to one husband**, that I may present *you as* **a chaste virgin to Christ**." (2Co 11:2)

The next scripture says His wife has made herself ready. Brides get ready for their groom and they wear white as a sign of purity. Putting on Yeshua our Messiah (Christ) in Baptism, is putting on Salvation. Putting on Yeshua is putting on the white robe of righteousness, making our selves ready for our groom.

- "I will greatly rejoice in the LORD, my soul shall be joyful in my God; ***for he hath clothed me with the garments of salvation [Yeshua],*** he hath covered me with the robe of righteousness, as a bridegroom decketh *himself* with ornaments, and as a bride adorneth *herself* with her jewels." (Isa 61:10)

- "For as many of you as have been **baptized into Christ have put on Christ**." (Gal 3:27)

- "Let us be glad and rejoice, and give honour to him: for **the marriage of the Lamb** is come, and **his wife hath made herself ready**." (Rev 19:7)

The bread and the wine, what most call communion, is just as important to get right as the one baptism. Communion is actually a part of our marriage ceremony to Christ, to the Lamb of God and is a Passover celebration. Jesus [Yeshua] is the Lamb of God, the Passover Lamb.

- "....For even **Christ our passover** is sacrificed for us:" (1Co 5:7)

Most of us know Jesus said: "Verily, verily I say unto you, Ye must be born again" but did you know Jesus also repeated the words, "*Verily, verily*" in John 6:53, just as He did when referring to "Ye must be born again".

- **"Verily, verily, I say unto you, Except ye eat the flesh of the Son of man, and drink his blood, ye have no life in you."** (John 6:53)

Eating the flesh of the Son of man and drinking His blood is just as serious as the one baptism for salvation, just as serious as ye must be born again. Here are our Saviour's words:

"50) This is the bread which cometh down from heaven, that a man may eat thereof, and not die. 51) I am the living bread which came down from heaven: if any man eat of this bread, he shall live for ever: and the bread that I will give is my flesh, which I will give for the life of the world. 52) The Jews therefore strove among themselves, saying, How can this man give us *his* flesh to eat? 53) Then Jesus said unto them, **Verily, verily, I say unto you, Except ye eat the flesh of the Son of man, and drink his blood, ye have no life in you.** 54) **Whoso eateth my flesh, and drinketh my blood,** *hath eternal life; and I will raise him up at the last day.* 55) For my flesh is meat indeed, and my blood is drink indeed. 56) *He that eateth my flesh, and drinketh my blood, dwelleth in me, and I in him.*" (Joh 6:50-56)

In this chapter, you will see that baptism is the seventh step in the Jewish wedding to our Jewish Saviour and lifting up the cup of communion (is the cup accepting our Saviour's blood covenant, sealing the covenant) the third step in the marriage to our Jewish Saviour.

The quotes in this chapter starting here are from: Cheryl Alvarado's Bible study: **Be Not Faithless But believing, Jesus The Mystery of God Revealed** [128] **Chapter 11 The Jewish Wedding** with her references: **A Mayim Hayim study on A Fresh Look At The Jewish Wedding** [1] and, **The Ultimate Wedding, Ancient Jewish Traditions and their Fulfillment in Jesus the Messiah** by Bill Risk [2] The references numbers in this chapter refer to her references.

...We find an amazing parallel, in which virtually every aspect of the ancient Jewish tradition is fulfilled. [2]

God gave the Jewish wedding customs and calls Himself our husband and the bridegroom in the Old and in the New Testament [Covenant]. Notice our husband's name is YHWH in Isa 54:5 and the husband we are espoused to is Christ in 2 Cor.11:2.

- **"For your husband is your Maker, whose name is** the LORD [**YHWH**] of hosts" (Isaiah 54:5) **"And I will betroth you to Me forever**; Yes, I will betroth you to Me in righteousness and in justice, in loving-kindness and in compassion, And I will betroth you to Me in faithfulness. Then you will know **the LORD [YHWH].**" (Hosea 2:19) [2] [betroth, espouse]
- **"And Jesus said** to them, "While the bridegroom is with them, the attendants of the bride do not fast, do they? So long as they have the bridegroom with them, they cannot fast. But the days will come when **the bridegroom** is taken away from them, and then they will fast in that day." (Mark 2:19-20) [2]
- 2 Cor. 11:2 says: " For I am jealous over you with godly jealousy: for **I have espoused you to one husband,** that I may present you as a chaste virgin **to Christ.**"
- "7) Let us rejoice and be glad and give the glory to Him, for ***the marriage* of the Lamb** has come and His bride has made herself ready. 8) And it was given to her to clothe herself in fine linen, bright and clean; for the fine linen is the righteous acts of the saints. 9) And he said to me, Write, ***Blessed are those who are invited to the marriage supper* of the Lamb.** And he said to me, These are the true words of God." (Rev. 19:7-9) [2] (John 1:29, 36 show that Jesus is the Lamb of God)

The marriage rite is a series of twelve steps. [1]

1) **The Bridegroom's Father chooses the Bride**, the Groom in most cases does not. [1]

- "No man can come to me, except the Father which hath sent me draw him: and I will raise him up at the last day." (John 6:44)

2) **The price was secured for the Bride**, and was usually something of great value. Lands, livestock, silver or gold. In the Believers instance the supreme price was paid, the precious Blood of Yeshua Messiah. Yeshua left His Home and the Glory of Heaven to come to earth to pay the ultimate price for a Bride. [1]

---

[128] Chapter 6's list of references from: Be Not Faithless But believing, Jesus The Mystery of God Revealed www.themysteryrevealed.info

129

- "Ye are <u>bought</u> with a price; be not ye the servants of men." (1 Co 7:23) [2]
- "Forasmuch as ye know that ye were not <u>redeemed</u> with corruptible things, as silver and gold, from your vain conversation received by tradition from your fathers; But with the precious blood of Christ, as of a lamb without blemish and without spot:" (1 Peter 1:18,19) [1]

3) **The Betrothal ritual is like an engagement party**. The promise was made and it was binding. The man and wife do not live together or have sexual intercourse at this time. **A cup of wine is lifted up and drunk by the Bride *to seal the Betrothal*.**[1]

The Betrothal (*kiddushin, or erusin*) was a much more formal concept in Jewish antiquity than our modern state of engagement. ***A betrothed couple was, for all legal purposes, considered to be married.***[2] Once the terms of the ketubah had been specified and the father of the bride had agreed to them, the prospective bridegroom would pour a cup of wine for the prospective bride. The wine would be blessed with the ritual prayer: "Blessed art Thou, Eternal our God, Creator of Heaven and Earth, who has given us the fruit of the vine, Amen." ***If she agreed to the match, she would drink from the cup, indicating her acceptance. In this manner, the covenant was sealed, and the couple was considered to be betrothed***. The betrothal period typically lasted one full year, commencing with the sealing of the covenant and ending with the nuptials themselves.[2]

- "**And I will betroth you to Me forever**; Yes, I will betroth you to Me in righteousness and in justice, in loving-kindness and in compassion, And I will betroth you to Me in faithfulness. Then you will know **the LORD [YHWH].**" (Hosea 2:19) [2] [betroth, espouse]

- "27) And he took the cup, and gave thanks, and gave it to them, saying, **Drink ye all of it**; 28) **For this is my blood of the new testament [covenant], which is shed for many for the remission of sins.** 29) But I say unto you, **I will not drink henceforth of this fruit of the vine, until that day when I drink it new with you in my Father's kingdom.**" (Matt.26:27-29)

Yeshua, when lifting the cup at the Passover, understood that in just a short time from that moment, He would also be lifted up on a CROSS. It would be for His Bride that He would suffer and do this![1]

Yeshua told His disciples He would not drink of the fruit of the vine until the day He drinks it with them in heaven, the eleventh step of the Jewish marriage ceremony. He lifted up the cup with His disciples, the first seal of the betrothal and when we lift up the cup (we call it communion today), we seal the covenant, the first seal of the betrothal, **to Yeshua, Yehoshua, YHWH-Salvation, YHWH, our God. Hosea 2:19** And I will betroth thee unto me for ever...

4) **Jewish marriages were legally formalized by a written marriage contract, called a *ketubah* (pl. ketubot)**, that stated the bride price, the promises of the groom, and the rights of the bride.[2]

The written marriage contract is drawn up and in it the Bride is promised that she will be provided and cared for in every way. It states that all of her needs will be fulfill by the Bridegroom. ***The Holy Scriptures are our marriage contract***. *It tells us all that our Bridegroom has done for us and will do for us and so much more!*[1]

- "And my G-d will provide, fulfill and meet all your needs according to His excellent riches in Messiah Yeshua." (Phil. 4:19) AGI [1]

5) **The Bride had to be in agreement with this marriage, and so it is with us**. By our free will do we enter into this contract. Today to enter into this Covenant I must accept Messiah Yeshua, and confess Him with my mouth to be L-RD of my life. However, making this decision is our choice.[1] **[L-RD = YHWH]**

- "... For we must all stand before the judgment seat of **The Messiah**. For it is written, "As I live, said <u>**MarYah [Lord Yah=YHVH=Yeshua]**</u>, every knee shall bow to Me, and <u>**every tongue shall confess Me.**</u>" Romans 14:10-11 from the Aramaic

- "... for we shall all stand before the judgment seat of **Christ**. For it is written, *As* I live, saith **the Lord,** every knee shall bow to me, and every tongue shall confess to God. Rom 14:10, 11 from the King James Version

6) At this point the cup was drunk from. This cup is also called the shared cup of the Brit, (Covenant). The two are now really married. The betrothed secured, (sealed). **<u>Gifts are now given</u>** to the Bride and her family from the Bridegroom or His Servant ...[1]

- For the wages of sin is death; but *the gift of God is eternal life* **through Jesus Christ [Yeshua HaMasiach] our Lord**. (Rom. 6:23)

Every time we share in the cup of Communion we are re-affirming our marriage Covenant with our Bridegroom Yeshua. We should always remember what it was that Messiah Yeshua our Bridegroom achieved for us personally, with the Covenant of "Communion in His Blood."[1]

7) **<u>The betrothal was, for the bride, a time of *purification* and *anticipation*</u>. The bride needed to undergo a ... purifying bath.**[2]

Purifying bath [Baptism, for the remission of sins, cleansing from sin]. We are told in Acts 2:38 to repent and be **baptized everyone of you in the name of MarYah Yeshua [Jesus] for the remission of sins [washing away of sins]** and ye shall receive the gift of the Holy Ghost. (See Acts 19:2-6)

- And such were some of you**; but you were washed,** but you were sanctified, but you were justified **in the name of the Lord Jesus Christ,** and in the Spirit of our God. (1 Cor. 6:11) [2]

See how God entered into a covenant with Israel and they became His.
- "Then I passed by you and saw you, and behold, you were at the time for love; so I spread My skirt over you and covered your nakedness. **I also swore to you and <u>entered into a covenant with you so that you became Mine</u>,**" declares the Lord GOD. "Then I <u>bathed you with water</u>, washed off your blood from you, and <u>anointed you with oil</u>**...** (Ezk. 16:8-14) [2]

Above it says you became mine, a reference to marriage. As in Ezk 16:8,9 bathed with water and anointed with oil, it is the same in the New Testament Acts 2:38, baptized, (cleansed) with water and ye shall receive the gift of the Holy Spirit (Anointed with oil. Oil is a symbol for the Holy Spirit).

8) **<u>At this point the Bridegroom would depart and go back to His Father's house to prepare a place for the wedding and his new Bride</u>.** My understanding is that **a pledge** is made by the Bridegroom affirming to his Bride that he will indeed return for her. Yeshua did the same! [1]

We read Yeshua's pledge in St. John's Gospel:

- "Do not let your hearts be distressed. Trust in G-d; trust also in Me. In My Father's house are many chambers; if it were not so, I would have told you. I am going there to make ready a place for you. And if I go and prepare a place for you, I will come back and catch you up to be with Me that you also may be where I am." (John 14:1-3) AGI These words above are the same words spoken in the ancient Jewish Wedding rite. Yeshua speaks to His followers as a Bridegroom, affirming to them that He would come to take them to Himself. [1]

- 9) **Now the time of waiting comes!** The Bride would prepare herself making all the preparations to be the best Bride she could be. She doesn't know the exact time when her Beloved will come for her, this time is "only" known by the Bridegroom's Father. When the Father sees that all of His Son's preparations for the wedding chambers (chadar) is ready, then He will allow His Son to transport His Bride to His home. [1]
- "But of that day or hour no one knows, not even the angels in heaven, nor the Son, but the Father alone." (Mark 13:32) [2]

10) **When the Bridegroom comes to get His Bride** it is more of a **willing kidnapping**. It could be called a **snatching** in the middle of the night. The Bridegroom and His friends would sneak up on the Bride suddenly. However, not without a shout first! Then there was a blast of the shofar sounding out, she must be ready to run to her Beloved, to flee with him with no hesitation or procrastination.

- "At midnight the **shout** went out: Here's the Bridegroom! Come out to encounter him!" (Matthew 25:6) AGI [1]

- "For the Lord Himself will descend from heaven with a **shout, with the voice of the archangel, and with the trumpet of God;** and the dead in Christ shall rise first. Then we who are alive and remain shall be caught up together with them in the clouds to meet the Lord in the air, and thus we shall always be with the Lord." (1 Thess. 4:16-18) [2]

The formal process of consummating the marriage in the "taking" of the bride was referred to as nissuin, which literally means "taking". [2] Having claimed the bride, the party would return to the bridal chamber where the nuptials themselves would begin. [2]

It is interesting and certainly worth remembering that one of the names for **the Feast of Trumpets according to Jewish literature, is "The wedding day of Messiah."** This whole marriage feast is a picture of the L-RD coming for His Bride before Yom Kippur, the day of Judgment.[1] [L-RD=YHWH]

Messiah has a "deed" for you, it's the Ketubah - the Betrothal Covenant. He is now our Master and our Husband. He has the rights to come to take us to His home because He paid the "Mohar" - the Bridal Price. [1]

11) **The Bridegroom with His strong open hand takes His Bride away to the place that he has prepared**...Blessings are said over the couple, this is call the Birkot Nisuin, the 7 blessings. **The second cup of wine is now drunk**, (...But I say unto you, I will not drink henceforth of this fruit of the vine, until that day when I drink it new with you in my Father's kingdom. Matt 26:27-29) **and this sets the second seal to the marriage Covenant.** We are waiting to drink this cup with our Bridegroom Yeshua. Now the new couple will spend 7 days together in the wedding room, the "Huppah." This starts the honeymoon cycle, this is where the Bridegroom will **cover her** with Himself. This part takes place in the Huppah. **This is also called the "Nisuin" or the "hometaking."** [1]

- "I will greatly rejoice in the L-RD, my soul shall delight in my G-d; for **He has clothed me with the garments of Salvation [Yeshua]. He has covered me with the Robe of Righteousness,** as a Bridegroom decketh himself with ornaments, and as a Bride adorneth herself with her jewels." (Isaiah 61:10) AGI [1]

12) **And now it is time for the Wedding Feast to begin!** Our Wedding Feast will be in the place that Yeshua has prepared. Right after the 7 days of the Huppah, the couple come out of the room and join their guests. These guests have a special name, they are called the **B'nai Huppah, "children of the Bridal Chamber."** They will join the Bride and Bridegroom to a very festive marriage feast. This is the meal that the couple share with their guest after the 7 days of being alone is over. This meal is called **Seudat Mitzyah**, a festive meal! [1] With how extravagant our weddings are, just imagine the marriage supper of the Lamb. ☺

- "Let us rejoice and be glad and give the glory to Him, for ***the marriage*** of the Lamb has come and His bride has made herself ready." And it was given to her to clothe herself in fine linen, bright and clean; for the fine linen is the righteous acts of the saints. And he said to me, "Write, ***Blessed are those who are invited to the marriage supper*** of the Lamb.'" And he said to me, "These are the true words of God." (Rev. 19:7-9) [2]

End of quotes from: Cheryl Alvarado's Bible study: <u>Be Not Faithless But Believing, Jesus Subtitle: The Mystery of God Revealed</u> Chapter 11, The Jewish Wedding, with her references: A Mayim Hayim study on <u>A Fresh Look At The Jewish Wedding</u> [1] and <u>The Ultimate Wedding, Ancient Jewish Traditions and their Fulfillment in Jesus the Messiah</u> by Bill Risk [2]

<u>When we take communion, we are lifting up the cup of the covenant, the 3rd step of the Jewish wedding.</u> It is so important to understand the mystery of God, the Godhead, that Yeshua is the head of the Church, the one YHWH God of the first commandment, that gave Himself for you and I, to reconcile us to Himself. He is the one YHWH God that did it all to save us. If you believe God is three separate persons or gods when you take communion you are being espoused to a different god than the one YHWH God of the first commandment, Yeshua=Yehoshua=YHWH-Salvation=YHWH.

- "***As for*** our redeemer, the LORD [YHWH] of hosts ***is*** his name, the Holy One of Israel." (Isa 47:4)

- "Then Jesus said unto them, Verily, verily, I say unto you, ***Except ye eat the flesh of the Son of man, and drink his blood, ye have no life in you. Whoso eateth my flesh, and drinketh my blood, hath eternal life; <u>and I will raise him up at the last day.</u>*** ... ***he that eateth of this bread shall live for ever.***" (John 6:53- 58)

Concerning, eating the flesh and drinking the blood of the Son of man, you do not have to take communion at Church, especially if you are at a Church that is partaking of the trinity [IHS] instead of the one LORD [YHWH] God of the first commandment [Remember, the cup is the first seal in our marriage ceremony to the Lamb of God, to YHWH]. You can buy Matzah bread, unleavened bread or you can make it. You can find the recipe on line but it must be unleavened bread because leaven represents sin. Our groom, our Saviour, the Lamb of God had no sin.

The next section explains by the scriptures, ***the great blessings*** we have, through eating the flesh of the Son of man and drinking his blood, through communion. With a chart of scriptures to use when you partake.

In this section there are quotes from: Cheryl Alvarado's <u>Be Not Faithless But Believing, Jesus Subtitle: The Mystery of God Revealed, The Bonus Chapter, Christ our Passover</u> [129] with her reference: <u>Health And Wholeness Through The Communion</u> by Joseph Prince[24]

... God brought me understanding of another doctrine, another very important doctrine when I read **Joseph Prince's Health And Wholeness Through The Communion.** [129-24]

Exodus 12 tells the story of God instructing His people to eat the roasted lamb and put the blood of the lamb on the door posts. Through the Passover God not only saved His people but gave His people **Protection**, **Provision**, and **Divine Health**.

"That ye shall say, It is the sacrifice of the **LORD'S [YHWH's] Passover**, who passed over the houses of the children of Israel in Egypt, when he smote the Egyptians, and delivered our houses. And the people bowed the head and worshipped." (Exo 12:27)

---

[129] Reference list from: Cheryl Alvarado's Be Not Faithless But Believing, Jesus The Mystery of God Revealed, The Bonus Chapter, Christ our Passover – 24 Joseph Prince's Health And Wholeness Through The Communion. www.themysteryrevealed.info

"He brought them forth also with silver and gold: and *there was* not one feeble *person* among their tribes." (Psa 105:37)

Yeshua is the Lamb of God, He gave His body and shed His blood for us. He is our Passover.
"The next day John seeth Jesus (Yeshua) coming unto him, and saith, **Behold the Lamb of God**, which taketh away the sin of the world." (Joh 1:29)
"And looking upon Jesus as he walked, he saith, **Behold the Lamb of God!**" (Joh 1:36)
Purge out therefore the old leaven, that ye may be a new lump, as ye are unleavened. For even (Messiah) **Christ our passover** is sacrificed for us: (1Co 5:7)

OUR PASSOVER- YESHUA! THE LAMB OF GOD.
The picture of the last super is a picture of Yeshua celebrating the Passover with His disciples. **Yeshua told His disciples:…"This is my body which is given for you"** and 1 Co 11:28,29, 30 says to examine ourselves that we are discerning the Lord's body that was given for us. Remember **Yeshua**=Yehoshua=YHWH-Salvation = YHWH, God's name forever, **the one YHWH God** of the first commandment, God manifest in the flesh, **gave His body for our healing.**

"23) For I have received of the Lord that which also I delivered unto you, That the Lord Jesus the *same* night in which he was betrayed took bread: 24) And when he had given thanks, he brake *it,* and said, **Take, eat: this is my body, which is broken for you**: this do in remembrance of me. 25) After the same manner also *he took* the cup, when he had supped, saying, This cup is the new testament in my blood: this do ye, as oft as ye drink *it,* in remembrance of me. 26) For as often as ye eat this bread, and drink this cup, ye do shew the Lord's death till he come. 27) Wherefore whosoever shall eat this bread, and drink *this* cup of the Lord, unworthily, shall be guilty of the body and blood of the Lord.[24] 28) **But let a man examine himself**, and so let him eat of *that* bread, and drink of *that* cup.[24] 29) For he that eateth and drinketh unworthily, eateth and drinketh damnation to himself, **not discerning the Lord's body.**[24] **30) For this cause many *are* weak and sickly among you, and many sleep.**" (1Co 11:23-30)

Partaking unworthily means not recognizing that the broken body of the Lord was meant to bring health and wholeness.[24] And by treating the Holy Communion as a ritual, they missed out on the blessings.[24]
Notice in the next chart, Yeshua repeats: "This is my body". **Yeshua**=Yehoshua=YHWH-Salvation=YHWH, ***YHWH God manifest in the flesh, gave His body*** for our healing. With His stripes we are healed. Notice Yeshua said in John 6:53, "Except ye eat the flesh of the Son of man and drink His blood, ye have no life in you." In other words, when we eat the flesh of the Son of man and drink His blood, we have the divine life of God with in us, His healing power within us. Also notice in Matt. 26:28 Yeshua says, "this is my blood of the New Testament, [covenant]". This is Yeshua=Yehoshua=YHWH-Salvation=YHWH's blood covenant. There is nothing stronger than the blood covenant of YHWH. Partaking worthily is recognizing that Yeshua [Jesus], *the one YHWH [LORD] God of the first commandment, gave His flesh and blood for you.*

The Bread
The Lamb's Body
The Body of Christ, our Messiah

(Mat 26:26) And as they were eating, Jesus took bread, and blessed *it,* and brake *it,* and gave *it* to the disciples, and said, Take, eat; this is my body.

(Mar 14:22) And as they did eat, Jesus took bread, and blessed, and brake *it,* and gave to them, and said, Take, eat: this is my body.

(Luk 22:19) And he took bread, and gave thanks, and brake *it,* and gave unto them, saying, **This is my body which is given for you: this do in remembrance of me.**

(Joh 6:51) **I am the living bread** which came down from heaven: if any man eat of this bread, he shall live for ever: *and the bread that I will give is my flesh, which I will give* for the life of the world.

(1Co 11:24) And when he had given thanks, he brake *it,* and said, Take, eat: this is my body, **which is broken for you**: this do in remembrance of me.

**Yeshua's body was Broken for me,
Broken me and my family,
Broken for our healing,
for our divine health!**

(1Pe 2:24) Who his own self bare our sins in his own body on the tree, that we, being dead to sins, should live unto righteousness: **by whose stripes ye were healed.**

(Isa 53:5) But he *was* wounded for our transgressions, *he was* bruised for our iniquities: the chastisement of our peace *was* upon him; **and with his stripes we are healed.**

(Ps 105:37) He brought them forth also with silver and gold: and *there was* not one feeble *person* among their tribes.

(2Co 8:9) For ye know the grace of our Lord Jesus Christ, that, though he was rich, yet for your sakes **he became poor, that ye through his poverty might be rich.**

The Wine
Blood of the Lamb
The Blood of the Covenant

(Luk 22:20) Likewise also the cup after supper, saying, This cup *is* the new testament in my blood, **which is shed for you.**

(1Co 11:25) After the same manner also *he took* the cup, when he had supped, saying, This cup is the new testament in my blood: this do ye, as oft as ye drink *it,* in remembrance of me.

(Mat 26:27) And he took the cup, and gave thanks, and gave *it* to them, saying, Drink ye all of it;

(Mat 26:28) **For this is my blood of the new testament, which is shed for many for the remission of sins.**

(Mat 26:30) And when they had sung an hymn, they went out into the mount of Olives.

**The song I like to sing after
taking the Bread and the Wine is:
Down at the Cross
Glory to His name, there to my life
is the blood applied,
Glory to His name.**

(Joh 6:53) Then Jesus said unto them, **Verily, verily**, I say unto you, **Except ye eat the flesh of the Son of man, and drink his blood, ye have no life in you.**

(1 John 5:20) And we know that the Son of God is come, and hath given us understanding, that we may know him that is true, and we are in him that is true, even in his Son *Jesus Christ. This is the true God, and eternal life*.

THE 2ND CUP OF THE WEDDING CEREMONY ☺ HALLEUYAH
(Mat 26:29) But I say unto you, I will not drink henceforth of this fruit of the vine, until that day when I drink it new with you in my Father's kingdom.

End of quotes from: Cheryl Alvarado's <u>Be Not Faithless But Believing, Jesus The Mystery of God Revealed,</u> <u>The Bonus Chapter, Christ our Passover</u> and her reference: <u>Health And Wholeness Through The Communion</u> <u>by Joseph Prince</u>

I exhort you, if you really love the truth, get the Bible study: <u>Be Not Faithless But Believing, Jesus</u> Subtitle: <u>The Mystery of God Revealed</u> by Cheryl Alvarado and do her quizzes at the end of each chapter. The quizzes really help bring understanding.

<u>When we take communion it is not only for our healing and to give us eternal life</u> (as John 6:53 and 54 says) but <u>we are lifting up the cup of the marriage covenant,</u> ***the 3rd step of the Jewish*** ***<u>wedding ceremony</u>***.

- "53) Then Jesus said unto them, Verily, verily, I say unto you, Except ye eat the flesh of the Son of man, and drink his blood, ye have no life in you. 54) **<u>Whoso eateth my flesh, and drinketh my blood,</u>** **<u>hath eternal life</u>**; and I will raise him up at the last day." (Joh 6:53,54)

- ***<u>If she agreed to the match, she would drink from the cup, indicating her acceptance. In</u>*** ***<u>this manner, covenant was sealed, and the couple was considered to be betrothed</u>***.

- "**<u>And I will betroth you to Me forever</u>**; Yes, I will betroth you to Me in righteousness and in justice, in loving-kindness and in compassion, And I will betroth you to Me in faithfulness. Then you will know **the LORD [YHWH]**." (Hosea 2:19) [2] **<u>Yeshua=Yehoshua=YHWH-Salvation= YHWH</u>** [betroth, espouse]

- "And he took the cup, and gave thanks, and gave it to them, saying, Drink ye all of it; **<u>For this is my</u>** **<u>blood of the new testament [covenant]</u>**, which is shed for many for the remission of sins. But I say unto you, **<u>I will not drink henceforth of this fruit of the vine, until that day when I drink it</u>** **<u>new with you in my Father's kingdom</u>**." (Matt.26:27-29) [When we drink the fruit of the vine in heaven with MarYah Yeshua, it is the second seal of the marriage covenant.]

<u>Baptism is the 7th step in the Jewish wedding ceremony, when the bride takes her groom's</u> **<u>name</u>**, not his titles; Father, Son, and not a description that He is the Holy Spirit. Legal agreements require a name, not the titles or roles played. **The New Covenant is our legal agreement, our marriage covenant, the blood covenant (see Luke 22:20), with the blood of our Saviour, that is recognized in the court of heaven, by the judge of heaven,** for the right to forgiveness of sins, remission of sins, salvation, **for eternal life, in Yeshua's name**.

- "And this is the record, **<u>that God hath given to us eternal life, and this life is in His Son</u>**... 13) These things I have written unto you that ye **<u>believe on the Name of the Son of God</u>**; **<u>that ye may</u>** **<u>know that ye have eternal life</u>** and that ye may **<u>believe on the Name of the Son of God</u>**." (1 John 5:11-13)
- "For I am jealous over you with godly jealousy: for **<u>I have espoused you to one husband</u>**, that I may present you as a chaste virgin **to Christ**." (2 Cor. 11:21)

<u>In Rev. 19:7 we read, his wife has made herself ready.</u>

- "Let us be glad and rejoice, and give honour to him: for the marriage of the Lamb is come, and his wife hath made herself ready." (Rev 19:7)

Have you took the cup of the covenant accepting Yeshua as your groom? Yeshua=Yehoshua=YHWH-Salvation=YHWH   Yeshua the one YHWH God as your groom? Remember: YHWH with vowels= Yahweh, Yahweh shortened is Yah. Mar is Aramaic for Adonai/Master So **<u>MarYah Yeshua = Master YHWH-Yeshua</u>**

Have you made yourself ready, repented [changed your thinking] and been baptized, in the name of MarYah Yeshua, our bridegroom [step # 7 in the Jewish Wedding], for the remission [cleansing] of sins, thereby confessing Yeshua as YHWH and Saviour?

- "Tell ye, and bring *them* near; yea, let them take counsel together: who hath declared this from ancient time? *who* hath told it from that time? *have* not I the **LORD [YHWH]? and there *is* no God else beside me; a just God and a Saviour; *there is* none beside me**." (Isa 45:21)

We must be ready, remember 5 of the ten virgins [5 of the brides of Christ] were not ready and the door was shut, in Matt. 25:10-12 and when they said, "Lord, Lord, open to us" Yeshua said. "I know you not". We must be ready.

- "And while they went to buy, the bridegroom came; and they that were ready went in with him to the marriage: and the door was shut. 11) Afterward came also the other virgins, saying, Lord, Lord, open to us. 12) But he answered and said, Verily I say unto you, I know you not." (Matt. 25:10-12)

Chapter 7 SOUNDING THE ALARM BEFORE IT'S TOO LATE
Come Out Of Her My People...

- "And I heard another voice from heaven, saying, **Come out of her, my people**, *that ye be not partakers of her sins*, and **that ye receive not of her plagues**." (Rev 18:4)   (*Her judgments*)

- "For the time *is come* that **judgment must begin at the house of God**: and if it first begin at us, what shall the end be of them that obey not the gospel of God?" (1Pe 4:17)

- "Therefore rejoice, *ye* heavens, and ye that dwell in them. Woe to the inhabiters of the earth and of the sea! for **the devil** is come down unto you, **having *great wrath*, because he knoweth that he hath but a short time.**" (Rev 12:12)

God's judgment begins with the House of God, with the great Church, Mystery Babylon.

If you read the book of Revelation in its chronological order you cannot understand the timing of this judgment, **the wrath of God, because the wrath of God is shown three times in the book of Revelations**, like the four Gospels: Matt, Mark, Luke and John, repeat the story of Jesus (Yeshua) four times. Only in the book of Revelations, the same story is shown ending with the wrath of God, three times: once in a long version, in a shorter version and a very short version. Understanding this is key. This was explained briefly in chapter 2. To understand fully, go to https://www.endtime.com/understanding-the-endtime/ and get Understanding the Endtime by Rev. Baxter Jr. It is really possible to understand the book of Revelations.

We need to understand now because we Catholics and Christians, will be here during the great tribulation. According to the sure word of God, we will see the antichrist sit (rule) in the Temple of God in Jerusalem (the abomination of desolation) which starts the great tribulation (See Matt. 24:15, 21). This is when the mark of the beast will start to be taken in order to buy and sell. We see in Rev. 15:1 the wrath of God is in the seven last plagues. And a few verses later in Rev. 15:7 it says the vials are *full of the wrath of God*. The seven last plagues are God's wrath. And God is still warning His people that the plagues, (His wrath- His judgement) is coming in Rev. 18:4. God's wrath has still not come yet in Rev. 18:4. Remember judgment must start with the house of God (See 1 Pe 4:17). When we read Revelations 17:1 we see this wrath is against the great whore, Mystery Babylon the Great, (the great Church-See Chapter 3). And we saw in Rev. 12:12 (above) it has been the devils great wrath because he knows his time is short.

- Rev 15:1) And I saw another sign in heaven, great and marvellous, seven angels having the seven last plagues; for in them is <u>filled up the wrath of God.</u>
- (Rev 15:7) And one of the four beasts gave unto <u>the seven angels seven golden vials full of the wrath of God</u>, who liveth for ever and ever.
- (Rev 17:1) And there came one of the seven angels which had <u>the seven vials</u>, and talked with me, saying unto me, Come hither; I will shew unto thee <u>the judgment of the great whore</u> that sitteth upon many waters:
- (Rev 17:5) And upon <u>her forehead was a name written, MYSTERY, BABYLON THE GREAT</u>, THE MOTHER OF HARLOTS AND ABOMINATIONS OF THE EARTH.

We must have understanding so we are prepared for this time of trouble. We must heed God's warning to come out of Mystery Babylon so that we be not partakers of her sins, do not receive her plagues, her judgments (and so that we do not take the mark of the beast), that we be not judged with her.

I have loved ones, family, who love God with all their heart, devout people, who love God, who are in the Catholic Church, unknowingly in Mystery Babylon. And I have loved ones, family, who are in Mystery Babylon's daughter churches, Churches that split off from the Catholic Church at the time of the reformation who unknowingly took Catholic, Babylonian, doctrines with them, (see Chapter 3). God is calling them, us, to come out of her, out of Mystery Babylon because He loves us. He put on flesh and died for us. He does not want us to receive Mystery Babylon's plagues, her judgments. But God always gives us a choice, free will. God's people, Israel, chose not to hear God's warning. We must heed His call to come out of Mystery Babylon. I pray God gives you and your family understanding for time is so, so, short. God is about to judge Mystery Babylon in this generation. This is the generation that will take the mark of the beast. This is the generation that must know the truth!

Scriptures show Mystery Babylon is riding on the back of the beast. The beast is the one world government that is ready to come into place now, called the United Nations. Soon the world will be deceived, not only by the false doctrines of Mystery Babylon, but also by the false prophet and false signs and wonders (Holograms mentioned in Chapter 2) and will take the mark of the beast.

God's word says, the devil deceives the whole world, (the whole world would and does include the Roman Catholic Church and Christians). He's been working on deceiving people, even God's people along time and is good at it. The devil actually deceives pretty much the whole world into worshiping him. When we are deceived into following doctrines of Babylon, we are following doctrines of devils. (See Chapter 3)

- "Now the Spirit speaketh expressly, that in the latter times some shall depart from the faith, giving heed to seducing spirits, and doctrines of devils;" (1Ti 4:1)

We are in a battle, a war. The war is for your soul! The devil used Mystery Babylon to bring in damnable heresies, doctrines of sun worship, Baal worship, doctrines of devils into the Church, to deceive God's people, to deceive the nations, and to deceive you.

God's word says, "narrow is the way" in Mat 7:13-14.

- "Enter ye in at the strait gate: for wide *is* the gate, and broad *is* the way, that leadeth to destruction, and many there be which go in thereat: 14) Because strait *is* the gate, and narrow *is* the way, which leadeth unto life, and few there be that find it." (Mat 7:13)

God says, "Narrow is the way". Mystery Babylon and her daughter Churches are not in the narrow way. God is warning His people to come out of her that they be not partakers of her sins, that they receive not her plagues, her judgments.

Putting all the puzzle pieces together:

Even though this book reveals who Mystery Babylon is, it is quite unbelievable if you don't have all the pieces connected, if the puzzle pieces are just laying all over the table in a pile. If you haven't read all the parts of this book, I encourage you, read every bit of it. You may want to read it several times because the more you read it, the mysteries becomes clearer and clearer, your vision, the revelation of the mystery becomes clearer and clear.

The Pope has the title *Pontifus Maximus*. *Pontifus Maximus* literally is the High Priest of the Babylonian Cult of Sol Invictus.

When Attalus, the Pontiff and King of Pergamos died, in B.C. 133, he bequeathed the headship of the "Babylonian Priesthood" to Rome. When the Etruscans came to Italy from Lydia, (the region of Pergamos), they brought with them the Babylonian religion and rites. They set up a Pontiff who was head of the priesthood. Later the Romans accepted this Pontiff as their civil ruler. Julius Caesar was made Pontiff of the Etruscan Order in B.C. 74. In B.C. 63, he was made "Supreme Pontiff" of the "Babylonian Order," thus becoming heir to the rights and title of Attalus, Pontiff of Pergamos, who made Rome his heir by will. **Thus the first Roman Emperor became the head of the "Babylonian Priesthood," and Rome the successor of Babylon. Each successor to Emperor from that point forward held the title** *Pontifus Maximus* **literally The High Priest of the Babylonian Cult of Sol Invictus** which was simply another incarnation of Mithraism stemming from the worship of Tammuz in Babylon. The Pope of Rome now carries forward that High Priesthood as Pontiff. 44

The Roman Empire began their official recognition of sun worship during the time of Aurelian when he instituted the cult of "Sol Invictus". There is virtually no difference between the cult of Sol Invictus and that of Mithraism or for that matter Catholicism/Christianity... In the year 307 A.D. Emperor Diocletian, a Sun Worshipper, was involved in the dedication of a temple to Mithra,... thus began the Roman version of the "Universal the Christo-pagan Mystery Religion." After the rein of Diocletian, **the Roman Emperor Constantine (the creator of modern day Christianity) maintained the title "***Pontifus Maximus***" the high priest of paganism**, and remained a worshipper of Apollo (Apollo is *Tammuz* in the Greek culture). His coins were inscribed: "SOL INVICTO COMITI", which is interpreted as "Committed to the Invincible Sun". During his reign pagan Sun worship was blended with the worship of the True Creator ... 44

It was just a short 300 years after the death and resurrection of our Hebrew Saviour, that the Roman Emperor Constantine maintained the title "*Pontifus Maximus*" the high priest of paganism, of the Babylonian Cult of Sol Invictus and

- In order to unite his empire, a world empire, the Roman Empire, and bring in the pagans into the Church, *he brought in the pagan sun-doctrines, sun worship, into the Church. He mixed Sun worship with true worship of YHWH (The LORD).* It is not a coincidence that the Catholic Church and Christianity have the Babylonian sun worship doctrines. (Chapter 3 shows 35 of the approximately 50 Babylonian Doctrines adopted into the Roman Catholic Church.)

- Although we have believed for close to 2000 years that we were celebrating Jesus birth (Christmas) and His resurrection (Easter), the traditions of our biggest holidays came from Babylonian sun worship. **Even the dates chosen for these holidays are from sun worship.** The Vatican set Yeshua (Jesus Christ) **the Son's birthday, on the birthday of the Unconquered Sun, Natalis solis invicti.** The celebration of Passover, to celebrate the Passover Lamb [Yeshua-(Jesus)], that God commanded to be observed forever, was replaced with the pagan Ishtar (Easter). The date of the true Passover was taken out and **Ishtar (Easter) being the goddess of the spring, the Vatican set the date the first Sunday after the full moon following the spring equinox.** Ishtar (Easter) the celebration of the spring goddess Ishtar's fertility, was mixed with our Saviour's resurrection and with the sun god Nimrod reborn as Tammuz. The dates and pagan traditions of the birthday of the sun and of Ishtar were kept but the names were changed to Christmas and Easter. (See Chapter 3)

- **Constantine's attempts to purge the church of its Jewish elements began with the Council of Nicaea (A.D. 325)** In a letter of Constantine to the bishops following the council ... Speaking of the churches observance of Passover, he wrote, "***Let us, then, have nothing in common with the Jews, who are our adversaries***...**this irregularity [observing Passover]** must be corrected, in order that we may no more have anything in common with the parricides and murderers of our Lord" From the excellent book of Dr. Robert D. Heidler The Messianic Church Arising Chapter 3 [130] We cannot take the Jewishness out, our Saviour was Jewish and all of our scriptures, the Bible, came from the Hebrews.

- **God commanded The Passover Feast to be** *observed forever.* **The Passover Feast is a great celebration of how YHWH (LORD) God** put on flesh, is our Passover Lamb, gave His flesh and blood to give us *Eternal life, healing, wholeness, provision, protection, deliverance, salvation.*

---

[130] Dr. Robert D. Heidler The Messianic Church Arising Chapter 3

The Hebrews have celebrated it since the first Passover, celebrating the great salvation God gave them (through the blood of the lamb) when God rescued them out of the hand of their enemy, the Egyptians and the Pharaoh, a fore shadow of Yeshua [Jesus], the Lamb of God bringing us out of the world and our victory over the devil. Yeshua celebrated the Passover with His parents (Luke 2:41-50) and was celebrating the Passover Feast at the last supper. Jews still celebrate the Passover today. We are grafted into the Vine, Yeshua and we are to celebrate what Yeshua, the Lamb of God, did for us on the cross. Today most of God's people do not know all of the blessings and rights that we have through His blood covenant or how to observe the Passover Feast.

(Exo 12:14) And this day shall be unto you for a memorial; and ye shall keep it a feast to the LORD [YHWH] throughout your generations; *__ye shall keep it a feast by an ordinance for ever.__*

- **Constantine took all of YHWH's Feasts, YHWH's appointed times to meet with His people, out of the Church. God commands His Feasts, His Holy appointments, to be kept forever.** This is a very important study, all of its own. I have listed five of YHWH's Feasts and the scripture address where commanded to be observed for ever.

  1) Passover Ex. 12:14
  2) Feast of Unleavened Bread Ex. 12:17
  3) Day of Atonement- Yom Kippur Lev. 16:29, 31, Lev. 23:31
  4) Feast of Tabernacles/ Booths Lev. 23:41
  5) Feasts of Trumpets Num. 10:8

- **Constantine replaced our Saviour's true name, Yeshua**, with three names for the second person of the Babylonian trinity, Tammuz, *the sun god*, that honors Zeus, which is another name for Satan. Shown previously but this is so important that I will show you how it was done again, shortly.

- **Two of the Ten Commandments which honor YHWH God were changed:**

1) The first commandment was changed by Mystery Babylon.
(Deu 6:4) Hear, O Israel: The LORD [YHWH ^{H3068}] our God *is* one LORD [YHWH ^{H3068}]
(Mar 12:29) And Jesus answered him, The first of all the commandments is, Hear, O Israel; The Lord [YHWH] our God is one Lord [YHWH]:

A short 300 years after our Saviour (Yeshua=Yehoshua=YHWH-Salvation=YHWH) God, gave His life for us, Constantine called for the Council of Nicaea, there was a vote and the Catholic Church (Mystery Babylon) established the doctrine of the Trinity, that God is three separate Gods, or three separate persons in one God. YHWH God's first commandment is to hear that YHWH is one YHWH but Constantine changed the worship of the one YHWH God to the worship of the Babylonian trinity. Over the past approximately 2000 years, the truth of YHWH God's first commandment that He is one YHWH God has been forgotten by most.

"... know that the LORD [YHWH] he *is* God; *there is* none else beside him." (Deu4:35)
"... know... the LORD [YHWH] he *is* God ... *there is* none else." (Deu 4:39)
"... know that the LORD [YHWH] *is* God, *and that there is* none else." (1Ki8:60)
"... I am the LORD [YHWH], and there is none else, there is no God beside me..." (Isa 45:5)
"... there is none beside me. I am the LORD [YHWH], and there is none else." (Isa 45:6)
"... I *am* the LORD [YHWH]; and *there is* none else." (Isa 45:18)

"... I, *even I, am* the LORD [YHWH]; and beside me *there is* no Saviour." (Isa 43:11)
"... I the LORD [YHWH]? and *there is* no God else beside me; a just God and a Saviour; *there is* none beside me." (Isa 45:21)
"As for our redeemer, the LORD [YHWH] of hosts *is* his name, the Holy One of Israel." (Isa 47:4)

141

"... I the LORD [YHWH] am thy Saviour..." (Isa 49:26)
"... I the LORD [YHWH] am thy Saviour..." (Isa 60:16)

The Jews understood [Jesus] Yeshua was claiming to be the one YHWH God of the first commandment. "Thou, being a man, makest thyself God" (Joh 10:33). This is why they crucified Him. They did not understand that He really was the one YHWH God. **It was hidden wisdom, a Mystery so that,** the Lord of Glory, the one YHWH of the first commandment, could do it all to save us (see 1 Co 2:7, 8).

2) The fourth commandment to remember the Sabbath, was changed by Mystery Babylon.
8) Remember the sabbath day, to keep it holy. 9) Six days shalt thou labour, and do all thy work: 10) But the seventh day is the sabbath of the LORD thy God: in it thou shalt not do any work... (Exo 20:8, 9, 10)

It is a sign between me and the children of Israel <u>for ever</u>: for in six days the LORD made heaven and earth, and on the seventh day he rested, and was refreshed. (Exo 31:17)

Remember we are grafted into the Vine, into Yeshua. The Sabbath, the seventh day, is a sign for ever between Him and His people, honoring Him as creator. God did not change this commandment. See the many quotes where Roman Catholics claim they made this change in Chapter 3 in the section called: Mystery Babylon Admits They Changed This!

When we keep the Sabbath holy, set apart, above the other 6 days, keep it special, and rest on the seventh day, we are acknowledging YHWH God as creator of heaven and earth, God rested on the seventh day after he created the heaven and earth. Constantine outlawed the observance of the Sabbath, punishable by death. He changed YHWH's day of rest from the seventh day, Saturday, to the first day of the week, Sun day to honor the Babylonian sun god.

- YHWH will soon be judging Mystery Babylon, who adopted Babylon's traditions. The Babylonians worshiped the Sun-god Baal, Bel (Belzubub), which is another name for Satan. The translators of the scriptures **replaced God's holy name YHWH with (LORD), 'LORD' = BAAL,** LORD is the English word for "Baal," a title meaning 'master, lord, or husband, frequently used as a title for pagan gods and leaders but **Baal is also a name for Satan**. (Shown previously but this is so important I will show you again shortly)

- **Much of the truth, for the masses, was lost.** Many died holding on to the truth in the inquisitions and there was forced ignorance when the Papacy made it against the law to have God's word in their own language at Council of Toulouse (1229 C.E.) and the Ruling of the Council of Tarragona (1234) [29]

- **Water Baptism, that Jesus [Yeshua] made a salvation issue** in Mar 16:16 when He said, "He that believeth and is baptized shall be saved" **was changed**. Many died over the issue of baptism. Many had their heads cut off and put on posts for miles.

- **Here are three historical references that tell us that the New Testament baptism was in the name of Jesus.**
  1) The New Testament knows only the baptism in the name of Jesus. Schaff – Herzog Religious Encyclopedia, Volume 1, page 435 [127-19]
  2) The early church baptized in the name of the Lord Jesus until the second century. Canney Encyclopedia of Religion, page 53 [127-20]
  3) Christian baptism was administered using the words, "in the name of Jesus." page 377. Baptism was always in the name of Jesus until time of Justin Martyr, page 389. Hastings Encyclopedia of Religion, Volume 2 [127-21]

- **Here are Two historical references that show baptism was changed:**
  1) <u>Britannica Encyclopedia</u>, 11th Edition, Volume 3, page 365 Baptism was changed from the name of Jesus to the words Father, Son & Holy Ghost in the 2nd Century (2nd Century = 101AD-200AD). [127-22]
  2) <u>The Catholic Encyclopedia</u>, 1913 Edition, Vol. 2, Page 263 Baptism was changed by the Roman Catholic Papacy when they declared: "it is also obligatory to mention the separate persons of the Holy Trinity." AND "**<u>Any ceremony that did not observe this form has been declared invalid</u>**." [127-16]

- The Roman Catholic Church (Mystery Babylon) totally changed the worship of the one YHWH (LORD) God, from how He commanded His people to serve Him,

  1) Replaced the first commandment, that He is one YHWH (LORD) to the Trinity (three in one),
  2) Changed the fourth commandment to keep the Sabbath the seventh day, to the first day, Sun day,
  3) Adopted close to 50 Babylonian doctrines of the sun god, who is actually Satan,
  4) Took out YHWH's Feasts - His commanded appointments for His people to meet with Him that are to be kept forever,
  5) And changed God's baptism- declaring any form that didn't follow their (Babylonian-Trinitarian) form was invalid. They changed the baptism which for salvation (Yeshua said: He that believeth and is baptized shall be saved) and is part of our marriage to the one YHWH God, Yeshua- shown in the fourth Chapter.
  And
- YHWH's name in Old Testament was replaced with LORD **which came from Baal** (Baal can mean Lord, master or husband and Baal is also short for Baal Zebuwb- a name for Satan) to be explained shortly,
- Yeshua's name in the New Testament was replaced with the name of the sun god Hesus, (Iesous in Greek)- which eventually became Jesus.

If you think about all these changes, you will realize that Roman Catholicism and the Christianity of today are not the true worship of YHWH as He gave it in His word and is not the true worship of Yeshua's disciples. *God's word says we must worship Him in spirit and truth.*

- "But the hour cometh, and now is, when the true worshippers shall worship the Father in spirit and in truth: for the Father seeketh such to worship him. **God *is* a Spirit: and they that worship him must worship *him* in spirit and in truth.**" (Joh 4:23-24)

Most, if not all organized Christian Churches today are the daughter Churches that sprang out of the Mother Church, the Roman Catholic Church, Mystery Babylon, when people left the Catholic Church, at the reformation 500 years ago. They all unknowingly took the Mother Churches Babylonian doctrines of sun worship, which are doctrines of devils, with them, when they left and started new denominations of Churches. 2017 is the 500th anniversary of the reformation. The mother Church, Mystery Babylon, is welcoming her daughter Churches back this year, back into the mother Church, back into Mystery Babylon. These are the end times we are living in. God is getting ready to judge in the time we are living in. God's word says judgment must start at the house of God (See 1 Pe 4:7) He is warning His people, us, in Revelations 18:4, come out of her, Mystery Babylon, that we receive not her judgement just four chapters from the end of the Bible.

Remember God is Love but He is also a judge. He judged His people in the Old Testament and divorced them. He is still a judge in these times. God gave His people many warnings in the Old Testament before He divorced them. He has given us many judgment warnings in our day. Rabbi Jonathan Cahn in his book: <u>The Mystery of the Shemitah</u> [1] explained 911 was a judgment warning and of America's need to repent. John McTernan's in his book: <u>As America has done to Israel</u> [6] *showed many judgement warnings*, (when America caused God's people, the Jews to die and or tried to divide their land), in our time, here are a few:

- 9-1938 Pres. Roosevelt called for conference, Chamberlain speech: "Peace in our time" caused Millions of Jews soon to die. **The Great Hurricane of 1938, Meteorological equiv. to Pearl Harbor**
- 10-30-1991 President George Bush announced USA official Policy to divide the land of Israel and make a Palestine state. **While President Bush gave that speech his house in Maine totally destroyed by the Perfect storm-A very strong warning.**
- 8-2005 President Bush met with Prime Minister Sharon in White House, pressuring him to pull out of Gaza, divide the land of Israel, President Bush congratulated Sharon for making the decision. **Hurricane Katrina formed. When the last Jew was out of Gaza, Sharon had stroke.**
- 7-16-2007 Pres. Bush gave speech regarding dividing land of Israel and Jerusalem, calling outpost illegal and America prepared to lead discussions. **7-20-2007 Stock Market Falls** worst decline in years, 2008 Housing crisis, Foreclosures, Illegal banking deals for houses/land
- 5-22-2011 President Obama gave speech, Israel to go back to 67 boarders- **Joplin Missouri Tornado**
- 3-11-2011 Japanese came against Israel, telling them to go back to pre-67 boarders **Great Earth Quake 2nd greatest in History**

Jesus [Yeshua=Yehoshua=YHWH-Salvation=YHWH], YHWH God put on flesh and die to pay our sin debt, to save us. We are not meant to have the wrath of God, God paid out debt. God has also given us freedom. We have a choice to obey God or not, to come out of Mystery Babylon or not. But remember God still judges and He is warning His people, us, to come out of Mystery Babylon before He judges her. The changes Mystery Babylon made, all the Babylonian doctrines brought into the Church and God's feasts- appointed times taken out, and God's name taken out of His baptism, and two of His commandments made of none effect. God hates these changes, these deceptions that have been done to His people, and God is going to judge Mystery Babylon in our time. We must heed God's warning to come out of Her.

I must explain again, the Replacing of our Hebrew God's name: YHWH and Yeshua with Baal (LORD) [Baal translated in English is Lord, but Baal is also an abbreviation for Baal Zebuwb.]

- "How long shall this be in the heart of the prophets that prophesy lies? yes, they are prophets of the deceit of their own heart; Which think to **cause my people to forget my name** by their dreams which they tell every man to his neighbor, **as their fathers have forgotten my name for Baal.**" (Jeremiah 23:26-27)

Babylon worshipped, Baal, *the Sun-god under the name BEL.*

The two oldest religions in the world are that of El and Bel (aka Baal). [God and Satan]

Beelzebub, Baʿal Zebub (Hebrew זבוב בעל) occurs in 2 Kings 1:2–6 as the name of the Philistine god of Ekron. **Beelzebub, also Beelzebul, is also identified in the New Testament as Satan, the "prince of the demons".**[n 15][n 16] [131]

... The word Beelzebub in rabbinical texts is a mockery of the Baʿal religion, which ancient Hebrews considered to be idol (or, false god) worship.[61] [131]

The Babylonians worshiped the Sun-god Baal, Bel (Belzubub), which another name for Satan, Lucifer.

#1167 ba'al, bah'al; from 1166; a *master*; hence a *husband*, or (fig.) *owner* (often used with another noun in modification of this latter sense):- + archer, + babbler, + bird, captain, chief man, + confederate, + have to do, + dreamer, those to whom it is due, + furious, those that are given to it, great, + hairy, he that hath it, have, +horseman, husband, **lord**, man, + married, master, person, + sworn, they of. [27]

---

[131] https://en.wikipedia.org/wiki/Beelzebub

Now, if these were the only uses of the word baal, we really couldn't complain, could we? Why? Because even Scripture reveals that YHWH was a husband to Israel (cf. Isa. 54:5; Jer. 31:32). This in Hebrew, would be, "YHWH is baal to Israel." Thus, baal is used in a good sense. But this is not the only usage of the word, as we shall show. [27]

#1168 ba'al, bah'al; the same as 1167; **Baal, a Phoenician deity:-Baal, (plur.) Baalim.**
...Ba'al was the founder of Babel (Babylon), according to secular history. He is identified with **Zeus,** Jupiter, Ammon, Asshur, Assur, Kronos, and Bel-Marduk. Morris Jastrow, Max Müller, and W. H. Roscher, all three agree: **Baal is the Babylonian sun deity**. [27]

The above reference says,
Baal is the Babylonian sun deity.
Mystery Babylon adopted all the sun worship doctrines of Baal the Babylonian sun god.

BAAL ZEBUWB OR BEELZEBOUL

#1176 (Hebrew) Baal Zebuwb, bah'al zeb-oob; from 1168 and 2070; Baal of (the) fly; Baal-zebub, a special deity of the Ekronites: Baal-Zebub. Remember when the Pharisees called Yahushua the Messiah Beelzebub (Mat. 10:25) and claimed that He cast out the demons by the prince of demons (Mat. 12:24, 27; Mk. 3:22; Lk. 11:15, 18, 19). [27]

Well, now go to Strong's Greek #954 and be ready for a shock!

#954 (Greek) Beelzeboul, beh-el-zeb-ool'; of Chald. Or. [by parody upon 1176]; dung-god; Beelzebul, **a name of Satan:** Beelzebub. [27]

- The shortened form of God's name, Yahweh is Yah. Example: Hallelujah means praise Yah.
- **Beelzeboul** (Greek) and **Baal Zebuwb** (Hebrew) are names of Satan and are also shortened to Bel or Baal
- **Baal in English is Lord.**
- **In Exodus 3:15 God tells us His name is YHWH (Yahweh), forever.** But in our English Bibles, **God's name, YHWH, was replaced with: LORD.** Lord which came from Baal. *Remember baal can mean* master; hence a husband, or, (fig.) owner, or *lord* (#1167) but baal is also short for the name: Baal= Baal Zebuwb (in Hebrew #1176), **(Baal for short) is another name for Satan, the Devil. The devil put his name, Baal (LORD in English), in place God's name, YHWH.**
- "And God said moreover unto Moses, Thus shalt thou say unto the children of Israel, The **LORD [YHWH]** God of your fathers, the God of Abraham, the God of Isaac, and the God of Jacob, hath sent me unto you: **this *is* my name for ever**, and this *is* my memorial unto all generations." (Exo 3:15)
- "How long shall this be in the heart of the prophets that prophesy lies? yes, they are prophets of the deceit of their own heart; Which think to **cause my people to forget my name** by their dreams which they tell every man to his neighbor, **as their fathers have forgotten my name for Baal.**" (Jer 23:26-27)
- As Jer 23:26,27 says, God's people have forgotten His name, YHWH, for LORD (Baal). Do most Christians you know, know that YHWH is God's eternal name or how to pronounce it?

And in the New Testament our Hebrew Saviour Yeshua [Jesus] is called Lord (Again Lord came from the word Baal which can mean lord, master, or husband but Baal is another name for Satan) The best way to give honor to our Saviour, Yeshua, is to use the Hebrew word: Adonai, which means master or owner. Some Jews also use Adonai instead of pronouncing God's name: YHWH.

How Constantine changed our Hebrew Saviour's name Yeshua to Jesus and the title Messiah was replaced with Christ:

In order to unite his empire, Constantine created a new god *from three Babylonian sun gods*, each representing Baal, sun worship. Each was an incarnation of the 2nd person of the Babylonian trinity.

(Shown previously in more detail in Chapter 3) [111] To make a very long and detailed story short, at the Council of Nicaea, they could not come to a decision on just one god they all could accept, so Constantine exercised his authority as Emperor and High Priest to consolidate the 3 primary gods that would effectively represent the Greek masses and the Eastern and the Oriental religions of the Roman Empire. Every one of these so called "gods" are nothing more than later incarnations of the Babylonian Religion whose savior was Tammuz the second member of the Babylonian Trinity and son/sun of "God". So, Constantine chose the following "gods" to unite his empire:

- To placate the powerful British factions he chose the great Druid god which was the sun god **Hesus**
- To placate the faction from Egypt he chose the Assyrian sun god **Horus**
- To placate the Eastern/Oriental factions he chose the Eastern Saviour-god, **Krishna** (Christ) (*Krishna is Sanskrit for Christ*) [111]

> **Krishna, which is Sanshrit for Christ, is not our Hebrew Messiah, Yeshua**. Krishna is the reincarnation of Vishnu. Vishnu is the second god of the Hindu trinity. The other two gods are Brahma and Shiva. Shiva is Satan, who is also called Zeus, which is another name for Nimrod or Tammuz. Krishna is the second member of the Babylonian trinity, Tammuz.

These three main sun god/saviors were then united into one composite deity called **Hesus Horus Krishna** which ***later became known in its English derived name as Jesus H. Christ***. Satisfying the Julius, Esu, Horus, and Krishna faithful who made up the vast majority of his empire. ***Constantine now had a "god" for his new religion which was not new at all but the rebirth of Babylonian sun worship.*** A "god" easily acceptable by all throughout his realm. [111]

More on the name Hesus, Iesous which eventually became Jesus:
Hesus is a later derivate of the name Esus pronounced "eh-soos". This is identically to the latin name Iesous where we get the English word "Jesus". Strong's #2424: Iesous (pronounced ee-ay-sooce'). [115]

When we simply take a step back and admit to ourselves what happened at the Council of Nicaea the similarities between Hesus and "Jesus" can easily be understood. They are one in the same as Hesus became "J"esus when the letter "J" was introduced into the vocabulary centuries later. [115]

The latin-greek word 'Jesus' sounds like Je-Zeus (hey-zoos). **Zeus or dios is the Greek Sun God...** "Soos" is Hebrew for "horse." This Pagan name 'sus' is used in many name-endings like Tarsus, Pegasus, Dionysus, Parnassus, etc. to honor Zeus phonetically... The Name of our Messiah in the "received" Greek is written: IESOU and IESOUS. The ending "S" is added because the Greek language requires male names to end in 's.'... The book 'Come Out Of Her My People' shows how several **ancient languages worshiped false deities under the names ESUS, ISIS, HESUS,** and others... [132]
So, 'Jesus' means nothing in Hebrew, the language it supposedly came from! **"Soos" is Hebrew for "horse"... Zeus was sometimes depicted as a HORSE-MAN**, or "centaur". The old Babylonian /Egyptian signs of the Zodiac/Zoo beasts in the skies included a centaur holding a bow and arrow, called Sagittarius - [which some interpret as] **Nimrod**... [132]

---

[132] http://yhvh.name/?w=1276

Mystery Babylon, the Roman Catholic Church, under Constantine and the Papacy, adopted the pagan sun gods of Babylon into one religion, and gave this god the name: Hesus (in Greek Iesous). *Hesus was the great Druid god* which was the sun god, Tammuz, the reincarnation of Nimrod, *who the Greeks called Zeus.* Hesus (Iesous) eventually came to be pronounced Jesus. Part of the mystery (Hidden wisdom) of Mystery Babylon is that our Hebrew Saviour's name, Yeshua, was replaced with Hesus, the Druid sun god, (in the Greek Iesous) to honor the Greek sun god's name, Zeus, another name for Satan.

- **"And no marvel; for Satan himself is transformed into an angel of light."** (2 Co 11:14)

The Pope, the leader of Mystery Babylon, is Pontiffs Maximus, the high priest of Babylon. The Pope calls himself the Vicar of Christ. Vicar of Christ means in place of Christ. Anti can mean *in place of,* so when he calls himself the Vicar of Christ, in place of Christ, he is calling himself the antichrist. The Vicar of Christ equals 666 in Roman numerals and is inscribed on the Popes crown. *The Pope shall stand in the temple of God (in Jerusalem) and claim to be God, this is the abomination of desolation.* He will not only claim to be the Christian God, Jesus Christ (Yeshua) but he will also claim to be the Muslim Messiah (the Mahdi), and the Jewish Messiah. When the abomination of desolation happens, as Yeshua (Jesus) explained in Matt. 24:15-21, "then shall be great tribulation".

Soon the devil's mark, the mark of the beast, 666 will have to be taken in the forehead or right hand to buy and sell. God's word says those who take it, the smoke of their torment will ascend up forever before the Lamb of God and the holy angles. This mark will be required three and a half years after the confirmation of the covenant by the antichrist, which is actually the peace agreement, between Palestine and Israel and the United Nations, a seven year, temporary agreement, that declares Israel's right to the land. This confirmation of this peace agreement by the antichrist is ready to take place now. This peace agreement may happen before the publishing of this book. As I explained earlier in the book, we Christians will still be here, when the antichrist stands in the Temple of God calling himself god and stops the sacrifices. The one true God (the God of the Bible) is calling His people out of Mystery Babylon before He judges her. God is not calling Jews, out of Mystery Babylon. He is calling Catholics and Christians to come out of Mystery Babylon, that we receive not her plagues, that we receive not her judgments. Satan has deceived the whole world, including those in Mystery Babylon, and her Christian daughter Churches into worshipping him, the sun god (called by many names) instead of the one YHWH (LORD). We must not take his mark, the mark of the beast. You can see the Roman Catholic Church openly worship Satan in Rome on You Tube, see my references 118,119, and 120.

- "And the great dragon was cast out, that old serpent, called the **Devil, and Satan, *which deceiveth the whole world...*"** (Rev 12:9)
- "And the third angel followed them, saying with a loud voice, ***If any man worship the beast and his image, and receive his mark in his forehead, or in his hand***, 10) The same shall drink of the wine of the wrath of God, which is poured out without mixture into the cup of his indignation; and he shall be tormented with fire and brimstone in the presence of the holy angels, and in the presence of the Lamb: 11) ***And the smoke of their torment ascendeth up for ever and ever:*** and they have no rest day nor night, who worship the beast and his image, and whosoever receiveth the mark of his name." (Rev 14:9-11)

Yeshua is our Saviour. We either believe that Yeshua is the one YHWH God of the first commandment, who was manifest in the flesh and died and rose again to save us, or that he is the second person of the trinity, the teaching that came from the mother church, Mystery Babylon, who changed the one baptism of the one Yeshua (Yeshua=Yehoshua= YHWH-Salvation=YHWH, the one YHWH, the one LORD) to fit her teaching that God is three separate Gods or persons in one.

1 John 5:7 says: "these three are one", not three in one. "These three are one", one which equals the one LORD, the one YHWH, the one Yahweh of the first commandment who is Yeshua [Jesus]. Mystery Babylon's doctrine of three separate Gods or three separate persons in one, equals a false god, equals spiritual adultery. God divorced the Hebrews for spiritual adultery, for going after other gods.

Unknowingly we have been indoctrinated with false teachings for close to 2000 years, that is why it is so hard to believe that we could be in spiritual adultery, but it is true. I showed you an abundance of proof in Chapter 3.

Read Yeshua's [Jesus] words in Rev. 2:18-24 about the fornication of the Church called Thyatira. They had the same doctrines of Baal (Satan) worship as Mystery Babylon and her daughter Churches do today. It is spiritual fornication. In Exo. 20:3-5 God tells us that He is a jealous God. In Revelation 2, He says to those that commit the (spiritual) adultery: *"I will kill her children with death"*, *"I will give unto every one of you according to your works."* i.e. according to what we do. And He says: *"as many as have not this doctrine, and which have not known the depths of Satan"*. (This fornication, is spiritual fornication, spiritual adultery against the one YHWH because we are YHWH'S Bride, His wife). The fornications are doctrines of Baal, doctrines of Satan, doctrines of Babylon and Mystery Babylon and her daughter Churches who took many of them with them at the reformation when they left the Roman Catholic Church.

(Rev 2:18-24) 18) And unto the angel of the church in Thyatira write; These things saith the Son of God, who hath his eyes like unto a flame of fire, and his feet *are* like fine brass; 19) I know thy works, and charity, and service, and faith, and thy patience, and thy works; and the last *to be* more than the first. 20) Notwithstanding I have a few things against thee, because thou sufferest that woman Jezebel, which calleth herself a prophetess, to teach and to seduce my servants to commit fornication, and to eat things sacrificed unto idols. 21) And I gave her space to repent of her fornication; and she repented not. 22) Behold, I will cast her into a bed, and them that commit adultery with her into great tribulation, except they repent of their deeds. 23) **And I will kill her children with death; and all the churches shall know that I am he which searcheth the reins and hearts: and I will give unto every one of you according to your works**. 24) But unto you I say, and unto the rest in Thyatira, **as many as have not this doctrine, and which have not known the depths of Satan**, as they speak; I will put upon you none other burden.

Now you know the truth, we are in the end times. God is our Father and He disciplines those He loves. God warns those He loves and He is a judge, (Judgement day is coming) and He even judges His own people. (I gave quite a few examples at the beginning of the book, and present time examples of God's judgments.) The Day of Judgment has not taken place yet in Rev 18:4, God is still warning His people to come out of Mystery Babylon in Rev. 18:4 that they be not judged. We will either heed God's word or the traditions of men. God's people, Israel, chose not to heed God's warning, they chose to serve Baal, spiritual adultery and God divorced them and dispersed from their promise land to all nations of the earth. They suffered a great deal, even the Holocaust. They were worshiping Baal (another name for Satan) when God divorced them. God told them He would not hear their cry because they worshiped Semiramis, also called the mother of God, the queen of heaven, but they refused to hear Him. (Shown in chapter 3) Will you hear His warning to come out of Mystery Babylon?

Four chapters from the end of the Bible God is warning His people to come out of her that we receive not her plagues, her judgments and **I am Sounding the Alarm now because we are in the end times now**. God warned His people, Israel, but they did their own will. They refused to hear God's warning. I pray you will heed God's call, His warning: **"*come out of her my people*"**, and take your Saviour's name, as His bride, in baptism, the cleansing bridal ceremony, in His holy name, Mar Yah Yeshua. (See: The marriage of the Lamb, chapter 6)

Yeshua's disciples preached according the revelation of the mystery, that Yeshua was the one (Lord) YHWH God manifest in the flesh and gave His life for us and said to repent and be baptized in His name for the remission of sins but Mystery Babylon kept that truth from us, teaching God's people the doctrines of Babylon. We are Yeshua's bride. A bride takes her groom's name. We take our Jewish groom's name, Mar Yah Yeshua (Master Yahweh Yeshua), ***trusting in His blood and His name***, in the Jewish wedding ceremony, baptism, the seventh step in the ancient Jewish wedding ceremony, that cleanses us from all sin, from all unrighteousness, making us ready for our groom, giving us our white robes of righteousness. Make up your mind now, to make yourself ready, by taking your Jewish groom's name now in the seventh step of Jewish wedding ceremony, baptism. (And don't forget **the cup of the marriage covenant, *the 3rd step of the Jewish wedding ceremony*** talked about in the sixth Chapter).

In Rev. 19:7 we read, His wife has made herself ready.

- "Let us be glad and rejoice, and give honour to him: for the marriage of the Lamb is come, and his wife hath made herself ready." (Rev 19:7)

Now is the time to make yourself ready, *repent* (a 180 degree turn, a change in your thinking), ask Him to come in your life if you haven't already and ask Him to help you live for Him, we can't do it without Him *and be baptized, in the name of Mar Yah Yeshua, (Master Yahweh Yeshua) for the remission (cleansing) of sins, and thereby confessing Yeshua as your LORD (YHWH=Yahweh) and Saviour*. It's the most important decision you'll ever make. None of us know the number of our days. God's word says: Today is the day of salvation. I exhort you, do the Bible Study: <u>Be Not Faithless But believing, Jesus Subtitle: The Mystery of God Revealed</u>, do all the quizzes, and come out of Mystery Babylon and her daughter Churches.

Yeshua called baptism a salvation issue. (Mar 16:16) "He that believeth and is baptized shall be saved; but he that believeth not shall be damned". (Act 10:43) "To him give *all* the prophets witness, *that through his name whosoever believeth in him shall receive remission of sins* (salvation)." As previously explained, baptism is a part of our marriage ceremony to our Saviour and we do not want to use a phrase or a translation of a name that honors the sun god, Satan, in the marriage ceremony. So next is a brief over view of our Saviour's Jewish name and then instructions on how to baptize in our Jewish Saviour's name. (Read Chapter 4)

- Strong's Hebrew 3444 yeshuah means salvation. Our Saviour's name real name Yeshua means salvation.
- Acts 4:12 says "there is none other NAME under heaven given among men, whereby we must be saved."
- **Yeshua** sounds like: (Ye-SHOO-a) [133]
- Our Saviour's name: **Yeshua is a contraction of Yehoshua. Yehoshua means Yahweh [YHWH] is salvation or the compound name: YHWH-Salvation.**
- Ex. 3:15 tells us *YHWH [Yahweh] is God's name forever.*
- "And God said moreover unto Moses, Thus shalt thou say unto the children of Israel, The LORD **[YHWH]** God of your fathers, the God of Abraham, the God of Isaac, and the God of Jacob, hath sent me unto you: ***this is my name forever***, and this is my memorial unto all generations." (**Exo 3:15**)
- "...and *all flesh shall know* that **I *The LORD [YHWH] am thy Saviour*...**" (Isaiah 49:26)
- <u>**Yah—short version of Yahweh**</u> *[YHWH=Yahweh]*
- **Example: Hallelujah** means Praise Yah
- **Mar** means master
- **MarYah—contraction of Mar and Yah, meaning 'Master/Lord Yah'.**
- "Then Shimon (Peter) said to them, Repent and be baptized, every one of you, in the name ***MarYah Yeshua*** (Lord Yah Yeshua= Master YHWH Yeshua) for the forgiveness of sins, so that you may receive the gift of the Holy Spirit (d'Rukha d'Qudsha in Aramaic, Ruach HaKodesh in Hebrew)." (Acts 2:38) [134]

After we hear and believe the gospel, the mystery of God, that Yeshua is the one YHWH God of the first commandment, that put on flesh and died to save us from our sins and rose again on the third day, the first thing to do is to pray, repenting, turning from of your sins, asking God to come into your heart and help you live for him, drink from the cup, (communion- you can do this at home see Chapter 6- I would not do it in a Trinitarian Church) indicating your acceptance of the proposal, of the one YHWH God and the marriage covenant is sealed, (the couple was considered to be betrothed, married - the 3rd step in the ancient Jewish wedding) then be baptized in His Holy name (His Hebrew-Aramaic name), Mar Yah Yeshua, for the remission of your sins and you shall receive the gift of the Holy Spirit. Then continue in His word and fellowship with like-minded believers.

---

[133] http://www.hebrew4christians.com/Names_of_G-d/Yeshua/yeshua.html
[134] Chapter 7's references from Be Not Faithless But Believing, Jesus [7]
http://ad2004.com/prophecytruths/Articles/DivineNameNT.pdf

To baptize:

You can use any body of water where you can be fully immersed: a tub, a pool, the lake, a river,
If our Saviour's name, Yeshua is new to you,
Practice saying our Saviour's full compound Aramaic name, Mar Yah Yeshua,
And practice saying: I baptize you in the name of Mar Yah Yeshua for the remission of your sins. (Acts 2:38)

Stand in a little over waste deep water, first making sure you can lower the person under the water and raise them back up. If the person is right handed, have them hold his left elbow with his right hand and hold his nose with his left hand. (Do the opposite for left handed people.)

Then tell them to repeat: in the name of Mar Yah Yeshua, after you say it,
then say, "I baptize you in the name of Mar Yah Yeshua for the remission of your sins",
they repeat "in the name of Mar Yah Yeshua",
and you lower them completely under the water (being buried with Messiah) and then raise him back up.

Congratulations, you just baptized them for the remission of sins, for salvation, part of the wedding ceremony to the Lamb of God, To Yeshua, who is YHWH, the one Yahweh.

- **"And I will betroth (a formal agreement to marry) thee unto me for ever**; yea, I will betroth thee unto me in righteousness, and in judgment, and in lovingkindness, and in mercies. 20) I will even betroth thee unto me in faithfulness: **and thou shalt know the LORD [YHWH]**." (Hos 2:19,20)

- **"For thy Maker is thine husband; the LORD [YHWH]** of hosts is his name; *and thy Redeemer the Holy One of Israel; The God of the whole earth shall he be called.*" (Isa 54:5)

A quick note about imperfect Faith

God's word tells us in His word that it is impossible to please God without faith.

- Heb 11:6 says, "But without faith *it is* impossible to please *him:* for he that cometh to God must believe that he is, and *that* he is a rewarder of them that diligently seek him."

My mother and my grandmother loved God and were women of devout faith. My grandma was a Catholic and believed in Jesus and I am sure she believed He was the second person of the Trinity. My mom grew up Catholic but later in life understood that God is one and was baptized in the name of Jesus. ***I believe I will see both of them in heaven.*** Although their faith may have been imperfect, God looks on our hearts. He knew their love and faith in Him. I suspect we all have imperfect faith.

When God gives us understanding we should walk in it (obey it) and when we do, He will give us more truth. Every time God revealed truth to me, I did my best to walk in it. I was baptized in the Trinitarian form, after I asked Jesus to come in my heart many years ago, then later I publicly confessed Him as my Saviour. Then when I understood that God is one, I was baptized in the name of Jesus. After I understood how His birth name, Yeshua was replaced, and I understood His Hebrew name was Mar Yah Yeshua I was baptized in the name of Mar Yah Yeshua for the remission of my sins. We must continue in each step of truth that God gives us.

Revelations 18:4 says: "Come out of her that ye be not partakers of her sins" thus we need to stop partaking of her many Babylonian traditions (sins). One way to do that, (after you have been baptized in our Saviour's name) is to look in chapter 3 at the list called: **Quick Overview**, or see the larger list at **http://remnantofgod.org/whoreofbabylon.htm** and check off the Babylonian traditions that you practice, the ones you partake in. Ask Yeshua to help you to stop partaking of them and follow His leading from His word.

Please share this book, everything in it, with your family, friends and with your Church, as many as will listen. Time is very short. Judgment is coming very soon. We are in the end times now. Our groom is coming to get us very soon, called the rapture, and we must be ready. Remember the parable Yeshua told in Matt 25: 1-12 about the ten virgins (Brides). Five of the 10 were ready but five of them were not ready. ***Half of His Church, His bride, was not ready and He told them, "I know you not"!***

Remember the revelation we discovered in the first chapter of this book about the trumpets. The first five trumpets have already sounded. The sixth trumpet is ready to sound, the war that will kill 1/3 of mankind that starts from the Euphrates River, also called World War III. We are in this war now. Then at the last trump, the seventh trumpet, Armageddon, our Saviour returns to get us His Bride and rescue His Jewish people. **We must be ready, even for a time as we think not.** What if we are in part of the 1/3 of the world that dies in the sixth trumpet war? We must be ready to meet Him in the sky (the rapture) for an hour we think not or if we die, we must be ready to meet our Groom.

- "Therefore be ye also ready: for in such an hour as ye think not the Son of man cometh." (Mat 24:44)
- "In a moment, in the twinkling of an eye, **at the last trump:** for the trumpet shall sound, and the dead shall be raised incorruptible, and we shall be changed." (1Co 15:52)

God word says: "My people are destroyed for lack of knowledge" But now that we have the knowledge that we need that will keep us from being destroyed. Sound the alarm, tell everyone what you've learned: who Mystery Babylon is and how to come out of her, **Sound the alarm**, tell our brothers and sisters to come out of Mystery Babylon, for God is calling in Revelation 18:4 ***"come out of her my people"***, that they receive not her plagues, and that they do not take the mark of the beast and that the smoke of their torment does not ascend up forever and ever before the Lamb of God and His holy angles (See Rev. 14:11). Join us who know the truth, and **Sound the Alarm, WARNING, WARNING, WARNING, come out of her my people.**

Give this book to everyone you know, for who would believe any of this, unless they are shown all of the puzzle pieces put together for them, that they may see the true image of Mystery Babylon, the beast and Mystery Babylon's leader the antichrist.

I wish you exceeding great blessings,
With Much Love,
Sincerely,
Cindy A. Alexander

Disclaimer:
There are many priests and pastors, faithful believers in Roman Catholic Church and in her daughter Churches who are dedicated to God, who love God with all their heart and serve God to the best of their ability and are God's children. God loves them greatly and so do I. God is calling them out of Mystery Babylon, (The Roman Catholic Church) and calling Mystery Babylon's daughter Churches (Christian Churches) out of her pagan doctrines, out of her Babylonian doctrines, that they be not partakers of her sins and receive her plagues (her judgments). I love God's people and that's why I put the puzzle pieces together in this book. The information contained in this book is here to bring truth to God's people about the large number of doctrines and traditions that clearly go against Scripture and where they came from so that God's people may see the full picture, in order to decide for themselves, what is truth and what is error, that they may heed God's call to come out of Mystery Babylon, that they be not par takers of her sins and that they receive not her plagues (that they receive not her judgments).

I am very, very grateful to all my references and resources. Thank you for sharing truth so that when all put together, the people God shed His blood for could see the truth, that we could see the full image of the beast. Not all of my references and resources believe everything I believe. And I do not agree with everything all my resources believe but I glean, I learn, many truths from them. We are all on our individual roads of revelation. May God Bless you all.

Chapter 4 The Mystery of God Revealed, Quiz Answers:
1) Understand, made, 1:20
2) Understanding, acknowledgment
3) Revelation
4) YHWH
5) YHWH, YHWH
6) Him
7) Father
8) One
9) One
10) Men, men
11) Hidden wisdom
12) Understanding
13) YHWH, none, no
14) None, YHWH, none
15) None
16) YHWH
17) YHWH
18) One
19) Are one, YHWH
20) Lord, God
21) Baptized, saved
22) All, name, remission of sins
23) For the remission of sins
24) 3000
25) Actions
26) I, Me
27) One, Christ

References and Resources:

Note: with web addresses that are longer than one line, you must be sure that the link is not broken, that it does not have extra spaces that are not supposed to be there, or it will not got the site.

1 The Mystery of the Shemitah by Rabbi Jonathan Cahn

2 Rev. Baxter's End times video: The Seven Trumpets

3 Rev. Baxter's https://www.endtime.com/ 1-800-Endtime

4 The End of Shemitah – You Tube (The Official 700 Club) https://www.youtube.com/watch?v=t6v2D36oCvc

5 Phil Richardson http://september2021.com/book-september-2021-graphs-and-images/

6 John McTernan's As America has done to Israel

7 Tim Spincer's Secret USA Navy Map

8 Ed Gray, Missouri State Emergency Management Agency (SEMA)
   http://www.showme.net/~fkeller/quake/maps3.htm

9 https://www.endtime.com/united-states-discovered-in-the-bible/

10 https://en.wikipedia.org/wiki/Fourth_Reich

11 http://www2.ministries-online.org/biometrics/rome.html

12 http://kenraggio.com/KRPN-Statue-Of-Nebuchadnezzar.html

13 https://www.endtime.com/understanding-the-endtime/

14 http://guide.discoveronline.org/discover/guide07/7sec4.htm

15 https://store.endtime.com/?s=from+here+to+armageddon+DVD

16 https://www.youtube.com/watch?v=61Ij8JcrSGY

17 https://www.youtube.com/watch?v=7NdC4a4tDD4

18 https://www.youtube.com/watch?v=el1TXBwfw3k

19 https://www.youtube.com/watch?v=BjqaMJrfq5U

20 https://www.youtube.com/watch?v=vHxqoDnmHlg

21 http://granddesignexposed.com/sun/baal.html

22 https://en.wikipedia.org/wiki/Seven_hills_of_Rome

23 https://www.worldslastchance.com/end-time-prophecy/who-is-the-beast.html

24 http://www.mindserpent.com/American_History/religion/pope/rc_images.html

25 http://remnantofgod.org/whoreofbabylon.htm

26 https://worldtruth.tv/mystery-babylon-exposed-2/

27 http://yahushua.net/baalgad.htm

28 https://en.wikipedia.org/wiki/Lucifer

29 Bernard Starr, author of Jesus Uncensored: Restoring the Authentic Jew
   http://www.huffingtonpost.com/bernard-starr/why-christians-were-denied-access-to-their-bible-for-1000-years_b_3303545.html

30 https://2017.lutheranworld.org/content/martin-luther-131

31 www.hope-of-israel.org/easter.htm

32 www.thinknot.net/easter.htm

33 http://www.remnantofgod.org/easter.htm

34 http://christianitybeliefs.org/end-times-deceptions/roman-catholic-church-is-mystery-babylon-lent-tammuz/

35 https://yrm.org/december-25-birthday-sun/

36 http://www.newadvent.org/cathen/03724b.htm (Under heading: Natalis Invicti)

37 http://www.fossilizedcustoms.com/Satan.htm

38 http://granddesignexposed.com/indexmystery/2chap/worship.html

39 http://missionignition.net/lynda/semiramis.php

40 http://granddesignexposed.com/indexmystery/2chap/worship.html

41 http://www.aloha.net/~mikesch/monstr.htm

42 https://philologos.org/__eb-ttb/sect43.htm

43 http://scripture-keywords.tripod.com/Babylon/07-Rome-Symbolism.html

44 http://www.sabbathcovenant.com/creationcriesout/HowRomeSunWorship.htm

45 http://amazingdiscoveries.org/S-deception_Pontifex_Maximus_Babylon#_

46 http://www.remnantofgod.org/whoreofbabylon.htm

47 https://grandislanddiaconate.wordpress.com/2012/02/22/why-is-incense-used-during-mass/

48 http://jesus-is-savior.com/False%20Religions/Roman%20Catholicism/blasphemy.htm

49 http://jesus-is-savior.com/False%20Doctrines/infant_baptism_exposed.htm

50 http://come-and-hear.com/editor/br_3.html

51 http://www.remnantofgod.org/whoreofbabylon.htm

52 http://vaticannewworldorder.blogspot.com/2012/04/roman-catholic-sun-worship-lucifer-sun.html

53 https://www.facebook.com/Zionians4Christ/photos/a.426638267420098.1073741825.4046900296149
22/912256952191558/?type=3&hc_ref=PAGES_TIMELINE

54 http://amazingdiscoveries.org/albums?view=album&code=SerpentDragonSymbols#_

55 http://www.markbeast.org/mark-beast-paganism.html

56 http://www.mindserpent.com/American_History/religion/pope/rc_images.html

57 http://vaticannewworldorder.blogspot.com/2012/03/r-eligious-symbols-religion-false.html

58 https://www.pinterest.com/pin/255368241341291122/

59 http://a-voice-in-wilderness.blogspot.com/2010/04/who-is-this-woman.html

60 http://www.bibletruth.cc/Easter.htm#Hot_Cross_Buns

61 http://endrtimes.blogspot.it/2012/04/pagan-roots-of-easter.html

62 http://www.newadvent.org (In The Catholic Encyclopedia under C for Christmas, then under the heading: Natalis Invictus)

63 http://assemblyofyahweh.com/wp-content/uploads/2015/03/Is-Our-Saviors-Birth-the-Origin-of-Christmas.pdf

64 http://www.mindserpent.com/American_History/introduction/footnotes/ft_sol_invictus_001.html

65 http://thetruthandthetruthalone.blogspot.co.uk/2009/01/ancient-romes-pagan-religion.html

66 https://worldtruth.tv/mystery-babylon-exposed-2/

67 https://en.wikipedia.org/wiki/Syncretism

68 http://aletheia.consultronix.com/7.html

69 http://ministeriomisionerodepoderenjesus.blogspot.com/2010/11/semiramis-priests-nimrod-tammuz-and-his.html

70 https://www.slideshare.net/kaondeandrew/the-secret-behind-the-wine-of-babylon-1-recovered

71 http://doubleportioninheritance.blogspot.com/2012/02/queen-of-heaven-why-does-church.html

72 http://www.pathofmary.com/daily-act-of-consecration-of-marys-own/

73 https://www.michiganchurchsupply.com/products/2-1-2-white-altar-bread-lm45?variant=39783022412

74 http://whale.to/c/isishorusseth.html

75 https://en.wikipedia.org/wiki/Halo_(religious_iconography)

76 http://scripture-keywords.tripod.com/Babylon/07-Rome-Symbolism.html

77 http://www.wisegeek.org/what-is-christmas.htm

78 http://www.oracionesparapeticiones.com/2013/07/oracion-la-virgen-de-la-medalla.html

79 http://new.exchristian.net/2012/06/great-virgin-isis-ancient-mythology-is.html

80 http://www.truthbeknown.com/mary.html

81 http://www.romeofthewest.com/2007/03/photos-of-immaculate-conception-church.html

82 https://biggestcults.wordpress.com/category/roman-catholicism/

83 https://www.sabbathtruth.com/sabbath-history/how-the-sabbath-was-changed

84 http://amazingdiscoveries.org/S-deception-Sabbath_Sunday_Catholic_Church

85 http://torch-of-salvation.blogspot.com/2011/07/man-with-number-666-that-is-mentioned.html

86 http://josiehagenministries.blogspot.com/2013/05/you-shall-offer-no-strange-incense-fire.html

87 http://www.new2torah.com/wp-content/uploads/2013/01/molech_sacrifice.jpg

88 http://www.scionofzion.com/mcr.htm

89 http://www.angelfire.com/la2/prophet1/maryolotry02.html

90 https://en.wikipedia.org/wiki/Purgatory

91 https://en.wikipedia.org/wiki/Gargoyle

92 http://www.aloha.net/~mikesch/wheel.htm

93 http://catholicreformation.yuku.com/topic/3123/Solar-Wheel-Mystery-Babylon-Vatican-and-One-World-Religion#.WRx6s4WcFqw

94 https://www.facebook.com/Zionians4Christ/photos/a.426638267420098.1073741825.4046900296149
22/912256952191558/?type=3&hc_ref=PAGES_TIMELINE

95 http://www.markbeast.org/mark-beast-paganism.html

96 https://en.wikipedia.org/wiki/Crosier

97 https://awarenessdeconstructingconsciousness.files.wordpress.com/2014/12/pope-serpent.jpg

98 http://nebraskaepiscopalian.org/wp-content/uploads/2013/08/cope.jpg

99 https://amazingdiscoveries.org/albums?view=album&code=SymbolsofGods#_

100 http://whale.to/c/churches_ill.html#All_seeing_eye_

101 http://worldtruth.tv/wp-content/uploads/2012/03/21kjedz1.jpg

102 https://rapsta24.wordpress.com/tag/catholic/

103 http://amazingdiscoveries.org/albums?view=album&code=SunWorshipSymbols

104 http://www.catholictradition.org/Christ/precious-bloodsh1c.jpg

105 https://www.catholicfaithstore.com/Store/Products/Cat/3bf/Sacred-Heart-Prints-and-Artwork/All.html

106 http://assemblyoftrueisrael.com/Documents/Sunworship.htm

107 https://en.wikipedia.org/wiki/Constantine_the_Great_and_Christianity

108 http://www.sabbathtruth.com/sabbath-history/how-the-sabbath-was-changed

109 http://www.themysteryrevealed.info/   Be Not Faithless But Believing, Jesus The Mystery Revealed by Cheryl Alvarado

110 https://www.scribd.com/document/176705397/Origin-of-the-Trinity-Ancient-Babylonian-Triad-Triune-Trinity-Chart

111 http://www.sabbathcovenant.com/christianitythegreatdeception/CouncilofNicea.htm

112 http://www.bbc.co.uk/religion/religions/hinduism/deities/vishnu.shtml

113 https://www.thoughtco.com/who-is-krishna-1770452

114 https://mythoughtsbornfromfire.wordpress.com/2013/10/17/shiva-bel-satan-set-and-typhon/

115 http://sabbathcovenant.com/christianitythegreatdeception/newgodcreated.htm

116
http://www.jesus-is-savior.com/False%20Religions/Roman%20Catholicism/satanism_in_the_vatican.htm

117 https://www.youtube.com/watch?v=x-y8jF25scU

118 https://www.youtube.com/watch?v=sUN-XEU6HUc

119 https://reptiliandimension.wordpress.com/2014/12/08/devil-worship-at-vatican-was-pope-francis-declared-son-of-lucifer-at-a-televised-roman-catholic-luciferian-worship-service/

120
https://www.bing.com/videos/search?q=you+tube%3a+full+blown+lucifer+worship+at+the+catholic+va
tican&view=detail&mid=DA29D82D9EC66E0639D5DA29D82D9EC66E0639D5&FORM=VIRE

121 http://www.aloha.net/~mikesch/666.htm

122 http://biblehub.com/greek/473.htm

123
https://www.bing.com/videos/search?q=you+tube+lutheran+church+called+pope+antichrist&view=
detail&mid=BE64507256B25AB7DE2DBE64507256B25AB7DE2D&FORM=VIRE

124 http://amazingdiscoveries.org/R-Papacy_aggressive_Pope_Catholic_Chiniquiy

125 Chapter 4's references from: Be Not faithless But Believing, Jesus by Cheryl Alvarado listed in the order that they are in this book:

    5 Wikipedia

    23 www.bible-history.com/map/south_palestine_judea.html

    3 http://www.e-sword.net/

    6 http://lexiconcordance.com/hebrew/3442.html

    10 http://lexiconcordance.com/hebrew/3091.html

    11 http://lexiconcordance.com/hebrew/3068.html

    8 Scripture List from Pastor Gary R. Dornbach II Refuge Church Liberty Missouri

    19 Schaff – Herzog Religious Encyclopedia, Volume 1, Page 435

    20 Canney Encyclopedia of Religion, (page 53?)

21 Hastings Encyclopedia of Religion, Volume 2

22 Britannica Encyclopedia, 11th Edition, Volume 3, page 365

16 The Catholic Encyclopedia, 1913 Edition, Vol. 2, Page 263

1 http://mayimhayim.org/JewishWedding.htm A Mayim Hayim study on A Fresh Look At The Jewish Wedding

126 https://www.oikoumene.org/en/resources/documents/assembly/2006-porto-alegre/1-statements-documents-adopted/institutional-issues/constitution-and-rules-as-adopted

127 Chapter 5 reference list from: Be Not Faithless But Believing Jesus The Mystery of God Revealed

16 The Catholic Encyclopedia, 1913 Edition, Vol. 2, Page 263

19 Schaff – Herzog Religious Encyclopedia, Volume 1, Page 435

20 Canney Encyclopedia of Religion, (page 53?)

21 Hastings Encyclopedia of Religion, Volume 2

22 Britannica Encyclopedia, 11th Edition, Volume 3, page 365

16 The Catholic Encyclopedia, 1913 Edition, Vol. 2, Page 263

128 Chapter 6's list of references from: Be Not Faithless But believing, Jesus The Mystery of God Revealed

1 A Mayim Hayim study on A Fresh Look At The Jewish Wedding

2 The Ultimate Wedding, Ancient Jewish Traditions and their Fulfillment in Jesus the Messiah by Bill Risk

129 Reference list from: Cheryl Alvarado's Be Not Faithless But Believing, Jesus The Mystery of God Revealed, The Bonus Chapter, Christ our Passover

24 Health And Through The Communion by Joseph Prince

130 Dr. Robert D. Wholeness Heidler The Messianic Church Arising Chapter 3

131 https://en.wikipedia.org/wiki/Beelzebub

132 http://yhvh.name/?w=1276

133 http://www.hebrew4christians.com/Names_of_G-d/Yeshua/yeshua.html

134 Chapter 7's references from Be Not Faithless But Believing, Jesus

7 http://ad2004.com/prophecytruths/Articles/DivineNameNT.pdf

135 http://members.tripod.com/sword_of_the_spirit/babylon.htm

136 http://www.biblehistory.com/babylonia/BabyloniaStriding_Lion.htm

137 http://www.ebay.com/itm/251793030692

138 https://www.buddhagroove.com/kuan-yin-and-infant-statue-19-5-inches-tall/

139 http://www.prayertoday.org/NamesofGod/Jehovah-names.htm

www.ingramcontent.com/pod-product-compliance
Lightning Source LLC
Chambersburg PA
CBHW062102090426
42741CB00015B/3305